A History of Macroeconomic Policy in the United States

Keynes asked whether his 'visionary' ideas would overcome the interests opposed to change. However, an examination of the histories of monetary and fiscal policies suggests that this is a false distinction. The interests and ideas associated with government policies are seldom opposed. The suspicion that the latter more often follows than confronts the former is supported by the experiences documented in this book.

Professor Wood's new title examines the controlling influences that drive macroeconomic policies in the United States. The book addresses the history of the interests, ideas, and practices of monetary and fiscal policies in the United States, although it also examines macro-policies in other countries, particularly the United Kingdom. Professor Wood argues that economic policies in the United States have been relatively predictable and stable historically, through a detailed examination of conflicts over taxes and monetary policy such as the whiskey rebellion, Magna Carta, the Stamp Act, the Banks of the United States, and the Federal Reserve. Issues covered also include property, economists' theories of stabilization, taxes, deficits, and monetary policy.

This book will be of interest to monetary and fiscal economists, both in the United States and the United Kingdom. It is also relevant to postgraduate and advanced undergraduate economics students.

John H. Wood is the Reynolds Professor of Economics at Wake Forest University in North Carolina, USA.

Routledge explorations in economic history
Edited by Lars Magnusson
Uppsala University, Sweden

1 **Economic Ideas and Government Policy**
   Contributions to contemporary economic history
   Sir Alec Cairncross

2 **The Organization of Labour Markets**
   Modernity, culture and governance in Germany, Sweden, Britain and Japan
   Bo Stråth

3 **Currency Convertibility**
   The gold standard and beyond
   Edited by Jorge Braga de Macedo, Barry Eichengreen and Jaime Reis

4 **Britain's Place in the World**
   A historical enquiry into import controls 1945–1960
   Alan S. Milward and George Brennan

5 **France and the International Economy**
   From Vichy to the Treaty of Rome
   Frances M. B. Lynch

6 **Monetary Standards and Exchange Rates**
   M.C. Marcuzzo, L. Officer and A. Rosselli

7 **Production Efficiency in Domesday England, 1086**
   John McDonald

8 **Free Trade and its Reception 1815–1960**
   Freedom and trade: volume I
   Edited by Andrew Marrison

9 **Conceiving Companies**
   Joint-stock politics in Victorian England
   Timothy L. Alborn

10 **The British Industrial Decline Reconsidered**
   Edited by Jean-Pierre Dormois and Michael Dintenfass

11 **The Conservatives and Industrial Efficiency, 1951–1964**
   Thirteen wasted years?
   Nick Tiratsoo and Jim Tomlinson

12 **Pacific Centuries**
   Pacific and Pacific Rim economic history since the 16th century
   Edited by Dennis O. Flynn, Lionel Frost and A.J.H. Latham

13 **The Premodern Chinese Economy**
Structural equilibrium and capitalist sterility
Gang Deng

14 **The Role of Banks in Monitoring Firms**
The case of the crédit mobilier
Elisabeth Paulet

15 **Management of the National Debt in the United Kingdom, 1900–1932**
Jeremy Wormell

16 **An Economic History of Sweden**
Lars Magnusson

17 **Freedom and Growth**
The rise of states and markets in Europe, 1300–1750
S. R. Epstein

18 **The Mediterranean Response to Globalization Before 1950**
Sevket Pamuk and Jeffrey G. Williamson

19 **Production and Consumption in English Households 1600–1750**
Mark Overton, Jane Whittle, Darron Dean and Andrew Hann

20 **Governance, The State, Regulation and Industrial Relations**
Ian Clark

21 **Early Modern Capitalism**
Economic and social change in Europe 1400–1800
Edited by Maarten Prak

22 **An Economic History of London, 1800–1914**
Michael Ball and David Sunderland

23 **The Origins of National Financial Systems**
Alexander Gerschenkron reconsidered
Edited by Douglas J. Forsyth and Daniel Verdier

24 **The Russian Revolutionary Economy, 1890–1940**
Ideas, debates and alternatives
Vincent Barnett

25 **Land Rights, Ethno Nationality and Sovereignty in History**
Edited by Stanley L. Engerman and Jacob Metzer

26 **An Economic History of Film**
Edited by John Sedgwick and Mike Pokorny

27 **The Foreign Exchange Market of London**
Development since 1900
John Atkin

28 **Rethinking Economic Change in India**
Labour and livelihood
Tirthankar Roy

29 **The Mechanics of Modernity in Europe and East Asia**
The institutional origins of social change and stagnation
Erik Ringmar

30 **International Economic Integration in Historical Perspective**
Dennis M.P. McCarthy

31 **Theories of International Trade**
Adam Klug
Edited by Warren Young and Michael Bordo

32 **Classical Trade Protectionism 1815–1914**
Edited by Jean Pierre Dormois and Pedro Lains

33 **Economy and Economics of Ancient Greece**
Takeshi Amemiya

34 **Social Capital, Trust and the Industrial Revolution: 1780–1880**
David Sunderland

35 **Pricing Theory, Financing of International Organisations and Monetary History**
Lawrence H. Officer

36 **Political Competition and Economic Regulation**
Edited by Peter Bernholz and Roland Vaubel

37 **Industrial Development in Postwar Japan**
Hirohisa Kohama

38 **Reflections on the Cliometrics Revolution**
Conversations with economic historians
Edited by John S. Lyons, Louis P. Cain, and Samuel H. Williamson

39 **Agriculture and Economic Development in Europe Since 1870**
Edited by Pedro Lains and Vicente Pinilla

40 **Quantitative Economic History**
The good of counting
Edited by Joshua Rosenbloom

41 **A History of Macroeconomic Policy in the United States**
John H. Wood

A History of Macroeconomic Policy in the United States

John H. Wood

Routledge
Taylor & Francis Group
LONDON AND NEW YORK

First published 2009
by Routledge
2 Park Square, Milton Park, Abingdon, Oxon OX14 4RN

Simultaneously published in the USA and Canada
by Routledge
270 Madison Ave, New York, NY 10016

Routledge is an imprint of the Taylor & Francis Group, an informa business

© 2009 John H. Wood

Typeset in Times by Wearset Ltd, Boldon, Tyne and Wear
Printed and bound in Great Britain by TJI Digital, Padstow, Cornwall

All rights reserved. No part of this book may be reprinted or reproduced or utilized in any form or by any electronic, mechanical, or other means, now known or hereafter invented, including photocopying and recording, or in any information storage or retrieval system, without permission in writing from the publishers.

British Library Cataloguing in Publication Data
A catalogue record for this book is available from the British Library

Library of Congress Cataloging-in-Publication Data
A catalog record for this book has been requested

ISBN10: 0-415-77718-6 (hbk)
ISBN10: 0-203-88356-X (ebk)

ISBN13: 978-0-415-77718-6 (hbk)
ISBN13: 978-0-203-88356-3 (ebk)

But though thus largely directed by practical needs, economics avoids as far as possible the discussion of those exigencies of party organization, and those diplomacies of home and foreign politics of which the statesman is bound to take account in deciding what measures that he can propose will bring him nearest to the end that he desires to secure for his country. It aims indeed at helping him to determine not only what that end should be, but also what are the best methods of a broad policy devoted to that end. But it shuns many political issues, which the practical man cannot ignore: and it is therefore a science, pure and applied, rather than a science and an art. And it is better described by the broad term 'Economics' than by the narrower term 'Political Economy'.

(Marshall 1920: 36)

It is universally acknowledged that there is a great uniformity among the actions of men in all nations and ages, and that human nature remains still the same in its principles and operations. The same motives always produce the same actions; the same events follow from the same causes.... Would you know the sentiments, inclinations, and course of life of the Greeks and Romans? Study well the temper and actions of the French and English: you cannot be much mistaken in transferring to the former most of the observations which you have made with regard to the latter. Mankind are so much the same in all times and places that history informs us of nothing new or strange in this particular.... Nor are the earth, water, and other elements examined by Aristotle and Hippocrates more like to those which at present lie under our observation than the men described by Polybius and Tacitus are to those who now govern the world.

(David Hume 1748: 92–3)

Contents

List of figures xi
List of tables xii
Acknowledgments xiii

1 Introduction 1

PART I
Fiscal policy 5

2 Interests: a history of tax conflicts 7
  The Magna Carta 8
  Ship-money 11
  The Glorious Revolution 15
  Contracts and commitments 20
  The Stamp Act: taxation without representation 23
  The Constitution of the United States of America 28
  The whiskey and other tax rebellions in the early United States 30
  Tariffs 33
  The missile gap? 39
  Conclusion 41

3 Ideas: the theory of stabilization policy 42
  The transmission of ideas 43
  The General Theory 47
  Acceptance and rejection 57
  The possibility of macroeconomic policy 63

4 Practice: the stability of Federal government deficits 67
  Popular explanations of the persistent deficits 68

x *Contents*

    An alternative explanation: military spending with tax smoothing 75
    Was Keynesianism ever practiced? 79

PART II
Monetary policy   81

5 The interests and institutions of monetary policy   83
    The Bank of England, 1694–1914 84
    The Banks of the United States 92
    The Independent Treasury 99
    Foundations of the Federal Reserve 100
    Conclusion 110

6 Knowledge, advice, and monetary policy   113
    Sources and limits of knowledge 115
    Ideas, experience, and action 117
    An economist's lament: 'What trade-offs?' 127
    Economists, bureaucracies, and policymakers 130
    Who's crazy? 137
    Policymakers and the public 145

7 The stability of monetary policy: the Federal Reserve, 1914–2007   153
    The Fed's variable reputation 153
    What they knew in 1914 155
    The Fed's model 162
    Qualifications 172
    Estimates 175
    A new theory 180
    Conclusion 181

PART III
Conclusion   185

8 It's interests after all   187

    Notes   191
    References   194
    Index   213

Figures

2.1	Tariff receipts as percentages of dutiable and all imports	36
3.1	Keynes's demand-determined income	65
4.1	Gross national product, actual and potential, and unemployment rate	74
4.2	Deficits, military, and other Federal government spending as proportions of GNP	75
7.1	Commercial paper rate and inflation, 1910–2007	171
7.2	Fed discount rate, short-term market rate, and free reserves, 1922–32	176
7.3	Fed discount rate, Fed funds rate, and free reserves, 1953–69	176
7.4	Fed discount rate, Fed funds rate, and free reserves, 1970–78	177
7.5	Fed discount rate, Fed funds rate, and free reserves, 1987–2007	177

Tables

2.1	Federal government revenue, spending, surplus, and debt: presidential terms, Washington to Jackson	34
2.2	Votes on the Tariff Bills of 1828 and 1833	35
4.1	Military spending and the deficit	68
4.2	Determinants of the full-employment surplus	70
4.3	Federal government budgets in selected years	73
4.4	The model	76
4.5	Regression estimates: dependent variable *def*	77
5.1	Congressional votes for and against the national banks	94
5.2	Selected reserve-requirement ratios of national and Federal Reserve member banks	108
7.1	Fed discount and Fed funds rate responses to free reserves	178
7.2	Taylor and Strong-free-reserves rules compared: dependent variable di_f	182

Acknowledgments

I have observed and tried to learn how macroeconomic policies are made since my days as a fellowship student at the Federal Reserve Bank of Chicago many decades ago, and have accumulated intellectual debts along the way to a great many officials, teachers (they were all my teachers), colleagues, and students, including George Mitchell, Andrew Brimmer, Lyle Gramley, George Horwich, Ernest Baughman, Bill Poole, Mike Grove, Ed Feige, George Kaufman, John Hughes, Rollin Thomas, Pat Hendershott, Dale Osborne, Frank de Leeuw, Dan Brill, Steve Taylor, Jack Guttentag, Terence Hutchison, Alan Walters, Uli Schlieper, Duane Harris, Mark Willes, Lee Hoskins, Ira Kaminow, Irwin Friend, John Boyd, Joe Lucia, Doug Vickers, Stuart Greenbaum, Gerry O'Driscoll, Ed Kane, Larry White, Cara Lown, Maureen O'Hara, Ed Prescott, Joe Burns, Tony Elavia, John Crihfield, Mike Lawlor, Jac Heckelman, Dan Hammond, Michael Bordo, Anna Schwartz, Bob Hetzel, Marc Quintyn, Donato Masciandaro, and Andreas Freytag, none of whom agree with everything in this book. I am also thankful for the facilities of Clare Hall, Cambridge, and the American Institute of Economic Research, Great Barrington, Massachusetts.

1 Introduction

> There is a naïve view among economists that 'we need to change this or that policy in order to improve economic welfare'. [T]his is impossible. The current values of policies reflect a delicate political equilibrium that balances all of society's conflicting interests. The current negative views of economists on the policy have already been embodied in its equilibrium. The policy is endogenous and is outside the control of any group, including the politicians. They are merely the agents balancing all of the conflicting interests....
>
> (Magee *et al.* 1989: xvi)

This book attempts a partial answer to the complex question: What determines monetary and fiscal policies? The answer prevalent among economists is clear and simple: economic theory. 'Academic thinking about monetary economics – as well as macroeconomics more generally – has altered drastically since 1971–73 and so has the practice of monetary policy', a prominent economist wrote in 2002. 'The former has passed through the rational expectations and real-business-cycle revolutions into today's "new neoclassical synthesis," leading the latter "into an era of low inflation that emphasizes the concepts of central bank independence, transparency, and accountability"' (McCallum 2002). The fluctuating inflations since World War II, a team of leading economists wrote, resulted from the applications of 'a crude but fundamentally sensible model of how the economy worked in the 1950s to more formal but faulty models in the 1960s and 1970s to a model that was both sensible and sophisticated in the 1980s and 1990s' (Romer and Romer 2002).

Economists were just as confident of their influence four decades ago. A former chairman of the president's Council of Economic Advisors and advocate of Keynesian interventions, wrote:

> Economics has come of age in the 1960s. Two Presidents have recognized and drawn on modern economics as a source of national strength and Presidential power. Their willingness to use, for the first time, the full range of modern economic tools underlies the unbroken U.S. expansion since early 1961. [W]e have at last unleashed fiscal and monetary policy for the aggressive pursuit of those objectives.
>
> (Heller 1966: 1–2)

2 Introduction

'By about 1980', however, after another revolution in economic theory, another Keynesian economist observed that 'it was hard to find an American academic macroeconomist under the age of 40 who professed to be a Keynesian' (Blinder 1988). The president elected that year seemed to share the next new policy view of economists when he said: 'Government is the problem' (Reagan, Inaugural Address: 20 January 1981).

Changing policies are often thought to be examples of the much quoted conclusion to J.M. Keynes's *The General Theory of Employment, Interest and Money* (1936: 383–4). After asking whether the application of his theory was more than 'a visionary hope', he answered that

> the ideas of economists and political philosophers ... are more powerful than is commonly understood. Indeed the world is ruled by little else. Practical men, who believe themselves to be quite exempt from any intellectual influences, are usually the slaves of some defunct economist. [S]oon or late, it is ideas, not vested interests, which are dangerous for good or evil.

These claims rest on weak foundations. Interests are more stubborn than Keynes assumed. The vanity of his hopes, and of theorists in general, is the thesis of this book. The interests – or incentives, to which we might expect economists to ascribe more influence – that govern the world have persevered. This alternative explanation of policy is supported by the record of actions of the monetary and fiscal authorities which form the substance of the pages that follow. Existing policies may not be 'delicate equilibria' as suggested in the opening quotation, but they are certainly endogenous and not easily manipulated by economists or politicians.

The case can be made more generally, but it is limited in this book to the United States, where it is shown that the direction of influence between economic theory and practice is primarily from the latter to the former. Notwithstanding their claims for innovation, economists have rationalized more than influenced policy. Ideas not supporting interests have been ignored in practice.

The lights of theory playing on public policies have oscillated – for example, from *Classical* to *Keynesian* to *New Classical* and *New Keynesian* – but the policies themselves have been more persistent than is generally recognized. Policymakers and policies have been more conservative than they have been given credit (or blamed) for. My purpose is neither to criticize nor defend the dominance of interests, but to record it in the hope of better understanding policy. In the process, we cannot help but find the opening epigraph by David Hume more helpful than Keynes's belief in the fragility and malleability of human thought and behavior.

The next six chapters explore the interests, ideas, and practices of fiscal and monetary policies. The general conclusions are quickly summarized. Economists dismiss the public's disapproval of the national debt as *Deficit Hysteria* (Benavie 1998) which fails to comprehend scientific explanations that public debts are like private debts, they arise from spending that promotes stabilization and growth, and the government's net worth is positive, anyway (Samuelson 1958: 350–62; Eisner 1986).

Opposed to this view of government budgets as applications of economic theory – instruments of macroeconomic policy – is the experience of tax conflicts that is virtually the history of the development of democratic government. Taxes have been about wealth and power, about government, in fact. We should be surprised if the powers for which interests have fought so long and so hard were given away to experts 'who have never won a precinct'. 'When you have decided upon your budget procedure you have decided on the form of government you will have as a *matter of fact*' (Fitzpatrick 1918). The pessimistic implications of the story told in Chapter 2 for the practice of discretionary stabilization policy are clear, and are shown in Chapter 4 to be realized.

The story of monetary policy is similar, although knowledge plays a greater part in its telling. Interests cannot be separated from knowledge. Central bankers, who function in the environment of the financial markets and have inherited with their banker cousins the belief that sound money is good for themselves and necessary to economic stability, resist the temptations of more removed and ambitious goals. They follow their interests, as they feel and understand them, as much as the congressmen who tax and spend. The money-market myopia of central bankers that is vilified by economists finds no place in monetary theory but explains their behavior. Fluctuating inflations have been due to governments wanting cheap finance – sometimes rationalized by equally fluctuating economic theories – rather than to instability in the knowledge or preferences of central bankers.

It is worth emphasizing that interests and customs are not the only impediments to the application of theory. The communication of knowledge is also fraught with difficulties. Even the understanding of a new theory – before its application can be considered – requires the breach of difficult, although sometimes invisible because they are in the mind, obstacles. The dissemination of theory among intellectuals might be thought a low hurdle, but it is seldom accomplished. Rhetoric is easy ('We are all Keynesians now.'), but intellectuals are as liable as practitioners to mold ideas in their own interests. Economists' rejection of Keynes's difficult general (including disequilibrium) theory of an uncertain money economy, preferring the familiar certainty-equivalent equilibrium of a costless real economy, is the subject of Chapter 3. The 'Keynesian revolution' is a case study of the difficulties of communication between groups in the policy chain.

Making the next step, although the purportedly Keynesian economists accepted (many had anticipated) Keynes's interventionist policy proposals, they had little influence on political minds. Applications even of the severely modified form that economists found tractable would have had to survive a complicated and itself uncertain political process that depends on the attitudes and energies of voters and their representatives attempting to manipulate viscous institutions.

The fundamental attitudes of policymakers – politicians and central bankers – have been distant from economic theory, and resistant to the volatile intellectual efforts to change them. The improvement in monetary policy the last three decades in fact has consisted of the government's subordination to the more persistent preferences of central bankers. Theory followed the Fed more than the other way around.

Chapters 5–7 do for monetary policy what Chapters 2–4 did for fiscal policy, giving a history of monetary policy that is another study in the stability of behavior, the mainly sensory determinants of that behavior, and an account of the persistent beliefs and conduct of the Federal Reserve.

Interests are probably sufficient barriers to the application of theories but the barriers are raised by the difficulties of communication – of the transmission of ideas between minds molded by divergent backgrounds, environments, and interests. Theorists and 'practical men' possess fundamentally different – closed vs. open, certain vs. uncertain – visions. The British empiricist philosophers and American pragmatists help explain a good part of the intellectual gap in terms of sensory differences arising from different experiences and environments which generate distinct ideas as well as interests. There are good reasons for the significant and enduring resistance of policy to theory. This book is not an argument that macro-policies ought to be conservative but rather a discussion of the forces that make them so.

Not all economists have believed that policies are straightforward applications of theory. Alfred Marshall distinguished 'economics' and 'political economy', the former being a science available to all regardless of ethical or political views. He believed that the coupling of 'political' with 'economics' wrongly implied 'political interests' that 'the practical man [distinct from the economist/scientist] cannot ignore' (Marshall 1920: 36; Marshall and Marshall 1879: 2; Cannan 1922: 43).

Marshall's interventionist successors have been unable to resist the mixture. Theories are explanations of economic relations that abstract from political, institutional, and cultural complications. However, the temptation to project theories onto actual economies has been irresistible. The distinctions between 'positive' and 'normative' economics, that is, between simplified general explanations and their applications to specific problems are often discussed but seldom taken seriously.

The field of 'public choice' is available to help qualify the exaggerated trust in the practical power of theory, but 'most economists have chosen to ignore the interaction between economic policy and politics' (Laffont 2000: 5). This book does not try to overcome these great problems by modeling the interactions. I only record that the practical influences of theory are small. Interests dominate policies, and largely mold the theories that rationalize them.

This does not mean that economic theory is uninteresting or useless. On the contrary, it provides considerable insights into economic relations. An example is its demonstration of the benefits of free trade, about which, probably more than any other issue, economists agree. So why don't we have free trade? The usual answer is in terms of interests realized through the political process (Riezman and Wilson 1995). Shouldn't this apply to other – fiscal and monetary – theories, as well?

Part I
Fiscal policy

2 Interests
A history of tax conflicts

> When a fellow says it hain't the money but the principle o' the thing, it's th' money.
> (Hubbard 1920)
>
> *Politics*, n. A strife of interests masquerading as a contest of principles.
> (Bierce 1911)

This chapter is a history of tax conflicts in England and the United States. I do not consider the efficiency of taxes directly but examine the interests affecting their adoption and collection. The history of taxes is also the history of the development of democracy. Property rights are personal rights. In his second *Treatise of Civil Government*, the ideas of which 'the principles of the American Revolution were in large part an acknowledged adoption' (Carpenter 1924: 180), John Locke wrote: 'The great and chief end ... of men uniting into commonwealths, and putting themselves under government, is the preservation of their property' (1690b: 180).

The political and social relations between groups of various locations and endowments have played important parts in tax struggles. The purpose of a tax may have been broadly national or imperial but its effectiveness was molded by the detailed political and social fabric of the nation or empire – of the English counties, the colonies, and in the new republic, the conflicting interests of enterprise and geography.

The keen, even violent, interests in government budgets belie those who would dismiss them as 'symbolic' or instruments of control. Governors and governed understood that wealth and power were at stake (Savage 1988: 7).

> it has long been recognized that the history of taxation is the history of 'the English constitution expressed in economic terms', and that 'the English constitution was developed by the necessaries of taxation'.
> (Dietz 1928)

The most famous as well as the most important episodes in the eternal conflict – the only certainties are death and taxes – are summarized in mostly chronological order. I am interested primarily in modern American fiscal policy, but since

8   *Fiscal policy*

American law and experience have grown out of the English, it is useful to begin with the Great Charter of 1215, before moving to the contest over Ship Money that led to the Civil War of the 1640s, the struggle over control of the public purse that was decided by the Glorious Revolution of 1688, and the Stamp Act and other differences between Great Britain and its American colonies leading to the War of Independence. These were followed by tax conflicts in the new republic when citizens sought to apply the principles of the Declaration of Independence from Great Britain to themselves vis-à-vis their state and federal governments. The most enduring tax conflict in the United States has been over tariffs. The continuing debate over defense spending and its finance is close behind. Disputes over both arose in the 1790s, and continue. Taxpayers do not always oppose taxes, such as during the 'missile gap' of the 1950s, when Congress complained that the president was not asking enough for defense.

These are not all the important tax conflicts, but I hope they will be sufficient to show why the economic implications of Keynesian stabilization theory were not accepted, or even considered by politicians or taxpayers, as opposed to intellectual activists. Even if the theory had been accepted, too much was at stake for economic and political interests to yield control.

The Magna Carta

> If any earl, baron, or other person that holds lands directly of the Crown, for military service, shall die, and at his death his heir shall be of full age and owe a 'relief', the heir shall have his inheritance on payment of the ancient scale of 'relief'. That is to say, the heir or heirs of an earl shall pay £100 for the entire earl's barony, the heir or heirs of a knight at most £5 for the entire knight's fee, and any man that owes less shall pay less, in accordance with the ancient usage of 'fees'.

Thus runs a translation of the second clause of the Great Charter that King John was compelled to accept by the nobles assembled at Runnymede, outside London, in 1215. John's imagination and ruthlessness in finding and collecting taxes, primarily for military efforts to retain his lands in France, had aroused dissension among the nobles, and his failures, especially the loss of Normandy, had reduced his status and opened the way to successful resistance.

The clauses are not numbered in the charter, but of the 63 issues that are usually identified, most are restrictions on the king's authority to command resources (Jennings 1965: 44–7). Prominent are limits on regular taxes, such as the inheritance fees noted above, and special levies for the king's military ventures. Procedures for assessing taxes are also specified, as in clause 12:

> No 'scutage' [payment in lieu of military service] or 'aid' may be levied in our kingdom without general consent, unless it is for the ransom of our person, to make our eldest son a knight, and (once) to marry our eldest daughter. For these purposes only a reasonable 'aid' may be levied.

Clauses on the administration of justice sought to secure property from arbitrary seizure. Court fines were limited to amounts 'in proportion to the degree of the offence', in the judgment of 'reputable men of the neighbourhood' (clause 20), and 'ordinary lawsuits shall not follow the royal court around, but shall be held in a fixed place' (clause 17). Further protections of property prohibited the king from seizing goods without payment, limited his ability to claim lands as his private forests, and protected towns and persons from being 'forced to build bridges over rivers except those with an ancient obligation to do so' (clause 23).

Clauses 48–62 promised to abandon or reverse several of the king's practices during recent hostilities between the king's men and his adversaries, such as the release of hostages, removal of foreign troops, return of forests and castles, and pardoning of opponents, the fulfillment of which was guaranteed by the provision that 'The barons shall elect twenty-five of their number to keep, and cause to be observed with all their might, the peace and liberties granted and confirmed to them by this charter.'

The document was evidently written in haste by many hands in the midst of bargaining. Most of its clauses dealt with particular grievances rather than general principles of law. It was an 'intensely practical document', F.W. Maitland (1902) wrote, 'the fit prologue for those intensely practical statutes which English Parliaments will publish in age after age'.

> It is worthy of its place just because it is no philosophical or oratorical declaration of the rights of man.... [I]t is a grand compromise, and a fit prologue for all those thousands of compromises in which the practical wisdom of the English race will always be expressing itself. Its very form is a compromise – in part that of a free grant of liberties made by the king, in part that of a treaty between him and his subjects.... And then in its detailed clauses it must do something for all those sorts and conditions of men who have united to resist John's tyranny – for the bishop, the clerk, the baron, the knight, the burgess, the merchant – and there must be some give and take between these classes, for not all their interests are harmonious.

This *'practicability'*, according to William McKechnie (1914: 121–2),

> is an English characteristic, and strikes the key-note of almost every great movement for reform which has succeeded in English history.... While democratic enthusiasts in France and America have often sought to found their liberties on a lofty but unstable basis of philosophical theory embodied in Declarations of Rights, Englishmen have occupied lower but surer ground, aiming at practical remedies for actual wrongs.

We will see that the English have not been free of the urge to try to collect taxes in the face of popular opposition.

Magna Carta was not the beginning of limited government in England. 'The traditional view' is that Magna Carta was a direct descendant of Henry II's

10 Fiscal policy

Coronation Charter (1154), which was an amplification of the old coronation oath sworn by William the Conqueror (1066), in terms borrowed from a long line of Anglo-Saxon kings until its origin is lost in the mists of antiquity (McKechnie 1914: 93). This does not deny its frequent lack of application under strong kings and in periods of disorder. Liberties (*liberties* of subjects to retain their property and *limits* of kings to take it were used interchangeably) were restored or improved when kings were in weak positions. John obtained the Pope's annulment of Magna Carta, but he died soon thereafter, and it was reissued with modifications by his infant son's (Henry III) advisors in 1216, and was confirmed many times, as in 1297, when several earls and the citizens of London refused to vote supplies to Edward I until he confirmed the Charter, particularly renouncing the right to tax the nation without its consent (Green 1887 i: 346).

The absence of machinery for enforcement was a shortcoming of the Charter. It was also subject to conflicting interpretations, and portions fell out of use. It was made a living document as much by its general thrust as by its specific clauses. The idea of limited government by common consent influenced Englishmen throughout the middle-ages even when they could not have recited any of the Charter's passages or even knew that several versions existed. More important than any clause was the idea of the 'rule of law' (Dicey 1908: 179). What men saw in the charter 'was not a body of specific law but that the King's action was bound and limited, and the community possessed the right to coerce him' (Adams 1912: 251).

Edward Jenks contended in 'The myth of Magna Carta' that as the product of selfish barons concern only with their own interests it was 'a stumbling block in the path of progress'. In fact his lament called attention to one of the Charter's strengths. Liberties are not granted. They are taken. It was left to commoners to follow the example of the nobles in exploiting the idea of limits on their governors in turn. Over time, as the ideas in the Charter took hold,

> For an aggrieved man, however humble, to base his rights upon [the charter] was to enlist the sympathy of all. Time and again, from the Barons' war against Henry III to the days of John Hampden and Oliver Cromwell, the possibility of appealing to the words of Magna Carta has afforded a practical ground for opposition; an easily intelligible principle to fight for.
> (McKechnie 1914: 128)

In 1770, Lord Chatham (the elder William Pitt) told the House of Lords that the barons deserved the gratitude of posterity for obtaining 'from their Sovereign that great acknowledgment of national rights contained in the Magna Carta [because] they did not confine it to themselves alone, but delivered it as a common blessing to the whole people', including colonists. He was responding to George III's opening address to Parliament that criticized the 'unwarrantable' conduct of Americans in resisting taxes (Almon 1792 ii: 7).

We may accept the barons' selfishness as well as their good example. Their behavior was as much an infection as an example, but every group must act for itself. The methods and goals of the barons anticipated those of our founding fathers. Writing of the New Jersey campaign, David Fischer (2004: 139) observed that

> Thomas Paine and the men of the Continental army shared a deep devotion to the American cause [in 1776], but they thought about it in different ways. From the greenest private to the commander-in-chief, most men in the army were American Whigs [defined below], fighting for their own rights. Paine was an English radical, fighting for everybody's rights.

Captain Alexander Graydon (1846: 188) remembered that Paine, who was welcome in the American camp, formed the impression that Washington

> embarked with him in the general cause of reforming, republicanizing, and democratizing the world; than which nothing was more foreign to the views of the General or those of the others who took a lead in the early stage of the contest. One of the most untoward consequences of a successful resistance of government is the unavoidable association in the undertaking of the worst men with the best, of fools, fanatics, system-mongers, reformers and *philosophers* with men of sense, moderation and virtue, who, wishing to stop when the true object of the controversy is attained, are seldom suffered to do it, or if fortunate enough to prevail, they are thenceforth viewed with suspicion and charged with apostacy. Thus General Washington is accused by this incendiary of having deserted his principles because of his not aiding and comforting him in his design of first revolutionizing England, and then France.

Ship-money

Though not asleep, Magna Carta was not in the forefront of politics after the thirteenth century until it was brought forward in the seventeenth century by a combination of legal scholarship and events. Justice Sir Edward Coke found ancient precedents to support the position that conflicts between statutes and the royal prerogative should be resolved by judges. This was potent intellectual ammunition for the taxpayers represented by Parliament in their disputes with Charles I (1625–49).

The House of Commons had grown out of the king's council, to which 'he summoned representatives', selected by their neighbors, 'to supply such direct information from the localities as would enable him to control the administrative machinery [and] to facilitate taxation'. The king at first sought information and advice, with no intention of surrendering any of his authority, but the growing wealth of the middle class gave them the power of the purse (Pasquet 1925: x).

This was the period of the Thirty Years War, and although England was not a major player, the young king and his first Parliament agreed on military intervention in the conflict. They differed on several points about the conduct of the war, however, as well as on domestic, especially religious, issues, and Parliament was niggardly in voting supplies. In that readable history of the development of English liberties, Winston Churchill (1956: 181) suggested that Parliament

> sought to use the money-power, of which they were the masters, to induce the king and his ministers to tread these dangerous paths. They knew well ... that the stresses of war would force the Crown to come to them.

They went further

> when they resolved that the customs duties of tonnage and poundage without which the King could not live, even in peace, should for the first time for many reigns be voted, not for the King's life, but for only one year.

Charles got only one-seventh of the money he requested, and when Parliament hinted at steps against his advisors he dissolved it in less than two months. His second and third Parliaments were also dissolved when they conditioned revenue on policy changes. Short of funds, he resorted to 'desperate measures'. Military service was required under martial law and soldiers were billeted in private homes. He called on the counties and boroughs for voluntary payments of funds that Parliament had conditionally offered, 'but from all parts of the country the answer came that money could not be granted "save in a parliamentary way"' (Tanner 1928: 59). Forced loans failed partly because judges found them illegal. Scores who refused to lend were imprisoned without *habeas corpus*, one being John Hampden, a Buckingham landowner and member of Parliament. 'I could be content to lend as well as others,' he told the Privy Council, 'but I fear to draw upon myself the curse in Magna Carta which is to be read twice a year upon those who infringe it' (Adair 1976: 53).

When Charles dissolved Parliament in 1629, he announced that another would not be called until 'his people shall see more clearly into his intents and actions' (*Parliamentary History ii*: 525). Over the next eleven years he tightened the Court's belt, ended his foreign adventures, borrowed as much as he could, sold crown lands and monopolies of doubtful legality, and interpreted the taxes with which he was left more broadly and collected them more aggressively (Wedgwood 1955: 156–61; Tanner 1928: 75–6). Ship-money 'practically saved the exchequer the entire cost of the navy' for a few years (Davies 1938: 80).

It had been the practice in wartime to require seaports to provide ships, or money in lieu thereof, for the king's use. Charles's first call for ship-money, in 1634, accorded with precedent in being limited to seaports and aimed at pirates (Gardiner 1906: 105–8). However, the 1635 call extended to inland counties, and when this was repeated in 1636, collection was resisted. Ship-money threatened to become a permanent tax, and the excuse of a wartime emergency had worn thin. There were always pirates. 'Sometimes resistance became violent; high words and cudgel blows were exchanged between [Squire] Thomas

Cartwright ... and the sheriff's men.' The king was wary of prosecuting resistors for fear of providing a platform from which to attack his policies. However, the 'defiance of subjects could not with safety be tolerated', and *Rex* v. *Hampden* was brought to the Exchequer Court in 1637 (Wedgwood 1955: 158). Hampden had refused to pay the £1 levied on one of his estates – a small sum for a wealthy man, the attorney-general pointed out (Adair 1976: 117).

It is worth saying something about the social and political framework of the country – or countryside – against which Charles I and later his younger son, James II, decided to do battle. The 'English countryside can be considered from many points of view other than that of landlord and tenant,' wrote David Ogg (1955: 122–3). Public office was a duty and privilege for the farmer/landowner. Denial except for reason, such as religious disqualification or on grounds of character, 'was tantamount to violation of his birthright'.

> In this way the county was, not inappropriately, referred to as the 'country', for it was a microcosm of the nation, having its armed force, the militia; its judiciary, the justices in petty or quarter sessions; its local parliaments, such as meetings of the lord lieutenant with the deputy lieutenants, where assessments for the upkeep of the militia might be determined; and the grand juries, which ... often gave expression to opinion on some question of the hour. ...
>
> The county was also a unit in the system of parliamentary representation; not only because it returned two knights of the shire; ... a majority of the parliamentary boroughs were within control of the landed gentry ... ; and to be returned as number one of the two knights of a county was the highest tribute that could be paid by a man's neighbours.

The idea that 'The history of England is the history of her local politics' (Ogg 1955: 122–3) anticipated Congressman Tip O'Neill's assertion three centuries later that 'all politics is local' (1994). Charles I and James II were brought down by the resistance of individual property and privileges that were inseparable from the national stage. Hampden's case was argued over six weeks at the end of 1637, and he was the most famous man in the country. His claim to immortality was strengthened in the next century by Thomas Grey, whose *Elegy in a Country Churchyard* included him among the giants of history:

> Perhaps in this neglected spot is laid
> ...
> Some village-Hampden, that with dauntless breast
>   The little Tyrant of his fields withstood;
> Some mute inglorious Milton here may rest,
> Some Cromwell guiltless of his country's blood.

Hampden's lawyers argued that except in emergencies only Parliament could raise money beyond the king's normal revenue, and the recent claims for ship-money had not been for emergencies. The Court found Hampden guilty by a vote of 7 to 5, agreeing with the prosecution that the king's powers were absolute. To the argument that the king was subject to 'fundamental law', Justice Sir Robert Berkeley said:

> The law knows no such king-yoking power. The law is of itself an old and trusty servant of the King's; it is his instrument or means which he useth to govern his people by. I never heard that lex was Rex; but it is common and most true that *Rex* is *lex*, for he is *lex loquens*, a living, a speaking, an acting law....

It was a maxim of the law of England, Berkeley declared, 'That the King can do no wrong.' Since he is 'bound to defend his people against foreign enemies', he must have the means to that end. Therefore the people are duty-bound 'to yield unto the King supply for the defence of the kingdom'. Being 'the sole judge of the danger', he 'ought to direct the means of defense' (Gardiner 1906: 121-3).

Charles's legal victory hurt him more than it helped. 'This decision marks the beginning of the collapse of the system of arbitrary government' that had begun with the dissolution of Parliament in 1629. The crown was getting by financially, and it is known that ship-money was honestly 'used to build a fleet of great ships which was to serve as the nucleus of the naval power of the Commonwealth in the First Dutch War' (1652-53) (Tanner 1928: 77). However, the 'habit of reverence for law which had been so thoroughly drilled into the English' was turned against the Stuarts. [E]ven in their most high-minded acts the Tudors were scrupulous in observing the forms of the law' (Macy 1909: 272). Charles's claim to the power to override the law on a fancied emergency gave him the reputation of a law-breaker (Tanner 1928: 78).

The Hampden decision 'caused a general loss of confidence in the courts of law'. In his *History of the Rebellion* written shortly thereafter, the Earl of Clarendon suggested that ship-money had been declared lawful 'upon such grounds and reasons as every stander-by was able to swear was not law'. The judges' reasoning 'left no man anything which he might call his own', and all 'found their own interest, by the unnecessary logic of that argument, no less concluded than Mr Hampden's' (1648 i: 87, 91). 'They had nothing to hope for from the judges...; and the only other place where salvation was to be found was in Parliament' (Tanner 1928: 78-9).

The decline in ship-money collections accelerated after the Court's decision. The Sheriff of Buckinghamshire did not press 'the matter because he listened too much to his kindred and friends', the Privy Council was told. None of the county's assessment for 1639 was paid (Adair 1976: 124).

Even so, Charles might have maintained his independence of Parliament if Scotland had not rebelled against his religious policies. Attempts to anglicize the Presbyterian organization of the Church of Scotland provoked expulsion of the 'pretended English bishops' in 1639, the organization of a government, and a declaration of war (Tanner 1928: 86). The two countries had been governed together in the Union of the Crowns since 1603, when James VI (of the House of Stuart) of Scotland became James I of England (Brown 1902 ii: 240).

In April 1640, unable to raise an army, Charles summoned the Short Parliament, so-called because it was dismissed after three weeks for demanding the redress of grievances before considering the king's financial needs. In less than six months he had to resort to another Parliament, which became the Long Parliament because it refused to be dissolved, asserted sovereignty, and waged war against the king.

Parliament won the Civil War, executed the king in 1649, and formed the Commonwealth. Parliament reigned by virtue of the army. In 1653, the head of the army, Oliver Cromwell, became lord protector. His difficulties with Parliament and the country were not unlike Charles's. Unable to deal with the myriad of religious and other issues to the general satisfaction, and with the declining legitimacy of unrepresentative Parliaments, taxes became increasingly difficult to collect. An official in London responded to a general's complaint from Ireland about arrears in pay: 'We are so out at the heels here that I know not what we shall do for money' (Tanner 1928: 210).

Fifteen months after the protector's death in 1658, General George Monk brought his army from Scotland to London to settle the differences between Parliament and its army. He called Parliament to meet in February 1660, on condition that it would reach a settlement with the army, dissolve itself within a month, and call a new Parliament for 20 April. Monk negotiated the Declaration of Breda, issued from Holland on 4 April by Charles II (eldest son of Charles I), promising

> that all our subjects may enjoy what by law is theirs, by a full and entire administration of justice,... a free and general pardon,... liberty of ... opinion in matter of religion, [and] all arrears due to the officers and soldiers of the army.
>
> (Gardiner 1906: 465–6)

Charles II was greeted by a royalist Parliament when he landed at Dover in May.

'The Great Rebellion ... had collapsed from within' (Woolrych 1958). The public's unwillingness to pay taxes levied otherwise than by a legitimate Parliament brought the Commonwealth down as it had the monarchy. The Stuarts were back but they had better be careful.

The Glorious Revolution

The restoration of the monarchy was popular but Parliament was determined to hold tight to the reins of finance for which it had fought. Progress had been made in securing the government's revenue the past twenty years, notably in new land assessments and excise taxes. The old occasional levies on personal wealth were replaced by monthly assessments collected by citizens after

16 Fiscal policy

Parliament fixed the liability of a county or borough, and 'Like so much of our present-day taxation', W.M.J. Williams (1908: 47) wrote, 'the Excise had its origin in the days of the Commonwealth and the Restoration.'

Parliament fixed the ordinary revenue of Charles II at £1,200,000, with £100,000 from Crown lands, £400,000 from customs, and £100,000 in place of the feudal dues over which King John and the barons had fought but no longer existed (Hill 1961: 148). Excises on beer, cider, tea, and other drinks would make up some of the difference, but more was needed, and a new tax called 'hearth-money' was levied on houses. A critic observed: 'Tis the general opinion of some that this Parliament, being most of all landed men and few traders, will never take away the excise, because their own burdens will thereupon become greater' (Hill 1961: 216–17). Tax historian William Kennedy (1913: 67) wrote: 'The acceptance in the seventeenth century of the doctrine that the poor man should pay taxation is one of the landmarks in English political opinion.'

Though not the heaviest, the most offensive tax was hearth-money.

> The discontent excited by direct imposts is, indeed, almost always out of proportion to the quantity of money which they bring into the Exchequer; and the tax on chimneys was, even among direct imposts, peculiarly odious: for it could be levied only by means of domiciliary visits; and of such visits the English have always been impatient to a degree which the people of other countries can but faintly conceive. The poorer householders were frequently unable to pay their hearth money to the day. When this happened, their furniture was distained without mercy.... The collectors [called chimney-men] were loudly accused of performing their unpopular duty with harshness and insolence. It was said that, as soon as they appeared at the threshold of a cottage, the children began to wail and the old women ran to hide their earthenware.
>
> (Macaulay 1855 i: 287)

The hearth tax was repealed after the Glorious Revolution 'in order', said the Act, 'to erect a lasting monument of their Majesties' goodness in every hearth in the kingdom' (Dowell 1888 iii: 167).

Regularization of the king's accounts did not end financial conflict. Charles II's needs exceeded his legislated revenues because of his lifestyle, a personal military force that grew to 8,700 men at the time of his death, and payments – called 'pensions' – to persons in public life with the expectation of their support (Tanner 1928: 224). Their extensive use, captured in the name given to the Pension Parliament of 1661–79, continued under James II and afterward. Samuel Johnson defined them in his *Dictionary* (1755):

> *Pension.* An allowance made to anyone without an equivalent. In England it is generally understood to mean pay given to a state hireling for treason to his country.[1]

In 1780, during an unpopular war and an escalating national debt, the House of Commons resolved 'that the influence of the Crown has increased, is increasing, and ought to be diminished', and affirmed its right to inquire into all areas of public spending. The 'economical reformers' led by Edmund Burke were helped by Cornwallis's surrender at Yorktown in October 1781. The king had pushed the war with the support of pensioners. The Commons were petitioned by London, Bristol, and other places complaining of depressed trade that required 'the abandonment of the war and relief to the burdened taxpayer'. In February 1782, the House moved to address the king against a continuance of the war, and the prime minister resigned. Government contractors were excluded from the House of Commons, several superfluous offices and clerkships were abolished, and the Pensions List was reduced and ordered to be reported to Parliament. George Veitch wrote in *The Genesis of Parliamentary Reform* (1913: 80) that 'Burke could have received no higher praise than a disgusted politician gave unwittingly when he complained that "Burke's foolish Bill" had made it a very difficult task for any set of men either to form or maintain an administration'.

Returning to the Merry Monarch, Charles II was as resourceful as his father in finding financial expedients. In addition to his greater willingness to compromise on religious and other issues, the son's pursuit of finance was assisted by the financial revolution that was underway. The Exchequer borrowed from the goldsmith bankers and anticipated tax receipts with interest-bearing paper issued for goods and services, redeemable for coin in order of their issue as taxes were collected. Charles's credit was insufficient for the unpopular and unsuccessful war against the Dutch that he joined with Louis XIV as a junior ally in 1672–74, and he defaulted on his debt. Partial payment was eventually resumed but Charles's credit never 'really recovered' (Feavearyear 1931: 104). This was one of the 'reasons why the City welcomed the Liberator [in 1688], under whom £1,300,000 was at last repaid to Charles II's bankers' (Hill 1961: 221).

The power of pensions was not unlimited, and in 1677,

> the House of Commons presented an address to the King praying him to make such alliances as would secure the kingdom, quiet the people, and save the Spanish Netherlands, and it was intimated that as soon as the desired alliances had been entered into, plentiful supplies would be forthcoming.
> (Tanner 1928: 237)

Charles was astonished and not above manufacturing history:

> You have intrenched upon so undoubted a right of the Crown that I am confident it will appear in no age ... that the prerogative of making peace and war hath been so dangerously invaded.
> (*Parliamentary History iv*: 899)

Of course those who control finance determine whether war is fought. That control was also fought over in the early (and later) United States. At first,

Congress voted appropriations in lump sums. The sole appropriations bill of 1789 was thirteen lines long and identified four items: civil and military expenses, the public debt, and pensions. Secretary of the Treasury Alexander Hamilton did not think more detail was necessary. This did not satisfy Congress, and although an inquiry found no dishonesty in the Treasury's accounts, 'there had been an application of some specific appropriations to objects other than those directed'. An act of 1800 directed the Treasury secretary to 'digest, prepare, and lay before Congress, at the commencement of every session, a report on the subject of finance, containing estimates of the public revenue and public expenditures...' (Dewey 1928: 116). In 1809, Congress ordered expenditures to be limited to the purposes for which they were appropriated (Bolles 1894 ii: 189–90).

The king was more strongly situated in 1677 than the American president the next century, and adjourned Parliament rather than capitulate. Renewed confrontation was avoided when Parliament resumed because the political situation had changed. The king 'was able of his own accord to announce an alliance with Holland and Spain against France' (Tanner 1928: 237). Charles was increasingly able to get along without Parliament because of his ability to borrow, the sale of Crown lands (most of the little that had been left by Charles I), and prosperity that brought increases in customs and excise. He also neglected security and other public services. The failures to protect British shipping from piracy or French threats, or 'even to provide convoys to bring coal from Newcastle reminded men how much better trade had been protected under Cromwell' (Hill 1961: 216).

When Charles died without legitimate issue in 1685, and was succeeded by his brother, James II, people grumbled about the new king's Catholicism. However, they desired political stability and gave him leeway. His main goal turned out to be the removal of restrictions on Catholics in public offices and the practice of their religion, which required friendly Parliaments, or better, independence of them. Two days after his accession he wrote to the French ambassador:

> I have resolved to call a Parliament immediately and to assemble it in the month of May. I shall publish at the same time a declaration that I am to maintain myself in the enjoyment of the same revenues the King my brother had.... It is a decisive stroke for me to enter into possession and enjoyment. For hereafter it will be much more easy for me either to put off the assembling of Parliament or to maintain myself by other means which may appear more convenient for me.
>
> (Speck 1988: 43)

Things went well for a while. James obtained what he hoped would be a malleable Parliament by active electioneering and liberal spending. Two hundred (of 513) members of the Parliament that assembled in May 1685 'were directly dependent on the king for their livelihood' and '400 had never sat in the House before'. Bribery was rampant. A minister felt justified in publicly reprimanding a member who had voted against the crown: 'Sir! Have you not got a troop of horse in His Majesty's Service?' 'Yes, my lord, but my brother died last night and has left me £700 a year' (Hill 1961: 230–4).

'Luck further strengthened James's hand' in the form of rebellions led by the Duke of Monmouth (an illegitimate son of Charles II) in the West Country and the Presbyterian Earl of Argyll in the Scottish highlands (Smith 1999: 162; Ogg 1955: 144–8). The country rallied behind the king, and in June Parliament voted him the revenues for life that it had granted his brother periodically. The customs and excise alone brought him more than Charles had received. 'So the government slipped from under the financial yoke which Parliament had intended to place upon it, thanks to the country's prosperity' (Hill 1961: 220).

The king's independence could not be stretched indefinitely, however. The more realistic Charles II had understood that his position rested on property, especially the Tory landed gentry that was committed to the established church. 'I will stick by you and my old friends', Charles had told a Tory supporter in 1680, 'for if I do not I should have nobody to stick to me' (Hill 1961: 232). 'Tory' was the name of one of the two main political parties, or more appropriately broad political views since party organizations did not exist. The other was 'Whig'. The names arose during the Exclusion Crisis of 1678–81 to distinguish those who wanted to exclude Catholics from the throne, the Whigs, from those who defended the lawful succession, the Tories. The Whigs favored the idea of a contract between the king 'under the law' and his subjects, who were entitled to resist misgovernment. They were found most often in the rising professional and commercial classes (Macaulay 1855 i: 257).

All were anxious to avoid another civil war:

> This is the essential if usually unspoken background to late seventeenth-century politics. The propertied classes could not forget the lesson [of military rule] they had learnt in 1646–60, just as kings did not forget the lesson of 1649 [Charles I's execution]. So political opposition was never pushed to extremes;... The House of Commons might criticize, but did not fundamentally oppose government, so long as government did not attack the interests of those whom the members represented.
> (Smith 1999: 61)

James's religious fervor drew him across these lines. His fall, Bishop Gilbert Burnet (1724 i: 341) wrote, was

> one of the strangest catastrophes that is in any history. A great king, with strong armies and mighty fleets, a vast treasure, and powerful allies, fell all at once: and his whole strength, like a spider's web, was ... irrecoverably broken at a touch.

The explanation lay in James's assault on his twin pillars of support, beginning with the open practice of his religion and the appointment of officials in defiance of the Test Act which required them to receive the Sacrament publicly according to the rites of the Church of England. Parliament refused James's requests to repeal the Test and Habeas Corpus Acts, and he prorogued it in November 1685, not to meet again during his reign.

Financially secure and with an army periodically concentrated near London to impress the populace, James felt free to pursue his religious and political objectives. He used his dispensing power to bring Catholics into the government, imposed them on the universities, and established an Ecclesiastical Commission to control the clergy. He also began to develop a party organization for support in the country. For this he needed the support of dissenters (non-Anglican protestants), in whose favor he dismissed uncooperative and often long-standing county and borough officials.

Having learned little from his father's experiences, James attacked the social as well as the economic fabric of England by assaulting the long-standing relationships on which local government depended. Leading gentry were dismissed from local offices 'unless they would pledge their support for repeal of the Test Act. And who replaced them? Ordinary persons both as to quality and estates (most of them dissenters).... It was too much even for Tory loyalty.' Lord Keeper Guilford had warned in 1684 that if the gentry were discontented, 'the whole use of the law is lost; for they are sheriffs, etc.' (Hill 1961: 236–7).

The king was 55 years old and the country seemed willing to wait for the end of his reign, when he would be succeeded by his Protestant daughter, Mary. However, on 10 June 1688, James's second wife, the Spanish princess Mary of Modena, gave birth to a son who would certainly be raised as a Catholic. On 30 June, Whigs and Tories sent an invitation to the Dutch William of Orange, Princess Mary's husband and a grandson of Charles I, to come to England with an armed force. William landed in November, and James, whose army had melted away, fled to France. The decision to place the army close to London had backfired as the camp became a popular gathering place.

> In truth the place was merely a gay suburb of the capital. The King ... had gravely miscalculated. He had forgotten that vicinity operates in more ways than one. He had hoped that his army would overawe London: but the result of his policy was that the feelings and opinions of London took complete possession of the army.
>
> (Macaulay 1855 ii: 758)

Contracts and commitments

The Glorious Revolution of 1688–89 has been seen as a triumph of property in which government was converted from oppressor to protector. The other side of the contract – property's payment – was the land tax.

William III (1689–1702) wanted England's support in the war that the Dutch and its allies were fighting against Louis XIV. The English leaders shared the desire for security against France and wanted a king who would provide stable government under the law. They had found that if they kept the king poor, as they tried with Charles II, public services and security suffered. On the other hand, if they allowed him sufficient funds, as they did for James II, he would be free to pursue unpopular policies. James had been more interested in a standing army to be used against his subjects than a navy for defense against France and the protection of trade. When he ordered the fleet anchored in the Thames to intercept the Dutch, the admiral responded: 'Your majesty knows what condition you left the fleet in.' The navy's reluctance to come to the king's aid might have been as much disloyalty as unreadiness, but in January 1688, an inspector had scraped rust 'as thick as a milled shilling' from gun bores (Ogg 1955: 216).

The Convention Parliament that assembled after James's flight was determined to correct these mistakes.

> William Sacheverell, a Whig, urged the Commons to 'secure this House, that Parliaments be duly chosen and not kicked out at pleasure, which never could have been done without such an extravagant revenue that they might never stand in need of Parliaments'. Paul Foley, a Tory, expressed similar views: 'If you settle such a revenue as that the King should have no need of a Parliament, I think we do not our duty to them that send us hither.'
>
> (Smith 1999: 61)

The new arrangements were credible because they provided for commitment by the parties. The Glorious Revolution aimed at a solution to one of history's dilemmas, 'the control of coercive power by the state for social ends' (North and Weingast 1989). Promises and good intentions are not enough. What is required is a self-enforcing constitution. The problems were essentially fiscal and consisted primarily of two parts: Englishmen wanted the king to be free of incentives to seize property, force or renege on loans, sell monopolies, or impose illegal taxes. They also wanted to ensure that government revenues would be applied to the purposes the taxpayers intended.

The solution also had two parts: satisfaction of the king's financial requirements as a matter of course instead of uncertainly and inefficiently in contests with Parliament; and parliamentary legal supremacy, or rather supremacy of 'the king in Parliament'. The method was substitution of the national debt for the king's purse. Instead of voting money to the king and hoping for the best, Parliament would allocate funds to the appropriate departments and monitor them.

This was easier resolved than accomplished. Parliament had adopted the principle of supply – taxation for specific uses – in 1665, but was unhappy with the government's practice of borrowing against future taxes to avoid its control. The fault was partly Parliament's because of the undependability of its votes, the uncertainty of customs and excise revenues, and the slackness of local officials reluctant or unable to collect assessments on themselves or their friends (Douglas 1999: 10).

However, even under the Pension Parliament discussed above, 'the great English revolution of the seventeenth century, that is, to say, the transfer of the supreme control of the executive administration from the crown to the House of Commons, was proceeding noiselessly, but rapidly and steadily' (Macaulay 1855 i: 131–2).

> no English legislature, however loyal, would now consent to be merely what the legislature had been under the Tudors…. The gentlemen who, after the Restoration, filled the Lower House, though they abhorred the Puritan name, were well pleased to inherit the fruit of the Puritan policy. They were indeed most willing to employ the power which they possessed in the state for the purpose of making their King mighty and honoured, both at home and abroad: but with the power itself they were resolved not to part.

Tax collections began to go to the Treasury instead of directly to the various departments. William was voted £700,000 a year for life, much less than Charles II or James II, for the courts and civil government – the civil list. A supporter complained that the king was kept 'as it were at board wages' (Grellier 1810: 22). Even they were scrutinized. In 1696, Parliament directed a commission to examine the government's accounts from 5 November 1688 (when William landed in England)

> to the intent that their Majesties and this kingdom may be satisfied and truly informed whether all the same revenues, moneys, and provisions have been faithfully issued out, disposed, ordered, and expended for the ends and purposes aforesaid; and that their Majesties' loyal subjects may thereby be encouraged more chearfully to undergo the like burthens for the support of their Majesties government and the farther prosecution of the war.
> (Grellier 1810: 24)

The weapon of finance had brought the king under the law, but that left Parliament. An exchange of dictators might not be an improvement. The new arrangement depended on diversity in Parliament and frequent elections. The Triennial Act of 1694 required a new Parliament at least every three years, although this was extended to seven years in 1715, in order, depending on the argument, to reduce the electoral burden or provide stability. The lives of Parliaments had been limited only by the king's pleasure. The king continued to be important in his power to dissolve Parliament and form ministries, that is, to take the lead in policy, which, however, to be effective required the support of the taxpayers' representatives.

The principal financial commitment of Parliament was the adoption of the land tax as a permanent measure. Land taxes were very old, and the major source of revenue locally. At the national level they had been reserved for war emergencies. They now began to be the main revenue nationally as well as locally, and because Parliament consisted principally of property owners, a large portion of the taxes they voted were on themselves (Grellier 1810: 18–20, 53–4). The king was constrained but assured of a living wage; Parliament was supreme but paid for it.

The composition of revenues changed as the century progressed, with customs and excise both overtaking the land tax (Mitchell 1962: 386–8), but the system proved sufficient for the government's needs. In spite – or because – of ministers' worries about the rising national debt resulting from major wars, interest rates were almost unaffected by government deficits (Barro 1987).

The Stamp Act: taxation without representation

Americans would have been surprised at being called impractical. They also saw their liberties in their interests. What are liberties except the freedoms to pursue one's interests? Although a considerable portion of the Declaration of Independence was devoted to principles – it was, after all, an appeal to 'the opinions of mankind' – two-thirds was addressed to immediate grievances such as 'quartering large bodies of armed troops among us [and] imposing taxes on us without our consent'. Taxation was at the heart of the American revolutionary struggle as much as those between King John and the barons and the Stuarts and Parliament. The *Instructions of the Town of Braintree to their Representative* to the Stamp Act Congress (written and carried out by John Adams, 1765) declared that in its intent to tax the unrepresented the Stamp Act was 'directly repugnant to the Great Charter itself'. Benjamin Franklin had warned the British government against taxing the colonies in 1754, telling the royal governor of Massachusetts that

> the People in the Colonies are as loyal as any Subjects in the King's Dominion's; that there is no reason to doubt the Readiness and Willingness of their Representatives to grant ... such Supplies for the Defence of the Country as shall be judg'd necessary, so far as their Abilities will allow.

They

> who are to feel the immediate Mischiefs of Invasion and Conquest by an enemy ... are likely to be better Judges of the ... Forces necessary..., and of their own Abilities to bear the Expence, than the Parliament of England at so great a Distance.
> (*Franklin* 1962 v: 444)[2]

George Grenville was blamed 'for inaugurating a policy towards the American colonies that resulted in their loss', although the prime minister who succeeded Pitt in 1763, after the expensive Seven Years War, was not the first British politician to think the colonies should be made to share the costs of their defense. They knew that taxing the colonies would not be easy. They did not wish to harm trade and realized that decades of managing their own affairs had given the Americans confidence in their self-government. A few saw the possibility of separation. Grenville was warned that the colonists 'entertain some extraordinary opinions regarding their relationship to and dependence on their Mother Country' (Bullion 1982: 2).

Collections of trade duties were trifling. It was complained in Parliament that 'smugglers of molasses instead of being infamous are called patriots in North America'. Customs revenues from America were less than the costs of collection. Those at home were not much better. Someone at the Treasury 'noticed in the account books that no goods from France or Italy legally entered Scotland between 1756 and 1762' (Bullion 1982: 99, 56).

The primary purpose of the customs service had not been revenue but trade regulation in the interests of British shipping and exporters (Dickerson 1951: 295). However, by new duties more rigorously enforced, the American Revenue Act of 1764 (called the Sugar Act because its duty on molasses drew the most attention) was designed 'for improving the revenue of this kingdom' (Pickering 1807 xxvi: 33–52).

This would be insufficient with even the most favorable results, and officials looked for something more. They settled on the stamp duty that had been employed in England since 1694 (Dowell 1965 iii: 286). The Stamp Act of February 1765, to become effective 1 November, required stamps on newspapers, pamphlets, and playing cards, as well as legal documents such as licenses, deeds, bills of sale, and affidavits. It was impossible (so the legislators thought) to do business without them. A Treasury secretary wrote that the stamp tax 'is not subject to the frauds to which Customs House duties are liable, nor to the severities of excise,… nor is it necessary to enter any man's doors for the purpose of collecting it'. Grenville told the House of Commons that it was 'the least objectionable' tax Parliament could impose on the colonies 'because it requires few officers and even collects itself' (Bullion 1982: 104).

A critic warned:

> The safety of this country consists in this with respect that we cannot lay a tax on others without taxing ourselves. This is not the case in America. We shall tax them in order to ease ourselves. We ought therefore to be extremely delicate in imposing a burden upon others which we not only not share ourselves but which is to take it far from us.
> (Sir William Meredith, House of Commons, 6 February 1765)

The bill passed with a large majority and received the Royal Assent on 22 March. The government had moved cautiously. It knew the tax would not be popular. However, neither it nor the opposition, nor even the Americans who had been consulted, foresaw the violence of the reaction in the colonies. Franklin, who had argued against the tax as a colonial agent in London, thought he would have to live with it and petitioned successfully for a friend for the position of stamp commissioner for Pennsylvania (Brands 2000: 363).

Protests erupted as soon as the news crossed the Atlantic. On 29 May, Patrick Henry offered five resolutions to the Virginia House of Burgesses, beginning:

> Resolved, That the first Adventurers and Settlers of this his Majesties Colony and Dominion brought with them and transmitted to their

> Posterity and all other his Majesties Subjects since inhabiting in this his Majestie's said Colony all the Privileges, Franchises and Immunities that have at any Time been held, enjoyed, and possessed by the People of Great Britain.

These rights had been affirmed by time and royal charters, and furthermore:

> That the Taxation of the People by themselves or by Persons chosen by themselves to represent them who can only know what Taxes the People are able to bear and the easiest Mode of raising them and are equally affected by such Taxes Themselves is the distinguishing Characteristic of British Freedom and without which the ancient Constitution cannot subsist.
> Therefore that the General Assembly of this colony have the only and sole exclusive Right and Power to lay Taxes and Impositions upon the Inhabitants of this Colony and that every Attempt to vest such Power in any Person or Persons whatsoever other than the General Assembly aforesaid has a manifest Tendency to destroy British as well as American Freedom.
> (Van Schreeven and Scribner 1973 i: 17–18)

The resolutions were adopted, and although the last was rescinded, the point had been made. Other colonial legislatures adopted similar resolutions and sent protests to England. In Virginia, the magistrates of Westmoreland County resigned rather than enforce the Act and those in Northumberland County operated without stamps on the ground that they were unconstitutional (Van Schreeven and Scribner 1973 i: 19–20).

The Sugar Act had sparked a step toward colonial unity in 1764 in Committees of Correspondence to share information and possibly develop a common policy. Delegates from nine colonies came to what was called the Stamp Act Congress in New York in October 1765, and agreed on grievances and declarations of rights essentially like Virginia's to be placed before His Majesty and Parliament (Weslager 1976: 59, 200–14; Thomas 1992: 66–8).

More effective than these formal protests were violent outbreaks throughout the colonies. In Boston, on 14 August, a mob burned the new stamp commissioner in effigy, demolished his house, and tore down the newly erected stamp office. The commissioner resigned, but over the next several weeks crowds attacked the houses of the governor and citizens thought to favor the Stamp Act (Morgan and Morgan 1995: 129–45). In Philadelphia, the stamp commissioner and Franklin's family had to plead with the mob to save their properties (Brands 2000: 366–7). By 1 November, there was no one in the colonies who would try to collect the tax. The ports of New York, Philadelphia, and Boston announced boycotts of British goods (Thomas 1992: 19).

Colonists rejoiced when Grenville was replaced in July 1765, although his fall owed more to a personal conflict with George III than to the Stamp Act's problems. The king agreed with Grenville and Parliament that the colonies were unreservedly subject to British law. On the other hand, Grenville might have made a more determined effort to apply the Act than the conciliatory Rockingham ministry that followed.

Before the end of 1765, it was clear the Stamp Act would not go into operation. The government's 'dilemma was that any concession would be unacceptable to British political opinion because it would be seen too obviously to be a surrender to mob violence' (Thomas 1992: 20). The debate on repeal showed three positions. Grenville contended that the Act should be enforced. William Pitt argued the principle that it was wrong to tax America. He agreed with those who asserted 'the authority of this kingdom over the colonies to be sovereign and supreme in every circumstance of government and legislation whatever'. However,

> It is my opinion that this kingdom has no right to lay a tax upon the colonies.... Taxation is no part of the governing or legislative power. The taxes are a voluntary *gift* and *grant* of the Commons alone.
>
> In ancient days, the Crown, the barons, and the clergy possessed the land ... and gave and granted to the Crown ... what was their own!

Since then the Commons had come to represent the wealth of the country.

> When, therefore, in this house we give and grant, we give and grant what is our own. But in an American tax, what do we do? We, your majesty's Commons for Great Britain, give and grant to your majesty – what? Our own property! No! We give and grant to your majesty the property of your majesty's Commons of America. It is an absurdity in terms.

Americans were represented by no one in the House of Commons, even *virtually*.

> The Commons of America represented in their several assemblies have ever been in possession of this, their constitutional right, of giving and granting their own money. They would have been slaves if they had not enjoyed it!
>
> (House of Commons, 14 January 1766)

The House supported the government's middle course 'that Parliament's undoubted right of taxation ought not to be exercised at the expense of British trade' (Thomas 1992: 20–1). The government tried to make the Stamp Act's repeal palatable at home by declaring Parliament's 'full power ... to bind the colonies ... in all cases whatsoever', making 'null and void' resolutions and votes in the colonies denying the power of Parliament (Thomas 1992: 69–70; Pickering 1807 xxvii: 19–20). The Declaratory Act passed with little opposition, although twenty-eight members of the House of Lords sent a dissent to the Commons complaining that the face-saving measure 'cannot possibly obviate the growing Mischiefs in America', and seems calculated only to deceive the People of Great Britain by holding forth a delusive and nugatory Affirmance of the Legislative Right of this Kingdom, whilst the Enacting Part of it does no more than abrogate the Resolutions of the ... Colonies, which have not in themselves the least Colour of Authority; and declares that, which is apparently and certainly criminal, only null and void.

(Simmons and Thomas 1983: 351)

British governments never found an American policy. They were unable to sustain an effort to make the colonies pay. What looked like attempts to raise revenue degenerated into assertions of authority, though to what purpose was unclear. Most of the customs duties enacted on the advice of Chancellor of the Exchequer Charles Townshend in 1767 were withdrawn in 1769 – 'upon consideration of such duties having been laid contrary to the true principles of commerce' (Thomas 1992: 72) – after colonial protests and small collections.

Only the tax on tea was kept. It was the most profitable and would help defray the expenses of government in the colonies, tea was not a British product, and the tax would be an outward but unobtrusive, it was hoped, manifestation of Parliament's authority. The government was again surprised by the reaction. Colonists were already upset by the growing tendency to free colonial administrations from financial dependence on local assemblies by paying the salaries of governors and other officials out of customs duties. They would rather pay the taxes necessary to government themselves, and have the control that went with it (Thomas 1992: 24, 33).

The attempt to sell taxed tea, even at a low cost to reduce the East India Company's inventory, led to the Boston Tea Party in December 1773, punishment of the town in the Coercive Acts that united the colonies behind Boston, and the meeting of the Continental Congress in September 1774. The Battle of Lexington and Concord followed in April 1775 (Labaree 1964: vi).

The Great Conservative, Edmund Burke, warned Parliament that, whatever the abstract rights and wrongs of the matter, it could not compel revenue from America, and that attempts to do so or even to declare that it had the right to do so, only produced enmity and strife.

I am not here going into the distinctions of rights, not attempting to mark their boundaries. I do not enter into these metaphysical distinctions; I hate the very sound of them. Leave the Americans as they anciently stood, and these distinctions, born of our unhappy contest, will die along with it. They and we, and they and our ancestors, have been happy under that system. Let the memory of all actions in contradiction to that good old mode, on both sides, be extinguished forever. Be content to bind America by laws of trade; you have always done it. Let this be your reason for binding their trade. Do not burthen them by taxes; you were not used to do so from the beginning. Let this be your reason for not taxing. These are the arguments of states and kingdoms. Leave the rest to the schools, for there only may they be discussed with safety.

(Burke 1774 i: 215)

28 *Fiscal policy*

The colonists had generally abided by the home government's regulations on trade because 'they found the burdens which it imposed counterbalanced by corresponding benefits', particularly access to the world's most advanced economy, legitimized, as Burke said, by tradition (Schlesinger 1918: 15). If you urge 'subtle deductions' enforced by 'supreme sovereignty ... they will cast your sovereignty in your face.... When you drive him hard, the boar will surely turn upon the hunters.... Nobody will be argued into slavery.' Burke did not deny the authority of Parliament when it could be exercised, that is, with the people's consent.

> Sir, whilst we held this happy course, we drew more from the colonies than all the impotent violence of despotism ever could extort from them. We did this abundantly in the last war ... and what reason have we to imagine that the colonies would not have proceeded in supplying government as liberally, if you had not stepped in and hindered them from contributing, by interrupting the channel in which their liberality flowed..., by attempting to take instead of being satisfied to receive? Sir William Temple says that Holland has loaded itself with ten times the impositions which it revolted from Spain rather than submit to.
> (Burke 1774 i: 218–19)

This would also be seen in the new republic during the Civil and Cold Wars discussed below.

The Constitution of the United States of America

> The Confederation ... gives the power of the purse too entirely to the State Legislatures. It should provide perpetual funds, in the disposal of Congress, by a land tax, poll tax, or the like. All imposts upon commerce ought to be laid by Congress, and appropriated to their use. For, without certain revenues, a Government can have no power. That power which holds the purse-strings absolutely, must rule.
> (Alexander Hamilton to James Duane, 3 September 1780 (1851 i: 154))

> The Congress shall have Power To lay and collect Taxes, Duties, Imposts and Excises, to pay the Debts and provide for the common Defense and general Welfare of the United States; but all Duties, Imposts and Excises shall be uniform throughout the United States.
> (US Constitution, Article I, Sec. 8)

The central government's power to tax was a leading issue at the constitutional convention in 1787. Since 1775, the government of the United States had consisted of a Congress in which each state had a single vote, acts required unanimity, and were without means of compulsion. These Articles of Confederation had performed well in many ways. They suited those who valued their independence from a distant central authority, and it financed and administered the defeat of a great empire. However, there were disadvantages. Treaties between the Confederation and foreign powers were not fulfilled because they depended on the cooperation of the states. The British were slow to vacate American territory partly because states did not indemnify Tories according to the peace treaty of 1783. Trade was complicated by the different state tariffs on foreign goods. The army was not paid and national debts left from the war remained in default without a means of payment. These problems led to the Annapolis Convention of 1786, which invited the states to send delegates to a meeting in Philadelphia for 'the sole and express purpose of revising the Articles of Confederation'. The constitutional convention was persuaded – barely – that the services they wanted from a central government required that it be given the power to tax.

This was the theme of Charles Beard's *Economic Interpretation of the Constitution* (1913), which argued that the founders were more than idealists. They also understood economic interests. James Madison followed Locke in *Federalist X* by pointing out that the protections of property and liberty are the same. Supporters of the Constitution particularly included public creditors who stood to benefit from the federal assumption of debts that was expected to follow its ratification. They were not disappointed, and in 1790, the first Congress under the Constitution narrowly approved Hamilton's plan that the federal government assume the interest-bearing debts of the states as well as those of the Continental Congress.

Criticisms of Beard provide a sample of the view that individual interests are, or should be, unimportant to political decisions. Beard was accused of Marxist sympathies (as if capitalists are uninterested in economics), suggesting 'unworthy motives' on the part of the founders, and reducing 'everything to a sordid basis of personal interest'. William Howard Taft wrote that people are 'used to muckraking in the case of living public men, but it is novel to impeach our institutions which have stood the test of more than a century, by similar methods with reference to the founders, now long dead' (Taft 1913: 3).

Later scholars criticized Beard's estimates, pointing out that some holders of public debt voted against the Constitution. However, a recent study that looked at the marginal effects of the various interests and characteristics estimated that constitutional convention 'delegates who were merchants, owned private securities, owned large amounts of public securities, were officers in the Revolutionary War, or represented more commercial areas nearer to navigable waters, other factors constant', were more likely to vote for issues in their interests and for those

> that strengthened the *national* government.... Conversely, delegates who were debtors, owned slaves, represented areas with heavier concentrations of slaveholdings, or represented less commercial areas farther from navigable water ... were more likely to vote for issues that strengthened the *state* governments and 'to vote against ratification of the Constitution' at state conventions.
>
> (McGuire 2003: 17–32, 209–10)

The whiskey and other tax rebellions in the early United States

The relations of citizens of the new republic to their governments resembled those of the colonists to London a few years before. They engaged in three violent acts of resistance to state and federal taxes. Shays's Rebellion, named for one of its leaders, took the form of a floating, irregular 'army' of several hundred citizens, mostly from western Massachusetts, that prevented several courts from sitting between August and December 1786. Their purpose was to prevent judgments against debtors whose difficulties were partly due to taxes levied to pay the state's war debt (Feer 1988: 46–7; Ferguson 1961: 246).

Fries' Rebellion in southeastern Pennsylvania in 1798–99 was against a property tax voted by the Federalist Congress concerned with the possibility of war with France. It was called the 'Window Tax' because it involved counting and measuring windows and the 'Hot-Water Tax' because housewives poured hot water on assessors. It reminded John Fries and other German settlers of the hated hearth tax in the old country (Davis 1899: 129–36).

The Whiskey Rebellion of 1791–94 was a renewal of colonial violence against excise taxes. Hamilton had used *Federalist XII* to try to allay fears that the proposed government would use its powers of taxation to collect the hated excise. He expected tariffs, properly administered, to be sufficient.

> An ordinary degree of vigilance would be competent to the prevention of any material infractions upon the rights of the revenue. A few armed vessels, judiciously stationed at the entrance of our ports, might at a small expense be made useful sentinels of the laws.
>
> [T]he people will ill brook the inquisitive and peremptory spirit of excise laws. The pockets of the farmers ... will reluctantly yield but scanty supplies.... In this country, if the principal part [of revenue] be not drawn from commerce, it must fall with oppressive weight upon land.... Thus we shall not even have the consolations of a full treasury to atone for the oppression of that valuable class of citizens who are employed in the cultivation of the soil.

However, the Tariff Act of 1789 proved insufficient for the government's needs (Table 2.1). Hamilton discovered that the customs service, even with new interception vessels, had as much trouble with smugglers and administration as the British government before him. An official wrote from Baltimore that 'the difficulties that have occurred in the Execution of the laws respecting the Customs have been infinite, and present themselves daily'. Duties were due before vessels could 'clear out' but owners paid 'with reluctance' or 'not at all without compulsion; and the law provides none'. Collections required bending the laws and 'indulging the Merchants' (Hamilton, A. 1987: v, 459–62).

After considerable debate, Congress accepted a portion of Hamilton's recommendation for higher tariffs along with excises led by a whiskey tax that would fall primarily on corn growers. Ferguson (1961: 290) wrote:

Nothing testifies more to the audacity of the founding fathers than their demand that the people relinquish what they had fought Britain to preserve [as Burke had predicted], and there is perhaps no more convincing evidence of a growth of national feeling than that the point was carried.

George Mason said of the move at the constitutional convention to give the national government unlimited taxing powers:

> Whether the Constitution be good or bad, the ... clause clearly discovers that it is a national government, and no longer a Confederation.... The assumption of this power of laying direct taxes does of itself entirely change the confederation of the states into one consolidated government.
> (Elliot 1859 iii: 29)

The whiskey tax was opposed on practical and idealistic grounds. It was an internal tax of the kind against which many thought they had fought the British, its revenue went to debt service rather than current benefits, and its burden fell disproportionately on grain growers distant from the large eastern markets. Distillation at the source was the most efficient way to market their product. Moreover, corn whiskey was in large part not a cash crop (and the tax had to be paid in coin), but part of the wages of farm workers.

Concessions shortly reduced the burden of the tax, including lower rates and the option of substituting for a tax on output the estimated monthly capacity of the still, which induced operators to improve their efficiency. Even so, it violated the principle of privacy that had overturned the hearth tax in England. William Pitt declared:

> The poorest man may in his cottage bid defiance to all the force of the Crown. It may be frail, its roof may shake; the wind may blow through it; the storms may enter, the rain may enter, but the King of England cannot enter; all his forces dare not cross the threshold of the ruined tenement![3]

Pitt's statement was more than an appeal to democratic sentiment. It conformed with the best legal precedents. Coke had written that 'A man's house is his castle' (1628: iv, 176–7). In 1761, the young American lawyer, James Otis, argued before the Superior Court of Massachusetts that recent writs enabling the authorities to search houses suspected of containing smuggled goods violated 'one of the most essential branches of English liberty, the freedom of one's house. A man's house is his castle; and while he is quiet, he is as well guarded as a prince in his castle' (Cuddihy 1979). Johnson's *Dictionary* expressed the popular feeling:

> *Excise.* A hateful tax levied upon commodities, and adjudged not by the common judges of property, but wretches hired by those to whom excise is paid.

32 Fiscal policy

Yet in 1794, 'The unproductiveness of the [whiskey] excise simply led Hamilton and his successor to urge and secure an extension of the system to a wider range of commodities.' Excises were levied on carriages, snuff, sugar, and auctions, and in 1797, taxes on legal transactions were collected through the sale of stamps to be attached to documents (Dewey 1928: 106–9).

Collections of the whiskey tax on the frontier from Georgia to Pennsylvania were nonexistent. Pennsylvania's notoriety arose from the problems of a determined collector in the western part of the state. Protest meetings were held and tax collectors were tarred and feathered. No taxes were collected from the area during the first year and a half of the excise, and the regional collector, John Neville, requested armed assistance. In 1792, his office was vandalized by citizens significantly dressed as Indians. Violence peaked in July 1794, when Neville accompanied a US marshal who served summons on distillers ordering their appearance in Philadelphia. They were met with hostility and Neville's guarded house was the scene of two battles with deaths on both sides.[4]

'Riots' and 'unrest' might be more descriptive than 'rebellion', but as with Shays's Rebellion, many in the East feared for the government. Hamilton urged strong action, and the administration prepared for military action. After a peace commission failed to get satisfactory promises of peaceful behavior and tax compliance from local assemblies, an army of 12,000 was sent over the mountains. When it got to western Pennsylvania in November 1794, most of the rebels had moved west or melted into the countryside. Of the twenty insurgents brought to Philadelphia on the charge of high treason for 'levying war against the United States', ten were tried. Two were convicted but pardoned by the president, who termed one a 'simpleton' and the other 'insane' (Ifft 1985; Slaughter 1986: 219).

The other rebellions were also suppressed, although the rebels may be said to have been victorious in all of them. Shays's Rebellion strengthened the case for the stronger central government embodied in the Constitution which led to the federal assumption of state debts and tax relief for Shays's soldiers. The opposition to internal taxes triumphed in Thomas Jefferson's election in 1800. In his first annual message to Congress, Jefferson said:

> there is reasonable ground of confidence that we may now safely dispense with all the internal taxes, comprehending excises, stamps, auctions, licenses, carriages, and refined sugars, to which the postage on newspapers may be added, to facilitate the progress of information, and that the remaining sources of revenue will be sufficient to provide for the support of government, to pay the interest on the public debts, and to discharge the principals in shorter periods than the laws or the general expectations had contemplated. War, indeed, and untoward events, may change this prospect of things, and call for expenses which the imposts could not meet; but sound principles will not justify our taxing the industry of our fellow citizens to accumulate treasure for wars to happen we know not when, and which might not perhaps happen but from the temptations offered by that treasure.

Internal taxes were accordingly eliminated in March 1802, and except for the War of 1812 (Table 2.1), did not return until the Civil War.

Going back to the 1790 fiscal plan, there is a real question whether the new taxes and consequent disorders were necessary. Hamilton had shifted the debt to perpetuities and the United States had the highest credit rating in Europe (Gordon 1998). The British government had found long-term bonds eminently suited to its needs. Its

> good record together with the capacity of lenders ... gave it unprecedented power and flexibility in the conduct of foreign policy and war.... It was never driven to a steep rise in current taxation for the purpose of financing war out of current revenue
>
> (Binney 1958: 105–6)

The US government failed to take advantage of its tax-smoothing capability in the 1790s, leaving its exercise to the supposedly less financially sophisticated Jefferson – aided by Secretary of the Treasury Andrew Gallatin – in connection with the Louisiana Purchase in 1803.[5]

Tariffs

> Ever since the time of Adam Smith an important body of opinion critical of the protective tariff has flourished among economists. Though the literature produced by these critics has been at once extensive and scholarly, one has only to look about him to see that it has not made a great impression on the course of events.
>
> (Schattschneider 1935: vii)

A key objective of the constitutional convention of 1787 was the centralized authority necessary to a national tariff. The first bill before the new Congress became the Tariff Act of 1789, with preamble beginning: 'Whereas it is necessary for the support of the government, for the discharge of the debts of the United States, and the encouragement and protection of manufactures that duties be laid.'

Tariffs were the principal revenues of the new government. Although Hamilton made a case for protective tariffs in his *Report on the Subject of Manufactures* (1791), they did not seriously come into play until after the War of 1812. Tariffs were raised to pay for the war, and some industries wanted to keep their protection. The fall in government revenues in the postwar depression was another reason for maintaining and even increasing tariffs. Secretary of the Treasury William Crawford 'distinctly voiced a protective note' in his 1819 *Annual Report*: 'It is believed that the present is a favorable moment for affording effective protection to that increasing and important interest [i.e., cotton, woolen, and iron manufacturers] if it can be done consistently with the general interest of the nation.' Political leaders acknowledged the benefits of free trade, but exceptions were justified by cheap foreign labor, the protection of articles needed in war, the future

Table 2.1 Federal government revenue, spending, surplus, and debt: presidential terms, Washington to Jackson (average millions of $ per annum)

Presidential terms	Revenue					Spending				Surplus[a]	Debt[ab]
	Total	Customs	Internal revenue	Public lands	Other	Total	War	Interest	Other		
Washington-I	3.2	3.0	0.1	–	–	3.5	0.7	2.1	0.7	–0.3	78.4
II	7.2	6.1	0.4	–	0.6	6.6	2.1	3.3	1.2	0.6	79.2
J. Adams	9.8	8.4	0.8	–	0.5	9.4	4.6	3.5	1.2	0.4	80.7
Jefferson-I	12.9	11.7	0.2	0.3	0.6	8.7	2.1	4.1	2.5	4.2	75.7
II	14.2	13.6	–	0.6	–	9.6	4.1	3.3	2.1	4.6	53.2
Madison-I	12.0	11.0	–	0.8	0.1	17.0	12.5	2.8	1.7	–5.0	81.5
II	26.9	19.0	3.5	1.5	2.9	30.0	20.6	6.0	3.4	–3.1	103.5
Monroe-I	19.7	16.3	0.3	2.2	0.8	18.8	8.4	5.4	5.1	0.9	93.5
II	20.5	18.7	–	1.2	0.6	16.5	6.0	4.9	5.6	4.0	81.1
J.Q. Adams	24.5	22.2	–	1.4	0.8	16.2	8.1	3.3	4.8	8.3	48.6
Jackson-I	29.8	25.9	–	3.0	0.8	17.7	9.2	1.1	7.4	12.1	4.8
II	33.3	17.5	–	12.8	2.9	26.1	14.4	0.1	11.6	7.2	3.3

Source: US Bureau of the Census (sec. Y).

Notes
Fiscal and calendar years were the same through 1842. The terms here begin with the first full year of the president (e.g. 1802 for Jefferson-I), which corresponds with his first Congress (the Congress elected end-1800 first met end-1801).
[a] Relation between surplus and debt is approximate because of changes in Treasury cash and other financial operations.
[b] Debt is at the ends of these terms, e.g. end-1805. Totals may not correspond because of rounding.

benefits of encouraging infant industries, and foreign duties and regulations (Hamilton 1790; Dewey 1928: 191–6; Taussig 1931: 1–7, 18–24).

Legislation was on sectional lines. The middle-Atlantic and western states favored protection and internal improvements under the American System articulated by Henry Clay (Peterson 1987: 68–84). The Northeast was divided between manufacturing and commercial interests, and southern planters opposed protection. A bill for increased tariffs was narrowly defeated in 1820, but they were raised in 1824 and 1828 (Dewey 1928: 174–80).

The latter was castigated as the Tariff of Abominations, and provoked a constitutional crisis when the South Carolina legislature adopted a nullification ordinance to the effect that it was not bound by the tariff. Collection of duties would not be permitted in the state after 1 February 1833.[6] Congress granted President Andrew Jackson's request for increased enforcement powers, but they were not needed after the compromise Tariff of 1833 (Holt 1999: 20). South Carolina nullified the Force Bill but accepted the tariff, which provided for lower rates while trying to meet the objections of protectionists by spreading the reductions over several years. The bill passed at the end of the session (1 March 1833) with Clay justifying his yea vote by observing: 'The hostile attitude assumed by a sister State towards the country had induced us to do what we are now bound to do, and a refusal ... would have endangered the integrity of the Union.' The measure was 'necessary for the peace of the country'. His supporters in the West changed with him, as indicated in Table 2.2.

The votes of the middle and southern states were more consistent. The former voted for the bill (an increase in tariffs) in 1828 and against the bill (a reduction in tariffs) in 1833. The South voted oppositely. New England opposed both times. Daniel Webster said at Faneuil Hall in 1820:

> I feel no desire to push capital into extensive manufactures faster than the general progress of our wealth and population propels it. I am not in haste to see Sheffields and Birminghams in America. It is the true policy of government to suffer the different pursuits of society to take their own course, and not to give excessive bounties or encouragements to one over another.

Table 2.2 Votes on the Tariff Bills of 1828 and 1833

	All	NE	Middle[a]	South[b]	West[c]	
1828	105–94	16–23	56–6	4–55	29–10	House
	26–21	6–5	8–0	1–15	11–1	Senate
1833	119–85	10–28	16–46	64–1	29–10	House
	29–16	6–6	4–4	13–1	6–5	Senate

Source: *Congressional Register*, 4/23 and 5/13/28, 2/26 and 3/1/33.

Notes
a NY, NJ, PA, and DE.
b Coastal slave states (except DE) and TN.
c OH, IN, IL, KY, and MO.

36 Fiscal policy

By 1828, however, he was arguing that 'since New England had accepted the act of 1824, and had entered upon manufactures with an earnest purpose, the nation was bound to fulfill the hopes which had been extended' (Dewey 1928: 175, 181).

Except for a brief increase in 1842, which was a response to falling government revenues in depression, tariffs continued to fall until the Civil War (Figure 2.1). Taxes of all kinds were increased in that war.

> The willingness if not indeed the open zeal of the people for taxation ... was noteworthy. A foreign minister remarked to [Secretary of State] Seward that he was learning something new about the strength of popular government. 'I was not surprised to see your young men rushing enthusiastically to fight for their flag. I have seen that in other countries. But I have never before seen a country where the people were clamorous for taxation.'

They 'rejoiced in taxation' (Dewey 1928: 304).

Protection did not end with the war. The bulk of Civil War tariffs was kept into the next century. Most internal taxes were eliminated after the fighting, but 'on almost all the articles with which the protective controversy is concerned the rates of the [tariff] act of 1864 were retained, virtually without change, for twenty years or more; and when changes were finally made, they were undertaken as if these rates were not in any sense exceptional, but were the normal results of an established policy'. The increases in the proportion of duty-free imports seen in Figure 2.1 followed the abolition of tea and coffee duties in 1872, and sugar in 1890 (replaced by a bounty to sugar producers) (Taussig 1931: 275–6).

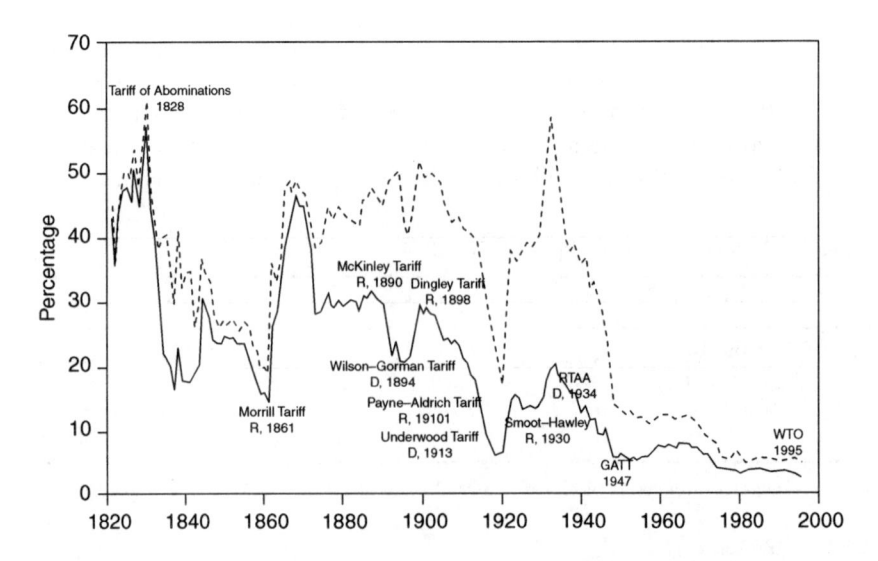

Figure 2.1 Tariff receipts as percentages of dutiable and all imports.

Strong protectionist sentiment remained, especially in the Republican Party, through and beyond the Smoot-Hawley Tariff of 1930. Instead of agreeing with economists and most of the founders about the desirability of free trade in principle, lobbyists now considered it an exception that required defending. Oppositions to particular duties before congressional committees typically began: 'We are in favor of protection but....' (Schattschneider 1935: 142).

'In tariff making', it has been said, 'perhaps more than in any other kind of legislation', the multiplicity of interests involved results 'in bills which no one intended'. When President Herbert Hoover called a special session of Congress to deal with agricultural problems, 'everybody [not just agriculture] got pretty much what he wanted' in Smoot-Hawley (Schattschneider 1935: 142; Taussig 1931: 491–5).

Pressures to reduce tariffs in the Progressive Era – by Republicans in the Dingley and Payne–Aldrich Tariffs of 1897 and 1909, and Democrats in the Underwood Tariff of 1913 – benefited from the belief that tariffs were responsible for rising prices (even though the rise was world-wide and a result of gold increases) and protected monopolies. Tariffs were raised when the Republicans returned to power in the 1920s, although the increase in the relative importance of free goods meant that the downward trend in effective overall rates was not reversed (Irwin 1998).

Determination of the right rates by a Congress with a mixture of contradictory goals – protection with competition for businesses and low costs for consumers – is a complicated business, and expert assistance was occasionally, if *pro forma*, called for. In 1882, Congress authorized a Tariff Commission to develop, in the words of President Chester A. Arthur, 'a substantial reduction of tariff duties [that] was demanded ... by the best conservative opinion of the country, including that which has in former times been most strenuous for the preservation of our national industrial defences'. However, the commission's recommendations for reductions averaging between 20 and 25 percent were 'treated by Congress with disapproval if not with contempt, as is frequently the case with expert findings in a democratic state' (Dewey 1928: 421).

The Tariff Act of 1897 authorized the president to negotiate bilateral reductions in certain duties up to 20 percent, subject to congressional approval. However, not one of eleven agreements negotiated made it past the committee stage. Tariffs were set 20 percent higher in anticipation of reductions, but none were forthcoming. 'In the end, the United States had a high bargaining tariff without having approved any of the bargains' (Irwin 1998). The Tariff Act of 1913 also authorized the president to negotiate tariff reductions, but again, no agreements were forthcoming.

The demand for experts grew with the desire for tariffs that offered protection without encouraging monopoly or a high cost of living. Americans were worried about cheap foreign labor, and Republicans spoke of equalizing costs of production. A Tariff Board organized in 1910 'made an energetic effort to collect data in regard to cost of production at home and abroad', although President Taft used it to thwart reductions by the Democratic Congress. He preferred to wait for the Board's 'scientific' recommendation (Dewey 1928: 485; Taussig 1931: 413).

The Tariff Board was terminated by the Democrats, but Woodrow Wilson's 'competitive tariff' was essentially the Republican formula (Schattschneider 1935: 8; Taussig 1931: 418–19). Neither is intellectually defensible. Both imply the 'simple prohibition and complete stoppage of foreign trade. Anything in the world can be made within a country if the producer is assured of "the cost of production together with reasonable profits"' (Taussig 1931: 363–4).

Congress accepted Wilson's proposal for a Tariff Commission in 1916, and in 1922 added quasi-legislative powers to modify rates under the cost-difference principle. Taussig (1931: 482, 521–2) wrote that its work was used

> chiefly for making points in debates or in Committee hearings, or for enabling a Congressman to see just what the figures meant for his party or constituents.... No sensible person conversant with our political ways could suppose that Congress would put into the hands of any such body the settlement of questions of policy.

Significant procedural changes came in the 1930s. '[U]p to the Great Depression Congress never seriously considered delegating its tariff-making powers to another agency' (Irwin 1998). The changes were in response to extreme conditions rather than changed tariff politics. The leadership of the Democratic Congress elected in 1932 was inclined, as on previous occasions, to cut tariffs 10 to 25 percent and negotiate further reductions. However, they could not muster the support necessary for a significant unilateral tariff cut under the conditions of high unemployment then prevailing, particularly since the depression had induced other countries to raise their tariffs and other barriers to imports (albeit partly as reactions to Smoot-Hawley). Congress compromised in the Reciprocal Trade Agreements Act (RTAA) of 1934, which authorized the president to negotiate tariff reductions up to 50 percent without congressional approval. By 1940, the United States had signed agreements with 21 countries that accounted for 60 percent of US trade, although most of the fall seen in Figure 2.1 was through price increases that eroded specific (fixed in dollars) duties.

Tariffs remained a partisan issue until after World War II, from which the United States emerged as the dominant exporter and potentially the greatest beneficiary of free trade. Forty-three percent of Republican senators, mainly from export states, voted for the renewal of the RTAA in 1945. The Republican Congress limited its renewal to one year in 1948, but tariffs were nonpartisan in the 1950s. The General Agreement on Tariffs and Trade (GATT) was organized as a framework for negotiations in 1947, but most of the work of cutting tariffs had been done. Continued low rates were encouraged by the desire to assist the Free World during the Cold War.

> It would be completely misleading to conclude that Congress, through its repeated delegation of trade powers to the president, abdicated any role in

the formation of trade policy. Although Congress never again wrote the tariff code ... it influenced the agenda by keeping the president on a short negotiating leash and enacting various forms of procedural escape clauses that were expanded over the postwar period.

(Irwin 1998)

The RTAA was effectively renewed through 1974, by which time non-tariff barriers (such as health and safety regulations directed at foreign goods and non-transparent import procedures) had become the major trade issue. Although the Act authorized the president to negotiate the reduction of 'any existing duty or other import restriction', Congress not only refused to enact legislation to implement an antidumping agreement negotiated in the Kennedy Round (1964–67) – 'the general view ... was that ... the president had overstepped his legislative power' – it 'enacted a provision which would nullify any provision of the antidumping agreement inconsistent with the U.S. law' (Sek 2001). The law was revised in 1974 to extend the president's so-called 'fast-track' authority – subject to extensive consultation with congressional committees – but lapsed in 1994, and has not been renewed.

In 1995, GATT was folded into the World Trade Organization, with a more formal structure to arbitrate disputes over violations of trade agreements and to authorize 'retaliatory measures' (trade sanctions) that Congress has largely ignored.[7]

The missile gap?

The armed forces were swiftly demobilized after World War II. Military personnel on active duty were cut from 12.1 to 1.4 million between 1945 and 1948. Military spending was cut from $86 billion to $9 billion, although it was still 5 percent of GNP the latter year, compared with about 1.4 percent in prewar years. The cutback was ended by the Soviet threat, particularly its possession of nuclear weapons.

Presidents Truman (1945–53) and Eisenhower (1953–61) had similar approaches to military budgets. They tried to treat the military services like other departments, all of which had to fit into what the presidents thought the country could afford and would accept. All had to go through the budget director, who worked closely with the president. Truman sought 'the proper relation between the long-range integrity of our debt management, the basic and pressing economic and social needs of the people of the United States, and the needs of our allies'. He resisted military pressures 'to force me to alter the budget which had been carefully worked out to achieve balance with the other needs of the government and our economy as a whole' (Schilling 1962; Truman 1956: 33–4). President Eisenhower similarly hoped to solve 'the 'great equation' of maintaining indefinitely a strong military force without bankrupting the country in the process (Snyder 1962).

Ike's first budget carried out his campaign promise to reduce government spending. Military cuts were consistent with the end of the Korean War but he was accused of putting money before security. Presidential strategies emphasized long-term preparedness rather than continuously at the crisis point. Planning for the long haul might not be enough, however. 'What's the use of being the richest man in the graveyard?' Senator Stuart Symington, Democrat from Missouri, asked. Defense should not be sacrificed to a balanced budget. 'Survival is more important than money' (Olson 2003: 299; US Congress 1956a: 971; Geelhoed 1959: 108).

The Democrats won control of Congress in the 1954 elections, and in 1956 a Senate Subcommittee on Airpower, extended to all branches of the military, was established under Symington's chairmanship to inquire into the nation's military readiness. The theme of the Hearings was established when Symington's ally, Washington Senator Henry Jackson, said to the first witness:

> Sometimes when some of us up on the Hill suggest that we ought to go all out on a certain program, we are told, 'Well, Senator, your idea is fine but the trouble is we are not in an all-out war.'
> The only answer that I have been able to give is that if we are involved in an all-out war, our industrial capability might be in an atomic ruin.
> (US Congress 1956a: 18)

The military chiefs admitted under questioning that their forces were limited by their budgets. Senator Barry Goldwater (a general in the air force reserve) testified that the problem had not been approached properly: 'we ought to say we need X number of airplanes and X number of men to do the job. I am convinced that if we can come up with a figure like that, the American public will back it and we can provide it' (231). The Subcommittee's *Report* concluded that American military deficiencies were worsening because 'Financial considerations have often been placed ahead of defense requirements' (McFarland 2001: 78–9).

Symington and Jackson were from states with large defense contracts but their concerns were shared by many of their colleagues. The airpower hearings were followed by an unrequested appropriation of $900 million for B-52 bombers, which, like the Truman administration in 1949, the Eisenhower administration did not spend (Kolodziej 1966: 233–8; McFarland 2001: 77–8; Adams 1961: 404; Schilling 1962: 46–7). The 1974 Budget Act later stripped the president of his right to impound appropriated funds. He can request rescissions but they require congressional affirmations that are seldom forthcoming and are usually ignored (Moore 2000).

Criticisms of the administration increased when the Soviet Union launched the first man-made satellite, Sputnik, in October 1957. The *New York Times* accused the administration of complacency toward the 'race for our survival'. The national debt ceiling 'is imposing a form of unilateral disarmament upon the United States'. 'There is abundant proof that red tape is needlessly but seriously impeding our weapons development program.... The Russians have a lead that could be exceedingly hazardous' (19 November 1957: 32).

The 'missile gap', a catch-all phrase for defense deficiencies, was a major issue in the November 1958 elections that resulted in a Democratic landslide. Symington was re-elected by the largest majority in a statewide race in Missouri history (Olson 2003: 337). John F. Kennedy associated himself with Symington's charges in his 1960 campaign, and at the beginning of his presidency he asked his secretary of defense to study the relative missile strengths of the United States and the Soviet Union. During a press briefing on 6 February 1961, Secretary McNamara said that 'if there was a gap, it was in our favor' (McNamara 1995: 21). The title of Linda McFarland's (2001) chapter – 'The making of a myth: Stuart Symington and the Missile Gap' – was apt. Nevertheless, one cannot be too careful, Symington said, backed by the president: 'If we are to err in an age of uncertainty, I want us to err on the side of security' (Olson 2003: 365–6; Sorenson 1965: 612).

Ike's intelligence, later confirmed, showed that the deterrent to any possible Soviet attack was more than sufficient. His Farewell Address, 17 January 1961, deplored 'the acquisition of unwarranted influence ... by the military-industrial complex' (Medhurst 1993: 189–93).

Conclusion

Government budgets are political outcomes of conflicts between interests. They are about power and the control of government, as much as immediate finance. Some are attempts to shift the burden of revenue, such as between excises and tariffs, and some because of opposition to the 'services' to be paid for by the tax, such as the intrusions of Kings John, Charles I, and James II, and the royally appointed officials to be financed by the Stamp Act. Sometimes, on the other hand, especially for war spending, taxpayers are ahead of the government. In any case, tax changes not supported by interests have little chance, including, as we will see in Chapter 4, those advocated by economic theorists.

3 Ideas
The theory of stabilization policy

Is the fulfillment of these ideas a visionary hope? Have they insufficient roots in the motives which govern the evolution of political society? Are the interests which they will thwart stronger and more obvious than those which they will serve?

I do not attempt an answer in this place.... But if the ideas are correct..., it would be a mistake, I predict, to dispute their potency over a period of time. At the present moment people are unusually expectant of a more fundamental diagnosis; more particularly ready to receive it; eager to try it out, if it should be even plausible. But apart from this contemporary mood, the ideas of economists and political philosophers, both when they are right and when they are wrong, are more powerful than is commonly understood. Indeed the world is ruled by little else. Practical men, who believe themselves to be quite exempt from any intellectual influences, are usually the slaves of some defunct economist.

(Keynes 1936: 383)

Economic theories of stabilization policy have been dominated by Keynes's *General Theory* since its publication in 1936. This is not to say that it was unambiguous or accepted in its entirety, but the *GT* has supplied the framework of macroeconomic debate for seven decades. Keynes's disciples ruled macroeconomic analysis into the 1960s, and although their authority was undermined by new ideas and events, their framework and often their specific models still take pride of place in textbooks and popular discussions. There is disagreement about what Keynes meant, and who are the true disciples, but I use 'Keynesian' for those who explain unemployment as a consequence of market imperfections and advocate remedies in the form of government intervention. Whether Keynesians adhere to the letter or spirit of the *GT* is another matter.

Competing models are also hung on Keynes's scaffolding. Monetarist and New Classical criticisms that emphasize the rationality of private agents and government rather than market failures employ the Keynesian system (Friedman 1970; Sargent and Wallace 1975). Even the modern form of the Classical model against which Keynes juxtaposed the *GT* was erected by him for the purpose.[1]

We can think of the connections between theorists and policy in two steps: from the original idea/model to its modifications by other economists to the effects of the resulting theoretical consensus (or *paradigm* in the terminology of

Thomas Kuhn's *Structure of Scientific Revolutions* (1962)) on policy. Chapter 6 below will look at the interactions of theory and practice in the determination of monetary policy. It is about the second step, that is, the relations of economists to policy. The present chapter is concerned with the first step, in particular the transformation of Keynes's economics into the form that was presented to policymakers. We will see in Chapter 4 that this model had less effect on policy than is popularly supposed. Its practical failure was in large part due to the inability or refusal of economists to follow up Keynes's efforts to incorporate time and uncertainty into the analysis. Whether this more challenging line of research would have increased Keynes's eventual influence cannot be known. It still would have had to overcome obstacles of communication with policymakers, practical implementation, and interests such as those reviewed in Chapter 2.

This chapter has four sections. The first compares Keynes's optimistic belief expressed at the top of the chapter with the mixed influence of ideas in practice. The second and third sections look at macroeconomic policy before the *GT*, the *GT*, and its reception by economists. Keynes was hardly the first economist interested in unemployment, although he offered what he believed was a more rigorous rationalization of existing policy proposals. We will see that the profession welcomed his endorsement of active government but rejected his difficult disequilibrium analysis of uncertainty in a money economy; or rather, perhaps it should be said, chose not to follow him in the attempt. The last section inquires into whether Keynes's policy hopes would have been better realized if his theory had been taken more seriously.

The transmission of ideas

Rhetoric

It is generally agreed that there was a Keynesian revolution. Not so generally agreed is what was revolutionized. Keynes himself expected revolutions in theory and policy. He wrote to the socialist George Bernard Shaw:

> I believe myself to be writing a book on economic theory which will largely revolutionise – not, I suppose, at once but in the course of the next ten years – the way the world thinks about economic problems. When my theory has been duly assimilated and mixed with politics and feelings and passions, I can't predict what the upshot will be in its effect on actions and affairs. But there will be a great change, and in particular, the Ricardian foundations of Marxism [and the Classics] will be knocked away.
>
> (Keynes, *Collected Writings* xiii: 492–3)

These expectations were ambitious, but on one level they were fulfilled or even exceeded. The *GT* was immediately and enthusiastically received by economists, and many pages of the leading journals were given to arguments about its meanings and ways of expressing them (Harris 1947). It was not long before textbooks claiming to incorporate Keynes's message were parts of the college curriculum. The new subject of macroeconomics was effectively interpretations of the *GT* (Tarshis 1947; Samuelson 1958). 'I have always considered it a priceless advantage to have been born as an economist prior to 1936 and to have received a thorough grounding in classical economics,' Paul Samuelson (1946) wrote on Keynes's death.

> It is quite impossible for modern students to realize the full effect of what has been advisedly called 'The Keynesian Revolution' upon those of us brought up in the orthodox tradition. What beginners today often regard as trite and obvious was to us puzzling, novel, and heretical.
>
> *Bliss was it in that dawn to be alive,*
> *But to be young was very heaven!*[2]

The confidence of the New Economists coming to Washington in 1961 was noted in Chapter 1. Keynes's image was on the cover of *Time*, 31 December 1964, and the cover story quoted 'the University of Chicago's Milton Friedman, the nation's leading conservative economist, who was Presidential Candidate Barry Goldwater's advisor on economics: "We are all Keynesians now"'.[3] Walter Heller (1966: 3) described the swearing-in of a new member of the president's Council of Economic Advisors. President Johnson said: 'Dr. Duesenberry, as we all know, is one of this Nation's leading economists. When I was growing up, that didn't seem to mean very much, but since I grew up we have learned the error of our ways.'

In little more than a decade, Keynesianism was dead. This is the usual story of the rise and fall of Keynesianism, which I propose to take a step farther by asking if Keynes ever lived in the sense that he or the Keynesians influenced policy? My answer begins with an historical review of the successes and failures of ideas. We know that the preponderance of practical economic ideas as expressed in new business ventures fail. It is the height of ambition, even arrogance, to expect a better fate for broad and complicated abstractions.

The force of reason

Philosophers and reformers have been notable for their trust in the power of ideas to change minds and behavior (Fonseca 1991: 7). John Stuart Mill contended that philosophy was decisive in human affairs: 'one person with a belief is a social power equal to ninety-nine who have only interests' (1861: 381).

> [S]peculative philosophy, which to the superficial appears a thing so remote from the business of life and the outward interests of men, is in reality the thing on earth which most influences them, and in the long run overbears every other influence save those which it must itself obey.
>
> (Mill 1838)

Karl Marx showed a similar faith in the power of reason when he criticized a fellow revolutionary's neglect of theory:

> To call to the workers without any strictly scientific ideas or constructive doctrine [is] equivalent to vain and dishonest play at preaching which assumes an inspired prophet on the one side and on the other only gasping asses.... People without constructive doctrine cannot do anything and have indeed done nothing so far except make a noise, rouse dangerous flares and bring about the ruin of the cause they had undertaken.
> (McLellan 1981: 13)

He argued that a social order is held together by a belief system, or 'ideology', and its replacement requires a new ideology that can be imposed only by reason.

Confidence in the susceptibility of beliefs to persuasion was carried into the twentieth century, reinforced by the successes of the new authoritarian systems and the high stakes for which the opposing intellectual camps contested. Conflicts between economic systems were intensified by the Great Depression of the 1930s. Many defenders and critics of free-market capitalism saw the battle predominantly as one of ideas – between pens rather than swords, missiles, or interests. Lionel Robbins blamed the depression not on any inherent flaw in the market mechanism but on self-defeating government policies that stemmed from 'ideas which have been put forward in the first instance by detached and isolated thinkers.... The measures of the last decade have been the result, not of spontaneous pressure by the electorate, but of the influence of a number of men whose names could be counted on the fingers of two hands' (1934: 199–200).

Ludwig von Mises wrote that politics

> is a purely intellectual matter.... In a battle between force and an idea, the latter always prevails.... It is ideas that group men into fighting factions, that press the weapons into their hands, and that determine against whom and for whom the weapons shall be used.
> (1962: 50)

F.A. Hayek wrote:

> Few contentions meet with such disbelief from most practical men ... as that, what is contemptuously dubbed as an ideology, has dominant power over those who believe themselves to be free from it even more than over those who consciously embrace it.
> (1973: 69–70)

He was appalled by the apparent easy successes of wrong ideas. 'Experts' as well as 'men in the street' fall prey to philosophical conceptions 'simply because they happen to be "modern"'. Consequently, 'it is our special duty to recognize the currents of thought which still operate in public opinion, to examine their significance, and, if necessary, to refute them' (1952: 206).

Not everyone was as confident of the power of ideas. Persuasion involved more than giving a soldier a musket. When David Hume suggested that 'belief is more properly an act of the sensitive than of the cogitative part of our natures', he was criticized for failing to teach the paths of virtue. William Paley believed that moral philosophy should teach 'men their duty and the reasons of it', and scolded Hume for failing to advance reasons 'sufficient to withhold men from the gratification of lust, revenge, envy, ambition, avarice, or to prevent the existence of these passions (Hume 1739: 183; Paley 1814 i: 1, 64; Fonseca 1991: 9). Hume had little hope for philosophy as a method of instruction. Instead of trying to alter beliefs or behavior by reason, he strove to explain how they were determined, and concluded that they rest more on sensory experiences than abstract reasoning. I will argue that, when it comes to the practical application of economic theory, we can learn at least as much from Hume's skepticism as Keynes's idealism.

Losses and misunderstandings

To be successful, ideas must be received by the potential actors. The production of a superior idea may be less than half the battle. Francis Bacon (1603: 93) observed that 'it is not a thing so easy as is conceived to convey the conceit of one man's mind into the mind of another, without loss or mistaking, especially in notions new and differing from those that are received'. This is so even for direct exchanges between sympathetic professionals sharing common backgrounds and goals. It is more difficult over gaps of time, interests, and cultures, and through layers of hierarchy. 'I hope to God you will be more successful than I have been in making people understand your meaning,' Charles Darwin wrote to the botanist J.D. Hooker. 'I am inclined to give up the attempt as hopeless. Those who do not understand, it seems, cannot be made to understand.' He wrote to the geologist Charles Lyell that 'the plainest case may be misrepresented and misunderstood.... I am beginning to despair of ever making the majority understand my notions' (1887: 110–11).

In 1907, William James wrote his friend and fellow psychologist/philosopher, Carl Stumpf:

> You will receive from me in a week or two the sole product of my *muse* this winter, namely, a little popular book called *Pragmatism*. In spite of what you say so gravely and even sorrowfully in [your] letter, I shall be surprised if, when I have read your quarto pages, and you my much smaller ones, we seem to each other as far apart in our thinking as you now suppose us to be. What staggers me in the recent controversial literature of pragmatism and humanism is the colossal amount of mutual *misunderstanding* that can exist in men brought up in the same language and with almost identical educations. It is

hard to believe! Language is the most imperfect and expensive means yet discovered for communicating thought.

(Perry 1935 ii: 203)

His surprise is surprising in view of his book's emphasis on experience as a primary source of knowledge, revealed more in behavior than words.

The sense of revolution was promoted by misunderstandings, innocent and otherwise, of pre-Keynesian economics. George Stigler, as much a student of earlier ideas as a contributor to the new, observed that 'the average modern reference to the classical economists is so vulgarly ignorant as not to deserve notice, let alone refutation' (1988: 214).

The receptions of the *GT* illustrate the forces that help and hinder the transmission of ideas. Eduardo Fonseca (1991: 19) suggested that 'the widely held notion that "Ideas rule the world of human affairs and its events"' – despite the usual disappointment of their originators – 'makes excessive and unwarrantable demands as regards both the transparency and transmissibility of highly abstract systems'. Was the 'Keynesian Revolution' an exception, and if so, in what ways? We will see that the success of the *GT*, although substantial in some ways, was disappointing in others. Of his two messages, one – the activist policy conclusion – was enthusiastically accepted, while the other – his vision of the economy, the *General Theory* itself – was rejected by his 'fellow economists', to whom it was 'chiefly addressed' (Keynes 1936: v). Even the success of the first must be severely qualified. It was well on its way to victory, if it had not already triumphed, when Keynes appeared on the scene.

His assault on the minds of economists is more than a case study of the transmission of ideas between scholars. We also learn something of the beliefs and behavior of policymakers and their relations with economists. Ironically, if the *GT* had been taken seriously by economists, it might have been more useful in the areas in which Keynes's hopes to persuade were least successful – in the minds and conduct of 'practical men'. The *GT* described the actions and often inaction of agents conditioned by habit and convention in the 'economic society in which we actually live' (Keynes 1936: iii). The implications of these descriptions were not pursued by economists, who were themselves propelled by habits and conventions too strong for Keynes, but they may help us understand the minds and conduct of market agents. Written from the viewpoint of a participant – Keynes traded in the financial and commodity markets – we learn much about markets from the *GT* and much about economists from their reactions to it.

The General Theory

Antecedents: the simultaneous development of laissez faire theory and interventionist policies

For two generations before the *GT*, government regulations of economic affairs advanced under the banners of Progress, Reform, and the New Liberalism while economists were perfecting a laissez faire theory in which government was irrelevant. Some managed to be in the front ranks of both parades, marching in opposite directions. Keynes wanted a logical reconciliation. His goal is succinctly stated: a theory which reconciled the contradictions between economic theory and social policies to enable economists, *qua economists*, to advance the prevailing social/political enterprise.

The problems addressed by the *GT* were not new. British unemployment rates exceeded 7 percent ten times and 10 percent three times between 1858 and 1893. American unemployment averaged 14 percent during the six-year depression of the mid-1890s. Price indexes fell one-third to one-half in the two countries between 1873 and 1896 (Mitchell 1962; US Bureau of the Census 1975). Alfred Marshall's 'Remedies for fluctuations of general prices' (1887), W.J. Ashley's 'sliding scale' for wages (1903), and Irving Fisher's *Purchasing Power of Money* (1922) are examples of the notice taken of price changes by economists. Their attention to unemployment is described below. The modern economist coming to the writings of his pre-Keynesian forebears is struck by the familiarity of concepts, problems, and proposed solutions.

The Keynesian Revolution was given a ride on the tide of social activism that had been building since the last third of the nineteenth century. Keynes argued in the 1920s that institutions and relationships had changed since the Great War in ways that demanded a greater role for the state. He argued in the opening of *The Economic Consequences of the Peace* (1919) that the pre-1914 laissez faire system owed its apparent success to fortuitous circumstances. The more difficult problems that followed the war required more active governments. His warnings against trust in the 'age-old poison' of laissez faire and 'doctrinaire delusions' of 'smoothly functioning automatic mechanisms' were presented as part of the New Liberalism, but his views were present in his father's generation (Moggridge 1992: 454; Clarke 1988: 78–83).

The growth of government was widely noted before 1914. Even at its peak in the mid-nineteenth century, laissez faire's influence on public policy was incomplete. The moves toward free trade and liberal incorporation laws were accompanied by compulsory public education and restrictive licensing laws. Banking and transportation had always been matters of public policy, and early in the century – in the Poor Laws and Factory Acts – 'the functions of the State were extended to the "welfare" of the people in the modern sense' (Spearman 1957: 105). What made the classical period notable in the history of regulation was the standard to which the state was held. The tour de force of the classical economists was their demonstration that resources might be allocated most efficiently by the invisible hand. 'Generally speaking', Jeremy Bentham wrote, 'there is no one who knows what is for your interest so well as yourself – no one who is disposed with so much ardour and constancy to pursue it' (1838: 33; Robbins 1952: 13). Economists and Parliament distrusted official interventions, which, Adam Smith (1776: 66–7) noted, were usually on the side of the powerful. They opposed an active paternalism, but protection of the weak and the provision of services for which private incentives were inadequate were held to be proper functions of the state. However, the burden of the case for action was on the interventionists.

Officials invoked laissez faire when the standard of intervention had not been met – or felt, which may be the same thing. It is hard to believe that the measures taken by the government in London to relieve the Irish famine of the 1840s would not have been greater if it had been closer to home. Ministers might not have been so confident that interference with natural causes did more harm than good if there had been a greater Irish interest in Parliament and an angry mob outside (Woodham-Smith 1962: 306, 406–10).

A.V. Dicey (1914: 119) saw in Mill's *Political Economy* (1848)

> already ... a modification, if not exactly of doctrine, yet certainly of tone and feeling. The doctrine of *laissez faire* ... and the mode of looking at life, and above all at legislation, loses a good deal of its rigidity and of its authoritative character.

Some have dated the end of laissez faire from W.S. Jevons' (1882: vii, 16) assertion of the futility of trying 'to uphold, in regard to social legislation, any theory of eternal fixed principles or abstract rights'. Every case involves 'a complex calculus of good and evil. All is a question of probability and degree', so that 'we can lay down no hard and fast rules, but must treat every case on its merits'. The burden of argument falls on no one. The change in attitude was reflected in the surge of legislation in the decades leading up to World War I. Much of it was directed against big business and toward the protection of labor and consumers, but hardly any aspect of economic life remained beyond the scope of government (Dicey 1914: Lecture VIII; Hutchison 1994).

Growing government interventions were accompanied by refinements in laissez faire theory. The 'marginal revolution' of Jevons (1871), Marshall (1920), and others added to the rigor of theoretical proofs of efficient and self-correcting free markets (Blaug 1996: ch. 8; Black 1972). Economics was steered onto a rigorous, mechanical, mathematical, amoral track by the same writers who in matters of public policy addressed the market imperfections from which their theories abstracted. Theory turned away from the moral line that Mill and Marshall hoped for. Mill had expected that the parts of his *Principles* – subtitled *with some of their applications to social philosophy* – that would have the greatest impact – he anticipated a 'tremendous outcry' – were the proposals relating to property, especially inheritance and bequest, which were designed to 'pull down all large fortunes in two generations'. To his surprise, a friend observed, 'this part of the book made no sensation' (Bain 1882: 89). (This should have given Mill some humility regarding the power of ideas.) Marshall rejected 'economic man' as the foundation of economics. In his *Inaugural Lecture* (1885) on assuming the Chair of Economics at Cambridge (*The Present Position of Economics*), he talked of turning the study of economics away from the supposition that man was a 'constant quantity' typified by Ricardo's 'city men'. In *Principles of Economics* (1920: 631–2), the work meant by those who used to say 'It's all in Marshall', he observed that economists were 'getting to pay every year a greater attention to the pliability of human nature, and to the way in which the character of man affects and is affected by the prevalent methods of the production, distribution and consumption of wealth'.

In fact, economic theories accepted only – an instance of the filtering of ideas – what advanced the analysis of 'economic man'. Jevons noted in his proposal for a 'General mathematical theory of political economy' (1866) that

> There are motives nearly always present with us, arising from conscience, compassion, or from some moral or religious source, which political economy cannot and does not pretend to treat. These will remain to us as outstanding and disturbing forces; they must be treated, if at all, by other appropriate branches of knowledge.

This simplification made possible, in his *Theory of Political Economy* (1871: 139), 'The keystone of the whole Theory of Exchange, and of the principal problems of Economics', which 'lies in this proposition – the ratio of exchange of any two commodities will be the reciprocal of the ratio of the final degrees of utility of the quantities of commodity available for consumption after the exchange is completed'. The new economics centered on this proposition enabled the development of a general equilibrium theory of an efficient market economy.

Keynes directed the *GT* against this smoothly adjusting system of time-invariant, rational, calculating, non-social agents,

> placing the emphasis on the prefix *general*..., to contrast the character of my arguments and conclusions with those of the *classical* theory..., upon which I was brought up and which dominates the economic thought, both practical and theoretical, of the governing and academic classes of this generation, as it has for a hundred years past.

He continued:

> I shall argue the postulates of the classical theory are applicable to a special case only and not to the general case, the situation which it assumes being a limiting point of the possible positions of equilibrium. Moreover, the characteristics of the special case assumed by the classical theory happen not to be those of the economic society in which we actually live, with the result that its teaching is misleading and disastrous if we attempt to apply it to the facts of experience.
>
> (1936: 3)

The Classics had not neglected the economic problems of their society, including unemployment. Some of them explained unemployment by inflexible wages in the presence of price deflation, some by inflexible interest rates, some by the lack of information about jobs in a dynamic system of growing and declining industries, and Marshall (1920: 591) wrote that depressions might be caused by failures of demand: 'Though men have the power to purchase they may not choose to use it.' Robin Matthews (1990) wrote on the centenary of the first edition of Marshall's *Principles* that

> The range of labour-market issues that were addressed by Marshall was not much narrower than the range that exists today...: unemployment, low wages, methods of wage determination, government regulation of hours and pay, social security, education and training – even inflation.

Keynes's father, Neville Keynes, anticipated the modern 'islands' rationalization of the Phillips Curve in evidence to the Royal Commission on the Depression of Trade and Industry (1886) by stating that depression was partly due to deflation, which 'discouraged enterprise' because of the trader's tendency 'to exaggerate his own loss by not taking sufficient account of the general fall in prices' (Skidelsky 1983: 231; Phelps 1969). A.C. Pigou, who succeeded Marshall to the Cambridge Chair of Economics, chose 'the great problem of Unemployment' as the text of his 1908 Inaugural Lecture, *Economic Science in Relation to Practice*, to illustrate 'the practical bearing of our science'. He criticized what came to be known as the 'Treasury view', according to which the employment effects of government spending were nullified by declines in the employment of firms whose production was 'crowded out'. He suggested a positive multiplier effect of government spending on production and employment. The dispute was mainly about how, not whether, government affected output. Ralph Hawtrey contended that the employment effects of fiscal expansions depended on their means of finance. The way to stimulate demand was monetary policy acting through short-term interest rates. He

> had become interested in the trade cycle when Joseph Chamberlain, in support of his case for tariff reform, compared British exports in 1903, a year of depressed trade and low prices, with those in 1873, a year of active trade and high prices

and began writing *Good and Bad Trade* in '1909, when the depression which followed the American crisis of 1907 was still unrelieved' (1913: vii).

Keynes's colleague Dennis Robertson also advanced monetary theories of the trade cycle in *A Study of Industrial Fluctuation* (1915) and *Banking Policy and the Price Level* (1926). These are examples of the attention paid to the problems of unemployment by Marshall and his Cambridge students. William Beveridge (1909, 1930) of Oxford and the London School of Economics focused on costs of information. He proposed public agencies to facilitate movements of workers from shrinking to expanding industries and regions. He was director of labor exchanges from 1909 to 1916. In the United States, Fisher (1922) explained unemployment by the failure of interest rates to adjust to price changes. Wesley Mitchell (1913) had embarked on his statistical study of business cycles. 'The rise of macro-policies' was, T.W. Hutchison (1964: 144) wrote, 'a long revolution'.

52   Fiscal policy

Most of his fellow economists shared Keynes's opposition to the Bank of England's policy of deflating to restore the international value of the pound, which in 1920 was about $3.50 compared with $4.86 before the war (Moggridge 1969: 25–34). In a riskless world of neutral money, all that was needed for a costless and successful policy was to reduce domestic money and prices. Writing the equation of exchange $M=kPY$, where $M=$money, $P=$the price level, $Y=$ output, and $k=$the public's demand for money relative to its income, Keynes wrote:

> The error often made by careless adherents of the quantity theory [is] that an arbitrary doubling of M, since this in itself is assumed not to affect k and Y, must have the effect of raising P to double what it would have been otherwise....
>
> Now 'in the long run' this is probably true. If, after the American Civil War, the American dollar had been stabilized and defined by law at 10 percent below its present value, it would be safe to assume that M and P would now be just 10 per cent greater than they actually are and that the present values of k and Y would be entirely unaffected. But this *long run* is a misleading guide to current affairs. *In the long run* we are all dead. Economists set themselves too easy, too useless a task if in tempestuous seasons they can only tell us that when the storm is long past the ocean is flat again.
>
> (Keynes 1923: 65)

Keynes was doubly unfair when he accused his contemporaries of neglecting unemployment because they believed the automatically adjusting full-employment classical model applied to the world in which they lived.[4] On the other hand, his claim that they did not have a theory of unemployment was valid. They had to treat macro-problems on an ad hoc basis as deviations from equilibrium caused by imperfections. 'Market failures' such as downwardly inflexible wages and slowly adjusting interest rates arising from the perverse behavior of workers and capitalists required attention, but explanations lay outside their models. Keynes wrote of Robbins' opposition to demand management: 'It is the distinction of Prof. Robbins that he, almost alone, continues to maintain a consistent scheme of thought, his practical recommendations belonging to the same system as his theory' (1936: 30).

An unfortunate consequence of these views, Keynes thought, was the effort wasted by economists and policymakers in trying to make the world conform to the flexible-price assumptions of the classical model instead of working on a consistent framework that accepted the world as it was. When the chairman of the Macmillan Committee on Finance and Industry suggested that the dole interfered with 'economic laws' by increasing the resistance of workers to wage cuts, Keynes responded:

> I do not think they are sins against economic law. I do not think it is any more economic law that wages should go down easily than that they should

not. It is a question of facts. Economic law does not lay down the facts, it tells you what the consequences are.

(Keynes, *Collected Writings* xx: 83)

The divergent paths of theory and policy may be attributed to economists' joint ambitions for scientific status and popular influence. The former is thought to lay in the direction of *general* results. Unfortunately, these have been intractable except in models of competitive agents operating in a frictionless laissez faire environment. Since departures from general equilibria must be due to violations of the assumptions of the theory, economists who would influence policy must step outside their theories. They teach rigorous general equilibrium theory in the morning and, with exceptions like Robbins, offer ungrounded policy advice in the afternoon. Keynes's goal in the *GT* was to resolve this contradiction.

He had long believed intuitively that economic stability and the full employment of resources required a forceful government freed of the restraints of the gold standard. We have seen that he was preceded on this path by other economists. Although the tide was rolling before Keynes joined it, he became a leading advocate of change, and was more willing than most to look outside the standard theory for solutions. However, he aspired to a more lasting contribution – a theoretical justification of the intuition that persistent unemployment and economic instability might be alleviated by government commitment to intervention. The popular success of the *GT* owed much to the political attractiveness of its policies. It lessened the stigma of money creation and public works, and pushed the socially divisive wage cuts implied by classical theory out of the minds of policymakers – although, as we will see, the theory itself was rejected and the separation between the scientific and policy efforts of economists continued.

The General Theory according to Keynes

The broadness of its scope and imprecision of its method and results make the *GT* a difficult book. Unlike the completely specified models of the Classics and modern mathematical economists, not all the possible influences are worked out. Keynes's system has no unique solution. In particular, there is no clear tendency toward a unique equilibrium, full-employment or otherwise.

> It is an outstanding characteristic of the economic system in which we live ... that it seems capable of remaining in a chronic condition of sub-normal activity for a considerable period without any marked tendency either towards recovery or towards complete collapse. Moreover, the evidence indicates that full, or even approximately full, employment is of rare and short-lived occurrence.
>
> (1936: 249–50)

Keynes argued that his *general* theory explained these phenomena because, unlike the classical model, it took account of institutions and the 'psychological

54 Fiscal policy

propensities' of agents as they actually are – especially the three propensities that determine aggregate demand.

He first considered the

> psychological characteristic of the community, which we shall call its *propensity to consume*. That is to say, consumption will depend on the level of aggregate income and, therefore on the level of employment N, except when there is some change in the propensity to consume.
>
> (28)

This propensity plays a key role in the determination of income because consumers change their spending by less than the full amounts of changes in their incomes, and firms produce for expected sales. The intersection between the aggregate demand (the propensity to consume plus investment) and supply functions is *the effective demand*. Production beyond this point results in excess supply and falling prices and profits because the rise in consumption is less than the rise in income. Thus, given the propensity to consume and the rate of new investment, there will be only one level of employment consistent with equilibrium.

The psychological propensity to invest is the most unstable part of demand. Although it ought to be a function of the rate of interest relative to prospective yields on projects, the latter depend on future events

> about which our knowledge is vague and scanty.... The state of long-term expectation, upon which our decisions are based, does not solely depend ... on the most probable forecast we can make. It also depends on the *confidence* with which we make this forecast – on how highly we rate the likelihood of our best forecast turning out quite wrong.... The *state of confidence*, as they term it, is a matter to which practical men always pay the closest and most anxious attention. But economists have not analyzed it carefully.... In particular it has not been made clear that its relevance to economic problems comes in through its important influence on ... the investment-demand schedule.

Consequently, 'moderate changes in the prospective yield of capital or in the rate of interest will not be associated with very great changes in the rate of investment' (147–9, 250). Keynes expanded on this point in a 1937 response to his critics. G.L.S. Shackle (1962) called it his 'ultimate meaning'. The Classics, he wrote, dealt

> with a system in which the amount of the factors employed was given and the other relevant facts were known more or less for certain. This does not mean that we were dealing with a system in which change was ruled out, or even one in which the disappointment of expectation was ruled out. But at any given time facts and expectations were assumed to be given in a definite

and calculable form; and risks, of which, though admitted, not much notice was taken, were supposed to be capable of an exact actuarial computation....

Actually, however, we have, as a rule, only the vaguest idea of any but the most direct consequences of our acts. Thus the fact that our knowledge of the future is fluctuating, vague and uncertain, renders wealth a peculiarly unsuitable subject for the methods of classical economic theory.... By 'uncertain knowledge' ... I do not mean merely to distinguish what is known for certain from what is only probable.... The sense in which I am using the term is that in which the prospect of a European war is uncertain, or the price of copper and the rate of interest twenty years hence, or the obsolescence of a new invention, or the position of private wealth holders in the social system in 1970. About these matters there is no scientific basis on which to form any calculable probability whatever.

(Keynes 1937)[5]

The hesitancy of private agents extends to policymakers, as we will see for central bankers in Chapter 7.

Finally, the rate of interest is also 'a highly psychological phenomenon' (202). In the Classical system the rate of interest is determined by the intersection of saving and investment, or what is the same thing, at the point of equality between the supply and demand for output as a whole. The rate of interest is key to the system's adjustment to equilibrium. A rise in saving, for example, depresses the rate of interest which stimulates investment until it has filled the gap opened by the fall in consumption, and the demand for output is restored to its full-employment supply. A flexible rate of interest transforms saving into investment. 'Parsimony, and not industry, is the immediate cause of the increase of capital', Adam Smith wrote. 'What is annually saved is as regularly consumed as what is annually spent' (1776: 321). Another way of putting this is Say's Law of Markets, according to which supply creates its own demand (Keynes 1936: 26).

Keynes rejected the demand-equilibrating theory of interest in favor of its determination by the demand for money, given its supply.

It should be obvious that the rate of interest cannot be a return to saving or waiting as such. For if a man hoards his savings in cash, he earns no interest, though he saves just as much as before. On the contrary, the mere definition of the rate of interest tells us in so many words that the rate of interest is the reward for parting with liquidity for a specified period.

(1936: 166–7)

The reward is uncertain, however. In fact, '*uncertainty* as to the future course of the rate of interest is the sole intelligible explanation of ... liquidity-preference', that is, of the demand for money in excess of that required for current transactions. A general fear of an increase in the rate of interest, meaning capital losses on non-money assets, induces a shift from those assets into money and therefore the fear's realization.

56 *Fiscal policy*

> It follows that a given M_2 [liquidity demand for money] will not have a definite quantitative relation to a given rate of interest of r; what matters is not the *absolute* level of r but the degree of divergence from what is considered a fairly *safe* level of r, having regard to those calculations of probability which are being relied on.
>
> (201)

> It might be more accurate, perhaps, to say that the rate of interest is a highly conventional, rather than a highly psychological, phenomenon. For its actual value is largely governed by the prevailing view as to what its value is expected to be. *Any* level of interest which is accepted with sufficient conviction as *likely* to be durable *will* be durable; subject, of course, in a changing society to fluctuations for all kinds of reasons round the expected normal.
>
> (203)

Effective demand and stabilization policy

What were the implications of Keynes's system for policy? Since there is no reason to expect *effective demand*, as determined by the propensities to consume and invest, to correspond to full employment, intervention by the authorities will usually be necessary. However,

> The difficulties in the way of maintaining effective demand at a level high enough to provide full employment, which ensue from the association of a conventional and fairly stable long-term rate of interest with a fickle and highly unstable marginal efficiency of capital, should be, by now, obvious to the reader.
>
> (204)

An implication for monetary policy is that if the central bank decides on expansion, it had better be firm because 'a monetary policy which strikes public opinion as being experimental in character or easily liable to change may fail in its objective of greatly reducing the long-term rate of interest' (203). This view informed Keynes's policy advice before and after the *GT*. Although that book focused on depression, his long-term concern was for economic stability and he did not neglect the evils of inflation. In an article on 'Dear Money' in the *Times* of 13 January 1937 (*Collected Writings* xxi: 389), written during a moderate expansion, he urged the avoidance of 'dear money' like 'hell-fire'. If demand had to be curtailed, 'we must find other means ... than a higher rate of interest. For if we allow the rate of interest to be affected, we cannot easily reverse the trend.... A low-enough long-term rate cannot be achieved' when needed

> if we allow it to be believed that better terms will be obtainable from time to time by those who keep their resources liquid. The long-term rate of interest

must be kept *continuously* as near as possible to what we believe to be the long-term optimum. It is not suitable to be used as a short-period weapon.

This lesson was not learned by the Keynesians, for whom a flexible long-term rate of interest was the main instrument of monetary policy.

Acceptance and rejection

> This book is chiefly addressed to my fellow economists. I hope it will be intelligible to others. But its main purpose is to deal with difficult questions of theory, and only in the second place with the applications of this theory to practice.
>
> (1936: v)

Keynes and the Keynesians

Michael Lawlor wrote 'that those models that emphasize the uncertainty that Keynes found so pervasive and influential an aspect of investing and asset holding, and so of capital and money markets, will be those most in the spirit of Keynes's own ideas' (2006: 5). Few and certainly not the most popular expositions or developments of Keynes met this test.

The method of the *GT* is distinguished from the classical economics by its dependence on three fundamental properties, as Keynes saw them, of a capitalist market economy: the limits to rationality imposed on decision-makers by an uncertain future; the importance of the financial markets, especially in the determination of the rate of interest, to macroeconomic outcomes; and the realization that contracts are in money rather than real exchanges equivalent to barter. Regarding the last, he wrote Pigou in 1930 that the primary difference between them 'arises out of a doubt as to whether the method of abstraction by which you first of all deal with the problems in terms of a barter economy, and then at a later stage bring in monetary considerations, is a legitimate means of approach in dealing with a short-period problem of this kind, the characteristics of which are, or may be, hopelessly entangled with features arising out of monetary factors' (Skidelsky 1992: 367). The 'real' approach had been expressed by Mill when he finally introduced money after having dealt with production, distribution, and exchange:

> There cannot ... be intrinsically a more insignificant thing, in the economy of society, than money; ...
>
> The introduction of money does not interfere with [is 'neutral' toward, in modern parlance] the operation of any of the Laws of Value laid down in the preceding chapters. The reasons which make the temporary or market value of things depend on the demand and supply and their average and permanent values depend on their cost of production, are as applicable to a money system as to a system of barter. Things which by barter would

exchange for one another, will, if sold for money, sell for an equal amount of it, and will exchange for one another still, though the process of exchanging them will consist of two operations instead of only one.

(Mill 1848: 488)

Jevons, the other marginalists, and economic theory in general formalized Mill's argument, which Keynes vigorously opposed. In a system of money contracts for future performance that is unavoidably uncertain and conditioned on conventions about money wages and interest rates, he wrote, 'neutral money' is 'a nonsense notion' (*Collected Writings* xiv: 93). He wrote in 1933,

> The theory which I desiderate would deal ... with an economy in which money plays a part of its own and affects motives and decisions, and is, in short, one of the operative factors in the situation, so that the course of events cannot be predicted in either the long period or in the short, without a knowledge of the behavior of money between the first state and the last. And it is this which we ought to mean when we speak of a *monetary economy*.
>
> (Keynes 1933)

He elaborated on this point in analyzing decisions in the face of 'uncertain knowledge'. In answer to the question how 'we manage in such circumstances to behave in a manner which saves our faces as rational economic men', he answered that 'we have devised for the purpose a variety of techniques'. Primarily, we assume that the present is the best available guide to the future, better, in fact, than is justified by past experience. 'In other words we largely ignore the prospect of future changes about the character of which we know nothing.' Furthermore, we rest this assumption on the authority of *existing* opinion, or *conventional* judgment. The implications for resistance to changes in wages and interest rates are clear. However, these conventions, 'being based on so flimsy a foundation, [are] subject to sudden and violent changes. The practice of calmness and immobility, of certainty and security, suddenly breaks down. New fears and hopes will, without warning, take charge.' What was unthinkable yesterday is conventional today.

> All these pretty, polite techniques, made for a well-panelled board room and a nicely regulated market, are liable to collapse. At all times the vague panic fears and equally vague and unreasoned hopes are not really lulled and lie but a little way below the surface.
>
> (Keynes 1937)

Robertson, now a critic, complained of Keynes's one-market-at-a-time analysis, particularly his focus on the money market as the sole determinant of the rate of interest:

> On the broader question of our respective attitudes to the work of our predecessors ... there *is* of course a difference of temperament.... [M]ay I

suggest that I – managing to keep throughout in touch with all the elements of the problem in a dim and fumbling way – have been a sort of glow worm, whose feeble glimmer lands on all objects in the neighbourhood: while you, with your far more powerful intellect, have been a light-house casting a far more penetrating, but sometimes fatally distorting, beam on one object after another in succession.

(Robertson letter to Keynes, 1 January 1938
(Keynes *Collected Writings* xxix: 166–8))

Robertson could not see why the rate of interest should not be jointly determined by the supply and demand for money at a moment in time (as Keynes's stock-of-financial-assets approach would have it) and the flow of the supply and demand for credit over time (saving and investment, which Keynes contended that the classics insisted on to the exclusion of the first). 'Such loose phrases as that interest is not the reward of not-spending but the reward of not-hoarding seem to argue a curious inhibition against visualising more than two margins at once' (Robertson 1938).

Robertson won the day eventually as the Keynesians dismantled the *GT*. An important difference between Keynes and his nominal followers was the latter's decision to continue the Classics' comparative-statistics analysis of models with unique equilibria. The modern view that the equilibrium rate of interest depends on saving and investment, with the money market having transitory effects, is Classical (Sayers 1953; Mill 1848: 405–6; Wicksell 1898; Fisher 1922).

Hicks' reconciliation of 'Keynes and the Classics' (1937) became the standard interpretation of the *GT*. The rate of interest equated the supply and demand for money (LM) *and* saving and investment (IS). Hicks' model was also noteworthy, like other Keynesian interpretations, for its abstraction from uncertainty and stable equilibria. A crucial element of Keynesian economics, implicit in the Hicks' *IS-LM* model but increasingly explicit in economics journals and texts, was its explanation of unemployment by the downward rigidity of money wages. This was the model that Keynes had tried to overturn, namely the classical theory of real price ratios and interest rates that eliminated excess supplies except in the presence of market failure. Instead of the classical system's automatic market-clearing tendencies toward full employment by means of flexible wages, prices, and interest rates, Keynes saw partial adjustments that only coincidentally produced full employment. Instead of the offsetting increase in investment responding to the fall in interest rates caused by an increase in the propensity to save, income adjusted downward to the reduction in aggregate demand – and stayed there pending a fortuitous arousal of animal spirits or government intervention. Saving and investment were coordinated by adjustments of income, not interest rates – with or without flexible wages.

The Keynesian dismissal of Keynes was made possible by their neglect of his keystone – uncertainty. If the future is known, investment decisions are straightforward, and liquidity preference as Keynes discussed it, that is, 'psychologically' or 'conventionally' persistent levels of interest rates driven by fears of

60 Fiscal policy

capital losses, is unknown. The admission of calculable risk does not affect the classical model. If the future is actuarially calculable, wages can be negotiated in light of their probable effects on future tradeoffs between work and leisure for workers and profits for employers. Efforts to hold on to conventional wages or interest rates as the safest course in the absence of information about the future cannot be rationalized in the classical system. The Keynesians threw out the baby (a theory of unemployment as a consequence of disorder) with the bathwater (the complications of uncertainty in a money economy). His biographer perceptively noted that in Keynes's 1937 response to his critics ('The theory of unemployment'), he 'is saying that his own theory is what the classical theory would have had to be had it taken uncertainty seriously' (Skidelsky 1992: 618).

The tractability of the Keynesian simplifications combined with Keynes's policy message to preserve its dominant position for four decades. '[T]he Keynesian economic system is essentially a machine which grinds out results according to where the several dials controlling the system are set', Lawrence Klein wrote in *The Keynesian Revolution* (1947: 153). Straightforward results followed from the assumptions of known probability distributions and *certainty equivalent* expectations (Theil 1961: 414–24).

Keynes saw the beginning of econometric models and did not like them. Asked by the League of Nations to review Jan Tinbergen's *Statistical Testing of Business Cycle Theories* (1939), Keynes was skeptical of the relations estimated by 'the method of multiple correlation'.

> Is it claimed that there is a likelihood that the equations will work approximately *next* time? With a free hand to choose coefficients and time lag, one can, with enough industry, always cook a formula to fit moderately well a limited range of past facts. But what does this prove? ... Is it assumed that the future is a determinate function of *past statistics*? What place is left for expectation and the state of confidence relating to the future?
> What place is allowed for non-numerical factors, such as inventions, politics, labour troubles, wars, earthquakes, financial crises?
> (Keynes letter to R. Tyler, League of Nations, 1938
> (*Collected Writings* xiv: 287))

It is ironic that the first Nobel Prize in Economic Science (1969) was shared between Tinbergen, for his applications of econometrics to Keynesian models, and Ragner Frisch, long-time editor of *Econometrica*. Klein won the prize in 1980.

The New Classics

Keynesians criticized Milton Friedman's reluctance to specify the model behind his monetary rule (Gordon 1974), but their own explicitness got them in trouble and contributed to Friedman's success. Monetarism was never adopted in practice or by the majority of economists in the sense of accepting the constant money-growth rule. However, the victories of the fundamental monetarist positions that free economies were stable and government money-creation caused inflation with no beneficial side effects were assisted by the rejection of Keynesianism made possible by its *falsifiability*. 'It is the fact that Keynesian theory lent itself so readily to the formulation of explicit econometric models which accounts for the dominant scientific position it attained by the 1960s' (Lucas and Sargent 1978). Keynesianism's strength was also its weakness. They 'had not suspected that radically anti-Keynesian conclusions were the logical outcome of [the standard and] seemingly innocuous maximizing assumptions' (Akerlof 2007).

A word about what was falsified is in order. Until 1960, Keynesian recommendations were limited to the government's influence on aggregate demand by taxing and spending (fiscal policy). It is amazing that money and prices were absent from these models, not only because they were the center of Keynes's theory but because one of the greatest inflations in history was underway. The Consumer Price Index more than doubled between 1933 and 1960. When Keynesians noticed them, prices were treated as given from outside their model in cost-push fashion by monopolistic firms and unions. The task of the little-noticed central bank was to accommodate fiscal expansions by increasing money to forestall the unemployment that would result from high real wages (Bowen 1960).

The Keynesian/interventionist model changed in the 1960s for several reasons. Interest in demand management had waned because political opposition in principle, as well as the practical selection and implementation of projects, had come to be recognized as insurmountable obstacles. Furthermore, the empirical validity of the classical assumption that consumption was a function of anticipated income implied that transitory fiscal changes would not significantly influence demand (Modigliani and Brumberg 1954; Friedman 1957; Eisner 1969). Keynesian fiscal policy was impractical and illogical.

Keynesians remarkably found in their failures a way to preserve their activist policy stance. The rediscoveries of inflation and money provided a policy opportunity in A.W. Phillips' (1958) observations of the negative correlation between unemployment and the rate of change of wages. This relation had often been noted but it became the basis of Keynesian policy proposals (Hume 1752; Fisher 1926). Paul Samuelson and Robert Solow (1960) claimed that the Phillips Curve contained a 'menu of choice between different degrees of unemployment and price stability'. By their estimates:

> In order to achieve the nonperfectionist's goal of high enough output to give us no more than 3 per cent unemployment, the price index might have to rise by as much as 4 to 5 per cent per year. That much price rise would seem to be the necessary cost of high employment and production in the years immediately ahead.

A hoped-for advantage of the Phillips Curve was that inflation could be manipulated by monetary policy, which was potentially more flexible than fiscal policy. In the event, it failed empirically and logically. The empirical failure was spectacular.

> [T]he models of the late 1960s predicted a sustained U.S. unemployment rate of 4 percent as consistent with a 4 percent annual rate of inflation. Based on this prediction, many economists at the time urged a deliberate policy of inflation. Certainly the erratic 'fits and starts' character of U.S. policy in the 1970s cannot be attributed to recommendations based on Keynesian models, but the inflationary bias on average of monetary and fiscal policy in this period should, according to all these models, have produced the lowest average unemployment rates for any decade since the 1940s. In fact, as we know, they produced the highest unemployment rates since the 1930s. This was econometric failure on a grand scale.
>
> (Lucas and Sargent 1978)

The logical failure of the Phillips Curve's 'menu of choice' arose from the Keynesian mixture of rationality and irrationality in different aspects of individual behavior. A 'policy' is systematic and therefore known. An x-percent inflation policy will presumably be taken into account – and thus undermined – in the wage contracts of actors who make rational decisions elsewhere.

Modestly defined, 'rational' expectations are simply consistent with the other assumptions of rational behavior in Keynesian models, thereby restoring the Classical conclusion that monetary policies are without real effects. Mill wrote:

> Another of the fallacies from which the advocates of an inconvertible currency derive support is the notion that an increase of the currency quickens industry. This idea was set afloat by Hume in his *Essay on Money* and has had many devoted adherents since. Mr. Attwood [of the Birmingham currency school] maintained that a rise of prices, produced by an increase of paper currency, stimulates every producer to his utmost exertions, and brings all the capital and labour of the country into complete employment.... I presume, however, that the inducement which, according to Mr. Attwood, excited this unusual ardour in all persons engaged in production must have been the expectation of getting more commodities generally, more real wealth, in exchange for the produce of their labour, and not merely more pieces of paper. This expectation, however, must have been, by the very terms of the supposition, disappointed, since, all prices being supposed to rise equally, no one was really better paid for his goods than before. Those who agree with Mr. Attwood could only succeed in winning people on to these unwonted exertions by a prolongation of what would in fact be a delusion; contriving matters so that by a progressive rise of money prices every producer shall always seem to be in the very act of obtaining an increased remuneration which he never, in reality, does obtain. It is unnecessary to advert to any other of the objections to this plan than that of its total impracticability. It calculates on finding the whole world persisting for ever in the belief that more pieces of paper are more riches, and never discovering that, with all their paper, they cannot buy more of anything than they could before.
>
> (Mill 1848: 550)

To the illogic of the Phillips Curve was added the fallacy of estimation subject to the *Lucas critique* (Lucas 1976). Effective policy cannot be conducted with a model estimated from data generated by another policy, including no policy. The model's parameters must be newly computed for each policy proposal because the behavior of private agents is conditioned on their expectations of policy. Econometricians might observe a Phillips Curve yet fail to provide the authorities with an output-inflation. For example, suppose the relations observed by Hume, Fisher, and Phillips were consequences of demand fluctuations producing covariations between money, prices, and employment. Changes in money independently imposed on the system will not yield the same relations; in fact, in the Keynesian system made logical such price changes do affect employment. We might observe a Phillips Curve and be unable to manipulate it. It melts in our hands.

Where does this leave macroeconomics and how have the Keynesians responded? Their capitulation has not been total although their advocacy of employment policy has moderated. 'New Keynesians' stress that economic decisions, especially wages and prices, adjust sluggishly – as distinct from the rapid market clearing of New Classical models (Gordon 1990; Romer 1993), although the system is too complex for beneficial government interventions. This recognition of an imperfect economy with unclear implications for government policy brings the New Keynesians closer than Keynes, the Keynesians, or even the New Classics to the Classical economists.

The possibility of macroeconomic policy

The *GT*'s review of past efforts to explain and remedy deficiencies in aggregate demand ended with a tribute to

> the brave army of heretics..., who, following their intuitions, have preferred to see the truth obscurely and imperfectly rather than to maintain error, reached indeed with clearness and consistency and by easy logic, but on hypotheses inappropriate to the facts.
> (Keynes 1936: 371)

Economists rejected Keynes's rationale for the brave army's intuition. 'Most people who admire Keynes accept the stimulus, take from him what is congenial to them and leave the rest', Joseph Schumpeter observed in 1937 (Skidelsky 1992: 26). 'Keynes's ideas became central to the policy discussion..., not because most of those concerned "bought" his *General Theory*, but because they fitted the preoccupations of the policy-making elite'.

This leads to the question whether the *GT*, had it been taken seriously, could have succeeded where the Keynesian departures failed? Two considerations suggest 'maybe'. First, the model of the *GT* may have been logically consistent (or at least not proved logically inconsistent) if only because it was left open and imprecise in several places. Unique states are excluded by psychological variations and uncertainty. Sub-normal activity might exist for considerable periods 'without any marked tendency either toward recovery or toward complete collapse'.

The second consideration is closely related to the first. While the *GT*'s argument was abstruse and difficult in places, in other places it presented situations that are more familiar to 'practical men' than to Keynes's 'fellow economists'. The genuine uncertainty discussed above is an example. Others are the recognition of bad times due to deficient demand and his emphasis on the short-term, especially in the financial markets that Keynes knew from experience. Bankers and other economic agents make money contracts in environments of incomplete information and uncertain futures. They see the world much as Keynes described it. As a speculator and student of the financial markets, he saw the world from 'the street' – Wall Street and Lombard Street as well as Main Street and the High Street – populated by agents with 'psychological propensities' who trust to 'conventions' in their engagements with uncertainty (Lawlor 1994; 2006). The *GT* might have been a better medium of communication between economists and practical men than was achieved by its textbook versions. The world of the *GT* has much in common with what might be called the 'folk model' of the person on the street who believes in effective demand, holds 'vague' and 'flimsy' views of the future, and resists wage and price cuts, enduring quantity adjustments in the process (Blinder 1997b; Lawlor 2000; Clower 1965; Leijonhufvud 1968).

On the other hand, applications of Keynes's model would have been difficult. He discussed its policy potential in his 1937 paper.

> It is not surprising that the volume of investment, thus determined, should fluctuate widely from time to time. For it depends on two sets of judgments about the future, neither of which rests on an adequate or secure foundation – on the propensity to hoard [which determines the rate of interest] and on opinions of the future yield of capital-assets.
>
> The theory can be summed up by saying that, given the psychology of the public, the level of output and employment as a whole depends on the amount of investment. I put it in this way, not because this is the only factor on which aggregate output depends, but because it is usual in a complex system to regard as the *causa causans* that factor which is most prone to sudden and wide fluctuation....
>
> This that I offer is, therefore, a theory of why output and employment are so liable to fluctuation. It does not offer a ready-made remedy as to how to avoid these fluctuations and to maintain output at a steady optimum level.... Naturally I am interested not only in the diagnosis, but also in the cure; ... But I consider that my suggestions for a cure, which, avowedly, are not worked out completely, are on a different plane from the diagnosis. They are not meant to be definitive; they are subject to all sorts of special assumptions and are necessarily related to the particular conditions of the time.
>
> (Keynes 1937)

The comparative-static general-equilibrium Keynesian models were worthless, even theoretically, as stabilization devices. That leaves the long run, which might have been Keynes's primary concern, anyway. His demand theory of output, especially when extended into the future, paints a dismal picture. It is shown in Figure 3.1, where the psychological propensity to consume (C) rises less than in proportion to income. Investment (I) is uncertain but often assumed constant as in the figure. The 'one level of employment consistent with equilibrium', where all output is demanded, is Y_e, which is usually short of full employment. The excess supply is denoted *Gap*. The economy cannot grow without outside help. If it is to grow,

> The State will have to exercise a guiding influence on the propensity to consume partly through its scheme of taxation, partly by fixing the rate of interest, and partly, perhaps, in other ways. Furthermore, it seems unlikely that the influence of banking policy on the rate of interest will be sufficient by itself to determine an optimum rate of investment. I conceive, therefore, that a somewhat comprehensive socialization of investment will prove the only means of securing an approximation to full employment; though this need not exclude all manner of compromises and of devices by which public authority will co-operate with private initiative.
>
> (Keynes 1936: 378)

Alvin Hansen (1939) extended this stagnation thesis in his presidential address to the American Economic Association. We can sympathize with such pessimism in the 1930s, in the midst of fears for the end of capitalism. Less understandable is its application by the president's Council of Economic Advisors in the 1960s, when they called for demand boosts regardless of conditions.

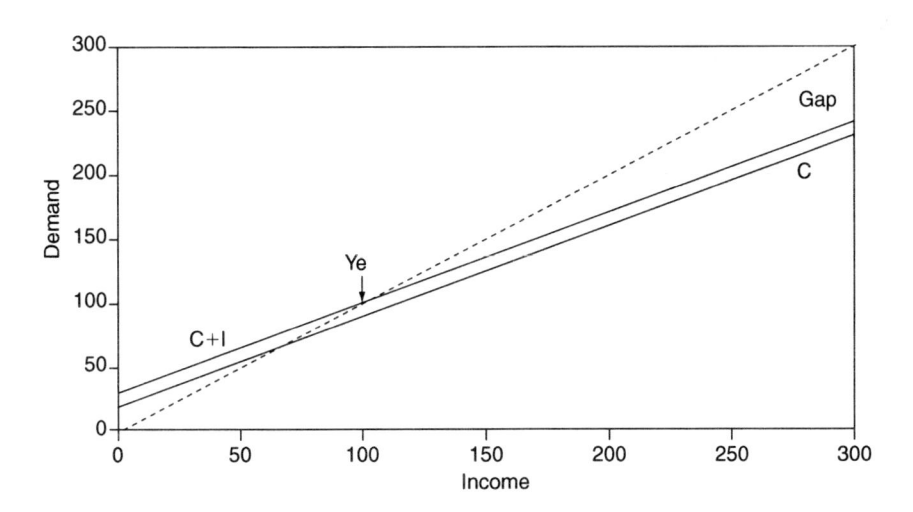

Figure 3.1 Keynes's demand-determined income.

In conclusion, neither long-run nor short-run Keynesian policies have been pursued. The reasons are many, including their illogicalities, empirical refutations, and difficulties of implementation. Demand has not been deficient – the modern concern is with inadequate saving – and socialism performs miserably. Considering politics, official agencies are not given the opportunity to pursue discretionary fiscal policies. Groups with political clout have not been persuaded that the probable benefits of these policies exceed their more certain costs. Congress's fear of an Executive empowered with an independent fiscal authority has not been overcome. We have learned that ideas and institutions share remarkable persistence. 'Share' is key here. As Jacob Viner (1944) wrote about Keynes's statement at the beginning of this chapter: 'I am ... impressed by the extent to which vested interests and going institutions seem to have the power to generate ideas congruent with themselves.' Without taking away from the heroism of the tax resistors in Chapter 2, their ideas did not conflict with their interests. Given persistence in the institutions, interests, and ideas of capitalism, we should be surprised to find revolutions in its fiscal and monetary policies.

George Washington understood the importance of interests in even the most idealistic of causes. Resignations of his officers threatened the 'very existence of the Army'. He urged 'their Country ... to make "a decent provision for their future support"'.

> Men may speculate as they will; they may talk of patriotism; they may draw a few examples from ancient story, of great achievements performed by its influence; but whoever builds upon it, as a sufficient Basis for conducting a long ... War, will find themselves deceived in the end. We must take the passions of Men as Nature has given them, and those principles as a guide which are generally the rule of Action. I do not mean to exclude altogether the idea of patriotism. I know it exists, and I know it has done much in the present contest. But I will venture to assert, that a great and lasting war can never be supported on this principle alone. It must be aided by a prospect of interest, or some reward.
> (George Washington, Letter from Valley Forge to Congressman John Bannister, 21 April 1778 (Washington 1944: xi))

4 Practice
The stability of Federal government deficits

> The high aspirations of American Keynesians to become discretionary managers of fiscal policy faded quickly. The powers to tax and spend, after all, are the meat and potatoes of the political process. Congress had no taste for delegating its authority over these matters to self-proclaimed experts who had never carried a precinct.
>
> (Barber 1996: 161)

Before the mid-twentieth century the US government ran deficits in war and paid the debt down in peace except when recessions depleted tax receipts. The budget was in surplus every fiscal year from 1866 to 1893, 1920 to 1930, and overall, 51 of 60 peacetime years between 1866 and 1930. By comparison, there were five surpluses between 1950 and 1997, none of them after 1969. What were the reasons for the change? The standard explanation or assumption in the economics literature is the diminished aversion to deficits arising from Keynesianism and the trauma of the Great Depression. This chapter suggests a different explanation that rests on traditional practices instead of new ideas: the principle of tax smoothing continued and deficits were due to war. The Cold War was small, but a war nevertheless. It 'was a real war, as real as the two world wars', with a major campaign – Korea – and several minor ones, a Soviet buildup in the 1970s that, like the German offensive in 1918, turned out to be the last burst of energy by the losing side, Reagan's military buildup, and again similar to World War I, a sudden and unexpected collapse (Friedman 2000: xi–xii). A simple model of choice between long-term budget balance and tax smoothing is developed. The estimates presented here are tentative – further research is needed – but they suggest continuity in government budget principles, particularly that spending shocks should be paid for over time. What was new after 1950 was significant military spending of unprecedented length, not its finance.

The inspiration for this approach was a pair of observations: the end of the Cold War about 1990 and the beginning of the War on Terror in 2001. The rise and fall of deficits with military spending is seen in Table 4.1. Beginning in 1954, after the Korean War, the long period of small D accompanied a long period of modest W (Figure 4.2). Their joint decline in the second-to-last column of Table 4.1 (subsequent to the Gulf War and the recession of the early 1990s)

68 Fiscal policy

Table 4.1 Military spending (W) and the deficit (D) (average annual percentages of GNP)

	1876–1916	1918–19	1920–30	1942–46	1954–89	1994–2001	2002–07	2008–12[a]
W	0.7	18.6	1.5	31.9	7.4	3.3	3.9	3.9
D	–0.2	14.3	–0.8	18.7	2.0	0.1	2.5	1.0

Sources same as Table 4.5.

Note
a Estimated.

resembled other shifts from war to peace. The next-to-last column is different. Unlike other wars, most of the rise in D during the War on Terror was due to tax cuts. However, rising revenue as time wears on suggests, in the absence of other fiscal changes, that the deficit will again be due to military spending. Projecting the budget and GDP to 2008–12 gives the estimates in the last column.

Keynesian and other popular explanations of the post-World War II deficits are summarized in the first section, which also presents evidence that academic discussions of fiscal policy in these years had little relation to practice. The second section constructs and estimates a model of government deficits. Robert Barro found them to be 'varied in order to maintain expected constancy in tax rates' for the period 1922–76, excluding World War II (1979; also 1984). The pre-1941 dummy had a significant negative effect, and inclusion of World War II reduced the fit, leading to the criticism (Shoven 1984): 'This is particularly destructive to the theory since these years provide, in some sense, "the real test" of the theory [because] battle casualties are the primary proxy for temporary government expenditures' (which was Barro's main explanatory variable). Brian Goff and Robert Tollison (2002) considered all years between 1889 and 1998, and also found that deficits corresponded with temporary government spending.

There is no reason to exclude war years once we recognize that military spending, during the Cold War as much as other wars, was the principal form of unusual spending. The sample is expanded to all periods since 1876, when quarterly estimates of GNP become available so that they can be used with fiscal years. (GDP has replaced GNP as the chief indicator of aggregate product, but the former is used for historical series.[1]) The last section reviews the fiscal-policy insignificance of Keynes and the Great Depression. In summary, a traditional budgeting model explains post-World War II deficits better than Keynesianism, the growing complexities of government, or cultural shifts.

Popular explanations of the persistent deficits

Skewed stabilization policy

The main thrust of Keynesianism has been the management of government budgets to stabilize aggregate demand. It should be noted that stabilization policy should be neutral with respect to government deficits over the business cycle. Deficits in recessions should be matched by surpluses in expansions. The long period of post-World War II deficits cannot be explained by stabilization policy unless the policy was skewed, that is, unless efforts to reinforce weak demands exceeded those restraining above-trend demands.

Unfortunately for Keynesian hopes, the effects of such predictable government actions are, because of the 'permanent income' hypothesis (discussed in Chapter 3), unlikely to be significant. The consumption effects of higher disposable income through lower taxes that are expected to be reversed later in the business cycle will be small. This 'life-cycle' approach to consumption decisions was well understood before Keynes (Fisher 1930: ch. 5; Ricardo 1821: 243–5). Ricardo's 'equivalence theorem', by which the wealth and consumption effects of a current tax or borrowing against future taxes are the same, is used in the budget decisions below. We saw in Chapter 3 that Keynes criticized the 'Classics' for ignoring all but 'calculable', or 'actuarial', expectations. His disciples ignored even these.

This chapter is less concerned with whether stabilization policy might have been effective than whether it was tried, and the answer, here too, is negative. Downturns attract political attention, but responses have been erratic and tardy. The sometimes favorable 'political climate' was not matched by its application (Salant 1989; Tobin 1987; Winch 1969: 312). The passage below records that in none of the nine recessions between 1948 and 1991 was a stimulus program adopted before the downturn ended. Any countercyclical stimulus of the 2001 tax cut was accidental because it was proposed for long-term reasons before the recession was predicted. The 2008 tax rebates were probably the most timely of the group.

A review of stabilization policy after World War II

In general, all such actions were taken after recovery had begun. Bruce Bartlett ['If It Ain't Broke, Don't Fix It', *Wall Street Journal*, Dec. 2, 1992] has identified the dates of passage for all of the postwar cyclical fiscal programs. None of them was finally enacted before the date the preceding recession ended, according to subsequent 'official' dating by the National Bureau of Economic Research. Specifically, for the recession beginning in November 1948 and ending in October 1949, President Truman proposed an 11-point program on July 11, 1949. Only one of the points was enacted, an *Advance Planning for Public Works Act*, signed in October, the month the recession ended. No fiscal action was taken to stem the recession of July 1953 to May 1954.

Congressional Democrats passed three countercyclical bills to deal with the 1957–58 recession, and President Eisenhower signed them. A highway bill was signed in April, the month the recession ended, and unemployment compensation and rivers-and-harbors bills were passed later that summer. The brief recession of April 1960 to February 1961 spanned two administrations. President Kennedy proposed several measures in February 1961, and an unemployment compensation bill was enacted in March. The *Area Redevelopment Act* was passed in May, and a Social Security Bill was passed in June.

The recession of December 1969 to November 1970 led to one major legislative act, the *Public Works Impact Program*, enacted in August 1971, almost a year after the recession had ended. The recession of November 1973 to March 1975 prompted several pieces of legislation, the first of which was passed the month the recession ended. That law included tax rebates and extended unemployment benefits.

No action was taken regarding the January–July 1980 recession other than to remove credit controls. However, the Reagan administration did adopt two countercyclically oriented programs for its [1981–82] recession. The *Surface Transportation Assistance Act* was enacted in January 1983 and the *Emergency Jobs Appropriations Act* was also passed in the year after the recession had ended. The recession of 1990–91 prompted a Democratic proposal, which President Bush vetoed. President Clinton's stimulus program, submitted after the recession was officially over, was defeated in Congress.

(Keech 1995: 160–1)

George W. Bush campaigned on a tax cut in 2000, and pointed to its countercyclical value when a recession was forecast. The cut was passed in May 2001, and the recession's trough was dated November 2001. The president signed the Job Creation and Worker Assistance Act in March 2002.

The tax rebates provided by the stimulus package of February 2008, could be the most timely effort of the group. A recession had probably not begun, although leading indicators had been predicting a recession for several months.

Estimates suggesting weak-to-no discretionary fiscal policy are reported in Table 4.2. The response of the full-employment surplus to changes in the GDP gap in the first column is statistically insignificant. That is, changes in output have not systematically induced budget responses. The gap is made significant,

Table 4.2 Determinants of the full-employment surplus (quarterly change relative to full-employment GDP) (1956:2–2001:4)

Constant	GDP gap(-1)	Budget surplus(-1)	R^2
0.003	−0.024		0.01
(0.040)	(0.016)		
−0.087*	−0.057***	−0.070***	0.04
(0.051)	(0.019)	(0.025)	

Source: Auerbach.

Notes
Standard errors in parentheses.
Adjusted R^2.
* Significant at 10% level.
*** Significant at 1% level.

but is counteracted, by the addition of the lagged budget surplus. This confirms the results of 'many authors [that] U.S. fiscal policy over the years has had the property that increased levels of national debt lead to higher subsequent budget surpluses' (Auerbach 2002).

A change in attitude

'Until the advent of the "Keynesian revolution" in the middle years of this century', James Buchanan and Richard Wagner (1977: 3) wrote, 'the fiscal conduct of the American Republic was informed by [the] Smithian principle of fiscal responsibility', that ' "What is prudence in the conduct of every private family can scarce be folly in that of a great kingdom" '; meaning that

> Government should not spend without imposing taxes; and governments should not place future generations in bondage by deficit financing of public outlays designed to provide temporary and short-lived benefits.... Keynesianism stood the Smithian analogy on its head. The stress was placed on the differences rather than the similarities between a family and the state, and notably with respect to principles of prudent fiscal conduct.

An example is the 'paradox of thrift', according to which increases in private propensities to save reduce realized saving by depressing aggregate demand and income (Samuelson 1958: 237).

These differences may be exaggerated. The tendency of government budgets to be in deficit during recessions and surplus during expansions, since their revenues depend on income, is consistent with the family behavior described by the life-cycle consumption model. Households smooth consumption by borrowing and lending in much the same way that governments incur deficits and surpluses in the course of smoothing taxes. This was the pattern of government budgets before Keynes. Although presidents and Congresses deplored recession deficits, politics and institutions inhibited remedial measures (Anderson 1986; Firestone 1960). Keynesian claims that governments had been obsessed with balancing the budget annually ignored the record (Smithies 1960).

Buchanan and Wagner were not complaining of stabilization policy itself. Surpluses in good times and deficits in bad times do not produce deficits on average. Rather, by making deficits respectable in recessions, Keynesianism eroded fiscal discipline in general. This is not proven. Buchanan and Wagner credit economists with more influence than the evidence supports. Public attitudes toward deficits do not seem to have changed. The distinction between the approval of economists and the disapproval of others is a common result of opinion surveys (Caplan 2001). Talk is cheap but it tells against the Buchanan–Wagner argument, which rests on the respectability of deficits, that is, on attitudes. People also express clear reasons for opposing deficits, such as to 'fight inflation' and 'reduce wasteful programs', and there is evidence that deficits influence votes. Statements of public officials also suggest that opposition to deficits has political value (Bratton 1994; Fair 1996; Blinder and Holtz-Eakin 1984). A report of the Office of Management and Budget, published by the Executive Office of the President, assured the public that 'Generally speaking, the Federal government plans its budget much like families do', and stressed 'fiscal discipline' (2001: 6, 21–32).

Also unchanged is the jealous watch of politicians over their spending and taxing powers. The history of conflicts between governments and the governed has been dominated by taxation. The forces reviewed above in Chapter 2 are still with us, as seen in Congress's continued refusal of executive discretion over taxing and spending. A 1993 executive-branch survey of the federal government reported that managers 'had too little flexibility because of extensive spending controls, many of which were imposed by Congress'. Agencies must obtain formal approval from the appropriate congressional committee before 'reprogramming' appropriated funds between activities (Wetterau 1998: 189–91). Congress's monitoring of Alexander Hamilton's Treasury continues.

Institutional complexity

It is argued that the continuing deficits resulted from a breakdown in the budget process due to the increased size and complexity of government, which, combined with individual preferences for spending over taxing, generated deficits that no one wanted. It is in this sense that government might differ from households. The complexity and unpredictability of the process are inevitable, agreed the long-term civil servant Alice Rivlin (1984), if for no other reason than that the budget implications of many programs depend on future events that are subject to the more-or-less optimistic forecasts of their supporters and opponents. However that neglects the fundamental question of political will, 'which an alternative set of procedures will not remedy'. It 'simply is not the case' that 'deficits are the sums of many small, uncontrollable items', Rivlin wrote. 'When the deficit arises from growth in a few big programs outrunning growth in revenues, there is no solution except to cut the growth in those programs or raise taxes, or both. Procedural changes will not make these choices easier.'

The attempt to centralize the budget process in the Budget and Impoundment Control Act of 1974 was preceded by the effort of the Budget and Accounting Act of 1921 to limit deficits that had become more frequent even before World War I and continued after the war (Keech 1995: 166–7) – possibly due more to recessions and the building of the Panama Canal than to weakening fiscal discipline. The earlier act seemed to work (helped by the economic expansion of 1921–24), whereas the latter, despite having helped to 'overcome a lack of coordination in budgeting..., has not solved the budget problem' (Gilmour 1990: 224–5). The 1990 Budget Enforcement Act's requirement that spending proposals be accompanied by reductions elsewhere or by revenue increases are overridden or ignored (Riedl 2005). President Reagan's budget director concluded that the process gives people what they want (Stockman 1986: 376) – a belief supported by the statistical insignificance of budget procedures.

The Stagnation Thesis

The warnings of Keynes and others that future demand would be increasingly inadequate for full employment were discussed in Chapter 3. The socialization of investment and manipulation of the tax structure to encourage consumption would be necessary. These fears reached crisis proportions at the Econometric Society's 1944 Round Table on Forecasting Postwar Demand that consisted primarily of concerns for the effects of the war's end on demand (Mosak 1945; Smithies 1945). An early indication that the government did not share these worries – notwithstanding the Keynesian rhetoric of the Employment Act of 1946 – was its postwar budget. Table 4.3 shows that the war-to-postwar budget shifted about as rapidly from deficit to surplus after the Keynesian Revolution as before. It went from a record deficit of 48 percent of GNP in 1945 to record surpluses of 4 percent and 12 percent in 1947 and 1948. The administration was less concerned with unemployment than 'bringing the boys home' and maintaining taxes to fight inflation (Truman 1956: 485–9; Witte 1985: 134). Figure 4.2 indicates that the deficit experience up to the mid-1950s, which included the Korean War and the 1948–49 and 1954–55 recessions, was not unusual.

Hopes for Keynesian practice were renewed in 1960 by the election of the youthful John Kennedy that coincided with the coming of age of economists whose education had included the New Economics. A new generation of politicians and economic advisors succeeded those whose aspirations had been developed in the classical era of limited possibilities. Together, they would 'get the country moving again'.

The interest in growth was encouraged by the obstacles to flexible fiscal policy. The chairman of Kennedy's Council of Economic Advisors (CEA) saw these obstacles as a major policy problem to be solved. Although 'we have ... learned the great aggregate lessons of modern economic policy,... we will not realize their

Table 4.3 Federal government budgets in selected years

Fiscal year	Outlays Total	Outlays Military	Receipts	Deficit	Deficit/GNP (%)
1916	0.7	0.3	0.8	–0.0	–0.1
1919	18.5	17.2	5.1	13.4	15.9
1920	6.4	4.5	6.6	–0.3	–0.3
1921	5.1	3.0	5.6	–0.5	–0.6
1922	3.3	0.9	4.0	–0.7	–1.0
1940	9.5	1.7	6.5	3.0	3.0
1945	92.7	86.5	45.2	47.5	20.9
1946	55.2	42.7	39.3	15.9	7.6
1947	34.5	12.8	38.5	–4.0	–1.7
1948	29.8	9.1	41.6	–11.8	–4.6

Sources: US Bureau of the Census (sec. Y); Balke and Gordon.

74 *Fiscal policy*

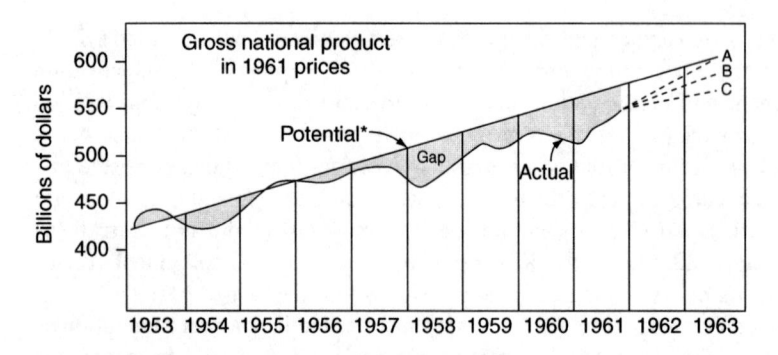

Figure 4.1 Gross national product, actual and potential, and unemployment rate (source: Council of Economic Advisors, *Annual Report*, January 1962).

Notes
A, B, and C represent GNP in mid-1963 assuming unemployment rates of 4 percent, 5 percent, and 6 percent, respectively.
*3.5 percent trend line through mid-1955.

full promise until we also learn, and apply, the lessons of timing and structure'. Kennedy asked for standby authority to make quick temporary tax cuts to fight recession. However, that request and a milder one by President Johnson were 'coldly received by a Congress jealous of its fiscal powers' (Heller 1966: 99, 101).

The CEA focused increasingly on growth, and continuously – as opposed to counter-cyclically – recommended the stimulation of demand. Its depiction of the long-term nature of the output gap is indicated in Figure 4.1. Most observers thought the economy boomed in 1955–56, but to the New Economists more stimulus was always needed. The stagnation problem was magnified by the dangers of falling behind the USSR. The continuation of recent rates of growth would make that country's GNP equal to America's before 2000, Seymour Harris (1964) predicted. This posed a threat 'especially since they, through their system, can achieve a much more effective use of their resources for the development of their military machine'.

Government budgets did not reflect economists' stagnation fears. In particular there was no move towards redistribution through income taxes. The 1964 tax cut reduced high brackets more than low brackets, in line with the long-term pattern of across-the-board cuts, especially for high incomes, from World War II levels. The largest tax change was the increase in the regressive social security tax.[2] Notwithstanding the CEA's advice, the Kennedy and Johnson presidencies did not run deficits beyond those predicted by military spending. Innovations in the tax code, such as the tax deferments allowed by investment accounts (IRAs), have sought to encourage saving. Stagnation, attitude changes, and other Keynesian reasons for deficits have little explanatory power. War is another matter.

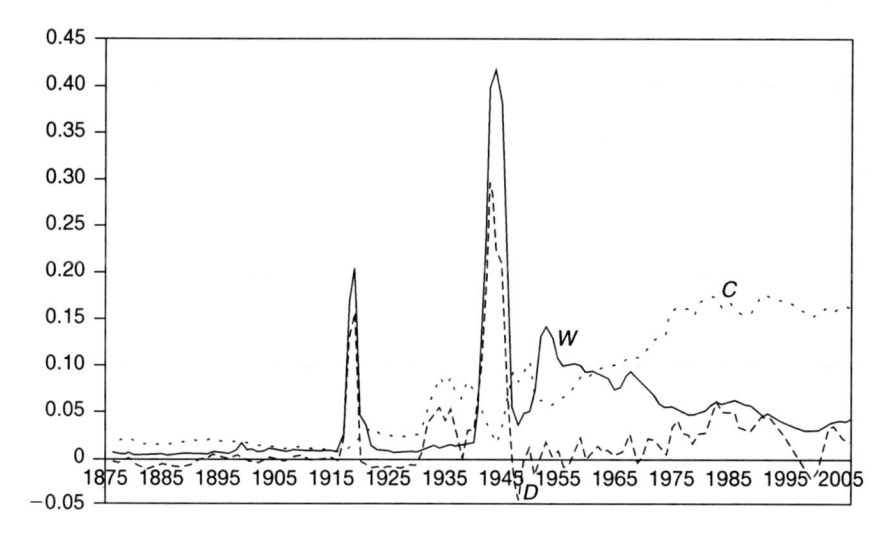

Figure 4.2 Deficits (*D*), military (*W*), and other (*C*) Federal Government spending as proportions of GNP.

An alternative explanation: military spending with tax smoothing

> When I was asked during the campaign about what I would do if it came down to a choice between defense and deficits, I always said national security had to come first, and the people applauded every time.... Defense is not a budget issue. You spend what you need.
> (President Reagan to Budget Director David Stockman (Stockman 1986: 274, 283))

These sentiments were expressed by one who had said, 'We can't give up on the balanced budget. Deficit spending is how we got into this mess' (Stockman 1986: 273). This section offers an explanation of the post-World War II deficits that is not based on changes in attitudes or institutions, but fits the traditional budgetary pattern of war and peace. Let's review the data. Except for wartime, military spending was continuously less than 1 percent of GNP between the Civil War and the 1930s, compared with 5 to 10 percent from World War II to 1990 (except 13 to 14 percent in 1952–54, during the Korean War, and a low of 4.7 percent in 1978–79). Peacetime surpluses before World War II averaged less than 1 percent of GNP. The change in the average peacetime so-called surplus from approximately 1 to 2 percent of GNP before and after World War II was accompanied by increases in average military spending by 6 percent. That is, borrowing accounted for half the increase in Cold War military spending, not very different from World War II. Figure 4.2 might justify surprise and satisfaction at the fiscal responsibility shown in the finance of the Cold War.

A model

The following estimates of the effects of military spending extend previous deficit explanations. It is assumed that political leaders (and presumably the voters) prefer constant tax rates and no debt, but trade-offs are necessary. Constant tax rates are efficient for taxpayers and government, for the former because labor and investment returns are made more predictable, for the latter because political and administrative costs of change are avoided. On the other hand, debt service is reduced by the credibility that arises from tax policies aimed to pay off the debt. Large temporary increases in spending rates, therefore, imply permanent but partial increases in tax rates, smoothed by efficiency considerations.

Let the welfare loss (L) as expressed by equation (4.1) in Table 4.4 be the sum of the efficiency loss from changes in the average tax rate, τ_t, and the loss due to its deviation from the rate, τ^R, which would eventually – like a perpetuity – pay off the debt at the current rate of spending, including interest on the debt. Current spending is assumed to be the best estimate of future spending so that τ^R is given by equation (4.2). Taxes and spending (military, w, and other, c) are expressed as proportions of GNP. The relative importance of smoothing is α. Minimizing L with respect to τ_t and rearranging gives the optimal tax rate, equation (4.3) and deficit, equation (4.4).

The model reflects Ricardian equivalence (hence the superscript R on τ) subject to the qualification that tax changes are costly. These costs are realized in the political arena. Differing commitments to war and conflicts over who should pay for it – political costs – combine with opposing principles of balanced budgets to produce compromise budgets. The last term in equation (4.4) accounts for the observed negative relation between military and other spending.[3] Figure 4.2 shows that this relation was strong during World War II and evident for most of the Cold War.

Estimates of the model, presented in Table 4.5, indicate that w was an important explanation of the deficit for the entire 1877–2007 period and for the three

Table 4.4 The model

$$L = \alpha(\tau_t - \tau_{t-1})^2 + (\tau_t - \tau_t^R)^2 \quad (4.1)$$

where

$$\tau_t^R = g_t = w_t + c_t \quad (4.2)$$

is military (w) and other government spending (c), including interest on the debt; (4.2) is equivalent to paying a perpetuity.
Minimizing L with respect to τ and substituting (4.2) gives

$$\tau_t = \frac{\alpha}{1+\alpha}\tau_{t-1} + \frac{1}{1+\alpha}g_t \quad (4.3)$$

Notice that τ_t tends to τ_{t-1} or g_t as the smoothing coefficient (α) dominates or is insignificant. Substituting into the deficit (d) and rearranging gives

$$d_t = g_t - \tau_t = \frac{\alpha}{1+\alpha}[d_{t-1} + (1-\gamma)\Delta w_t] \quad (4.4)$$

where $\Delta c_t = \gamma \Delta w_t$ and Δ denotes one-period change.

subperiods containing the major wars (World War I, World War II, Cold War). The significance of the lagged deficit, *def1*, indicates a smoothly changing deficit.

An automatic stabilizer – output relative to its natural rate, *y/yn* – is added, although it is not significant until the last period, when government spending relative to GNP is greatest. The second regression considers a Keynesian dummy (1 for 1946–80) that is insignificant, as was the (unreported) dummy for the entire post-World War II period. Considering the *constant* and *y/yn* (which averages close to unity), the deficit has no trend. Not reported in Table 4.5, but consistent with the discussions above, dummies for political alignments and procedural changes in the budget process (listed at the bottom of the table) are insignificant. Deficits seem to have been stable between 1877 and 2007 in the sense that they were explained by military spending throughout.

The first regression implies a relative strength of the tax-smoothing component in the loss function of $\alpha=7$, and $\gamma=0.17$, the latter compared with a regression estimate of *dc* on *dw* of 0.11 reported in note 3.

The subsample regressions indicate that the deficit's response to *w* has fallen over time, possibly for one or both of two reasons. The first is strengthening revenue capabilities of the government. Increases in revenue relative to spending during the Civil War and World Wars I and II were 19, 25, and 40 percent, respectively (Wood and Wood 1985: 686). This with the absence of a time trend

Table 4.5 Regression estimates: Dependent variable *def*

	1877–2007		1877–1920	1921–46	1947–2007
constant	0.019	0.020	0.003	0.010	0.136*
	(1.5)	(1.6)	(0.3)	(0.4)	(3.0)
def1	0.875*	0.877*	0.911*	0.862*	0.742*
	(32.6)	(32.5)	(50.2)	(14.3)	(9.3)
dw	0.729*	0.734*	0.884*	0.708*	0.512*
	(22.6)	(22.3)	(51.7)	(10.7)	(6.3)
y/yn	–0.018	–0.020	–0.003	–0.006	–0.135*
	(1.3)	(1.4)	(0.3)	(0.2)	(2.9)
DK[a]		0.002			
		(0.9)			
R^2	0.915	0.915	0.988	0.940	0.638
h	–1.42	–1.48	–3.21	–1.82	0.438

Sources: Balke and Gordon; Bureau of the Census (1975); Council of Economic Advisors, *Economic Reports of the President*; Federal Reserve Bank of St. Louis *National Economic Trends*; Congressional Budget Office, *Monthly Budget Review*.

Notes
a = 1, 1946–80, 0 otherwise. R^2 adjusted for degrees of freedom; absolute t-statistics in parentheses; * significant at 5% level; Durbin's *h* does not reject the hypothesis of no serial correlation in the residuals in most cases.
Insignificant dummies are not reported for changes in budget procedures (1921, 1974, 1985 [Gramm-Rudman], and 1992 Budget Acts) or political-party compositions of government (Democratic House; split Congress; Democratic president; split government), generally consistent with Goff and Tollison.

78 Fiscal policy

suggests that the size of government did not raise deficits relative to GNP. The opposite was more nearly the case. A second reason is the long-term commitment to the Cold War. Recognition that 'the cold war is in fact a real war in which the survival of the free world is at stake' came in National Security Council Paper NSC-68 in April 1950. The country had to look to 'the long haul' rather than 'the year of maximum peril' (Hammond 1962).

Military budgeting is different

There is another reason, beyond tax smoothing, why military spending might induce frequent deficits. The size and uncertainty of spending do not, by themselves, imply persistent deficits. It is reasonable to ask why the expected contributions of military spending to deficits are not zero. An answer might lie in their perceived necessity. Although the unpredictability of threats and weapons developments make security costs uncertain, other programs also face uncertainties. However, the latter are usually subject to genuine spending limits. Not defense. Uninterrupted security is essential in a nuclear or terrorist age. Waste is guarded against, but less than the best is unacceptable. 'The second-best airplane is like the second-best poker hand', General Tooey Spatz said. 'No damn good' (Wildavsky 1987: 356). The military, supported by Congress, was appalled by the intrusive role of the president's budget directors. 'Has the time come when you, the representatives of the people, sit here merely to be Charlie McCarthy's for the Bureau of the Budget?' asked the chairman of the House Naval Affairs Committee (Kolodziej 1966: 52).

What are Congresses and presidents who wish, in President-elect Eisenhower's words, to solve 'the "great equation" of maintaining indefinitely a strong military force without bankrupting the country in the process' (Snyder 1962) to do? They cannot write a blank check to the generals and admirals, who never feel secure. The response has been a short but elastic rein. 'Responsible' budgets are set in light of the political costs of taxes and benefits of competing programs. Then, very often, a new threat, weapons advance, or cost overrun calls for additional funds – which cannot be denied without endangering national security. 'The defense budget was not derived as part of a coherent strategy within realistic fiscal limitations. Rather, it was a series of ad hoc adjustments to strategic and fiscal realities' (Kanter 1982). It was not the result of explicit maximization but of a democratic process of balancing tax burdens and unfolding security needs. If Congress had appropriated expected (rather than optimistic) needs, we would have experienced budget balance on average at the cost of possibly inadequate defense half the time.

When Congress inquired into corruption in World War I finance, the former head of supply in France (and later vice president of the United States), Charles Dawes, responded:

> Sure we paid. We didn't dicker. Why, man alive, we had to win the war. We would have paid horse prices for sheep if sheep could have pulled artillery

to the front. Oh, it's all right now to say we bought too much vinegar and too many cold chisels, but we saved the civilization of the world. Damn it all, the business of an army is to win the war, not to quibble with a lot of cheap buying. Hell and Maria, we weren't trying to keep a set of books, we were trying to win the war.

(Sullivan 1935: 203–4)

'You're dealing with a government that is run by continuing resolution', complained a senator (Wildavsky 1987: 388). This process may also help explain the positive (though small and statistically insignificant and unreported in Table 4.5) coefficient on the post-World War II dummy, that is, during the period in which it was understood that readiness was essential.

Was Keynesianism ever practiced?

'Now I am a Keynesian', President Nixon announced when he submitted a deficit budget instead of the usual projected surplus derived from optimistic forecasts (*New York Times* 7 January 1971). Keynesian rhetoric was shared by Republicans and Democrats, but the actions of both fit the pre-Keynesian tradition of wartime deficits. The data suggest that *The General Theory* and Great Depression did not affect deficits. Popular explanations such as changes in attitudes and an out-of-control budget exaggerate the importance of new ideas relative to historical political relations. The demobilization after World War II and explicit recognition of the Cold War place the fiscal events of the last 60 years within the experience of pre-Keynesian governments. Congress did not follow up its ambitious pronouncements of macroeconomic objectives. It gave up none of its control over taxing and spending, and established no institutions for the management – as opposed to the discussion – of economic stabilization or growth (Holmans 1961: 12–13). Those who said: 'Because public investment, unlike private investment, is directly under social control, it is easy to turn on the tap and to turn it off again', had 'never tried to close a military base or terminate a crop support program' (Tarshis 1947: 513; Elzinga 1992). Government has grown, but the vaunted 'fiscal revolution' (Stein 1969) never happened. If there was a 'narrowing of the intellectual gap between professional economists and men of affairs' (Heller 1966: 1), as an advisor alleged, it has not been reflected in practice.

Part II
Monetary policy

5 The interests and institutions of monetary policy

> I am humble Abraham Lincoln. I have been solicited by many friends to become a candidate for the Legislature. My politics are short and sweet, like an old woman's dance. I am in favor of a national bank. I am in favor of the internal improvement system and a high protective tariff. These are my sentiments and political principles. If elected, I shall be thankful; if not it will be all the same.
>
> (1 March 1832)

This is the entirety of Lincoln's first campaign speech, consisting of the three planks that made up the Whig Party platform.[1] The first of these planks concerned the government's role in money. The Bank of the United States was the foremost political issue of the day, the opposite sides being led by Senator Henry Clay for the Bank and President Andrew Jackson against. The particular institutions of American public policy have been variable, the interests behind them less so. This is especially true of monetary policy. Government sponsorship of a national bank was controversial from the beginning of the republic. Those for a strong central government wanted a national bank. The attitudes of existing banks and the public toward government involvement in money depended on the net benefits expected. Northern commercial centers wanting finance were the leading supporters of the first Bank of the United States until the developing local banks began to oppose the competition of a government agency. The less industrialized South and West were suspicious of centrally supported finance. Support for a government bank also varied over time in response to the government's need for finance, which was greatest in war. The charters of the first and second Banks lapsed in 1811 and 1836, and nothing more of the kind was accomplished until Woodrow Wilson's New Freedom accommodated the various groups in the Federal Reserve: noncompetitive support for the money-center banks which voluntary membership allowed the regional banks to avoid.

This chapter supplies part of the basis for understanding the monetary policy of the Federal Reserve, which will be examined in Chapter 7. We find significant historical continuities in the Fed's behavior that can be traced to the interests that created it and continue to shape its policy. We find that the ideas of the monetary authorities, whatever their institutional detail, have been stable, especially their concern for the health of the financial sector. In monetary as in fiscal policy, ideas and practices have been aligned to interests.

We begin with the Bank of England for several reasons. Its foundation and behavior developed from interests that were to be repeated in the United States, including the private pursuit of profit and the government's desire for cheap finance; it was the model for the first American central banks, as well as important parts of the Federal Reserve; and the principles of money and central banking are transatlantic. The current issues of central bank independence and its role as lender of last resort originated with the Bank of England.

The Bank of England, 1694–1914

> They raised in the City ordinary personal loans from every one who would lend. They issued tallies upon the excise and upon other revenues until there were several millions of pounds' worth outstanding and payments were two years in arrear. They raised a million upon a tontine.... They issued a lottery loan of a million.... Finally, and almost as a last resource, they founded the Bank of England.[2]
>
> (Feavearyear 1931: 114–15)

Origins in the accommodation of private interests and government finance

England and its allies were at war with the powerful France of Louis XIV, and the government's credit was not good. Kings Charles I and II (1625–49 and 1660–85) had repudiated debts or paid them tardily, and financial problems were not solved by the Glorious Revolution's replacement of James II by the constitutional monarchs William and Mary in 1688. The government was settled but finance remained scarce. The 'Government created by the Revolution ... could hardly expect to be more trusted with money than its predecessor' (Bagehot 1873: 91).

Proposals for a national bank had failed because of fears of its weakness and strength: investors' fears that their assets would be seized by the government and a concentration of financial power that would rival or be abused by government (Petty 1682; Horsefield 1960). Reflecting on Charles I's 'stop' of the mint in 1640, when he seized the private coin kept there for safekeeping, diarist Samuel Pepys wrote on 17 August 1666: 'The unsafe condition of a bank under a monarch, and the little safety to a Monarch to have any City or Corporacion alone ... to have so great a wealth or credit ... makes it hard to have a bank here.'

These fears were overcome by a combination of the government's 'desperate want of money' and the protections of property promised by the new limited monarchy discussed in Chapter 2. In 1694, Parliament offered a corporate charter to the Governor and Company of the Bank of England for a loan of £1,200,000 at 8 percent. The government took advantage of the superior credit of private investors, to whom it offered the security of 'Rates and Duties upon

Tunnage of Ships and Vessels, and upon Beer, Ale and other Liquors' (hence the name of the Tunnage Act that founded the Bank) and undertook to pay £4,000 annually for 'management' of the government's finances. The charter would expire on payment of the loan, with a year's notice, but not before 1706. Addressing fears that the Bank would enable the government to circumvent Parliament, future loans to the government required legislative approval and the Bank was prohibited from buying Crown lands, whose sale had helped Charles I avoid Parliament's oversight of his government (Clapham 1944 i: 14–19).[3]

The loan was not repaid and the charter was renewed seven times between 1697 and 1800 in exchange for cheap finance (McCulloch 1858; Wood 2005: Table 3.1). The connection was profitable for both parties. The government got funds on favorable terms and the Bank got the government's business and competitive protections in the exclusive right of corporate banking and the prohibition against companies of more than six partners from issuing notes. The Bank was threatened by several crises in its first century but it survived and was useful to the government and the public (Clapham 1944 i: ch. 7; Wood 2005: 42–7). Speaking for the renewal of its charter in 1781, during another war, the prime minister defended the bargain: a £3,000,000 loan to the government at 3 percent for the continuation of the Bank's privileges.

Critics objected that the bargain's terms were 'by no means equal to what the public had a right to expect for the great and obvious benefits' to the Bank. The desperate terms on which the charter had first been granted were no reason for their continuation. The prime minister responded that those who would 'institute a new company' that might 'give more ... had not well considered the subject'. Breaking up the present company and attempting to form a new one might have 'dreadful consequences'.

> [T]he Bank, from long habit and the usage of many years, was a part of the constitution, or if not a part of the constitution, at least it was to all important purposes, the public exchequer; all the money business of the Exchequer being done at the Bank, and as experience had proved, with much greater advantage to the public than when it had formerly been done at the Exchequer. Besides, the Bank was always in advance to the public very considerably; at present, the public were indebted about seven millions to the Company.
>
> (Lord North, House of Commons, 13 June 1781)

He asked whether it might not 'be many, many years before a new company could establish its character and its credit, in so eminent a degree, as that to which the present Bank had raised itself'. The new charter passed by a vote of 109 to 30.

Suspension, paper money, and the theory of central banking

The French wars of 1793–1815 were eventful for the Bank's operations as well as for the theory of how it, now recognized as a central bank, should behave.

86 Monetary policy

The modern theory of central banking originated in this period, stimulated by the fiat-money system that existed between 1797 and 1821. The government's pressure for finance depleted the Bank's bullion (gold and silver) reserve, and in 1797 provoked a run on the Bank. The government permitted (or prescribed) suspension of the convertibility of Bank notes, and during the next 16 years, money and prices, financed by Bank credit, rose 75 percent.

In 1809, the Bank's critics secured a parliamentary committee of inquiry into the high price of bullion (depreciation of the paper pound). Bank officials denied responsibility for the inflation on the grounds that their lending had continued to follow the same principles as before 1797. Lending continued to be based on real (collateralized by goods) bills of exchange. The *real bills doctrine* asserts that, for given V (velocity of money), tying M (money) to T (the rate of transactions) stabilizes P (the price level). However, this assertion is invalid because lending on goods depends on their expected prices, so that M and, therefore, P depend on expected prices, P^e. The price level is what it is expected to be.

$$MV = PT \qquad M = P^e T \qquad P = MV/T = P^e V$$

The real bills doctrine has had many adherents (Mints 1945), and it is sometimes assumed that because the Federal Reserve Act of 1913 prescribed real bills as collateral for Fed lending, its monetary policy was based on that fallacious theory (Timberlake 1993: 224–9, 259–60; Meltzer 2003: 22, 57–8). In fact, as we will see, the Act's purpose was to make a market for bank liabilities, and it is evident from central bankers' behavior (see Chapter 7 below) that although real bills were preferred collateral, they have not determined the quantities of bank credit or money.

The Bank's restraint (average annual inflation was 3.1 percent between 1797 and 1810) suggested that the influence, if any, of the real bills doctrine was small (Cannan 1925: xiii). Nevertheless, the Bullion Committee argued that monetary restraint required the discipline of convertibility, and proposed the resumption of the gold standard.

The proposal had little chance of overcoming the government's need for finance, however, and the prime minister said it constituted an admission that the country was unwilling to 'continue those foreign exertions which they had hitherto considered indispensable to the security of the country [and] in adopting it would disgrace themselves forever, by becoming the voluntary instruments of their country's ruin (*Hansard*, 7–8 May 1811). The *Bullion Report* was overwhelmingly rejected, and nothing was done until Napoleon's defeat in 1813.

Succeeding decades saw monetary instability, erosion of the Bank's prestige, and threats from its competitors. The resumption of convertibility was lengthy and uneven. It was finally accomplished in 1821, along with deflation and depression, to be succeeded by a boom and then a panic in 1825, for which the Bank was blamed (Acworth 1925). It had supported the rush to invest in the newly independent countries of South America, and when the collapse came, its reserve dangerously low, the Bank refused assistance to its customers. It 'acted as unwisely as it was possible to act', Walter Bagehot (1873: 190) wrote. When dozens of country banks and London houses stopped payment and the Bank was on the verge of joining them, it appealed to the government for help in the form of credit or, as in 1797, permission to stop payment. The government refused, telling it to be ready to 'pay out to the last penny' (Feavearyear 1931: 220–1).

The Bank reversed course. Instead of harboring its reserve in the hope of surviving the collapse, it began to assist the financial market 'by every possible means, and in modes that we never had adopted before', and 'we were not on some occasions over nice' regarding loan collateral, a director recalled (Bagehot 1873: 192–3). The panic ceased, and in a few weeks the Bank's reserve began to increase. This episode is important in the history of the concept of 'lender of last resort' because, Frank Fetter (1967) wrote, it was 'the principal historical ... case upon which [Bagehot] built his argument'.

The Bank's privileges had always been resented, and the recent instability joined with growing wealth and investment opportunities to increase the political strength of its actual and potential competitors. Negotiations begun in 1822 for the renewal of the Bank's charter, which in 1800 had been extended to 1833, broke down and were not resumed until expiration was imminent. In 1826, Parliament opened the door to joint-stock banks of issue as long as they did not have offices within 65 miles of London, and the Bank was warned 'that it would be useless to ask for an extension of their Charter as the price of the concession, as "such privileges were out of fashion"' (Acres 1931: 423).

The joint-stock banks expanded into London when they realized that the prohibition of companies of more than six partners issuing 'bills or notes payable on demand' did not exclude banks of deposit (Joplin 1822; Feavearyear 1931: 423). The development of deposits as the preferred means of payment quickly enabled several banks to pass the Bank of England in size.

The Bank had to fight for its remaining privileges, and even its life, during the next 20 years. The government was no longer in 'desperate want of money'. Waterloo was 18 years in the past at the end of the Bank's charter, and the government's budget was in surplus, with no war on the horizon. After much debate, the Bank Charter Act of 1833, extended the charter to 1844, and put the Bank and government at arm's length. It was admitted, with the emergency past, that the wartime inflation had been caused by the Bank acting under pressure from the government. Chancellor of the Exchequer Lord Althorp admitted to the House of Commons 'that the blame which was often attributed to the Bank was often attributable to the action of the Government upon the Bank' (9 August 1833).

To show that the government no longer depended on the Bank, the Act ordered payment of a substantial part of the public debt owed to the Bank and the regular publication of the Bank's accounts. Its accounts had been secret and it had been (correctly) accused of violating legal limits on loans to the government. The new transparency was intended to make such trespasses more difficult by making the Bank more accountable (because more transparent) to Parliament and the public.

Of course the government had less need of the Bank than formerly. We will see that similar changes occurred at the same time and for the same reasons in the United States, and in both countries at the end of the next century. Whether a central bank is independent, or sometimes even allowed to exist, depends on the financial needs of the government.

The search for stability

The two main monetary issues in nineteenth-century Britain, as always and everywhere, were the question of the standard – gold, silver, a combination of the two, or a managed paper currency – and financial stability – especially the avoidance of panics. Regarding the first, after some debate during the period of resumption, England continued on the gold standard until World War I, meaning that the price level was governed by the relative costs of producing gold and other goods. The gold standard has the reputation of stability, but price indexes fell 25 percent between 1821 and 1851, rose 40 percent between 1851 and 1857, following gold discoveries in California and Australia, and fell 43 percent during the Great Deflation of 1873–96, before rising 47 percent between 1896 and 1913, after more discoveries and technological advances in mining gold (Mitchell 1962: 471–5).

Long-term price stability was impressive, the 1913 price level being within 12 percent of 1821's, and short-term changes were small compared with the twentieth century. Nevertheless, the system was severely criticized by economists. We saw their concern for price stability above in Chapter 3. Alfred Marshall (1887) wrote: 'The evils of our present monetary system are great. It is ... a great evil that whenever a man borrows money to be invested in his business he speculates doubly. In the first place he runs the risk that the things which he handles will fall in value relative to others – this risk is inevitable, it must be endured. But in addition he runs the risk that the standard in which he has to pay back what he has borrowed will be a different one from that by which his borrowing was measured.'

Marshall urged contracts indexed to the price level, and symmetallism (an amalgam of gold and silver) in place of the gold standard. Bimetallism – coins and bank reserves separately in gold and silver – had been advocated because fluctuations in the value and quantity of money might be less than if money consisted of one metal (Bordo 1987). It was difficult to keep both in circulation, however, because their relative market value often deviated from the mint ratio. This problem might be overcome by a fixed combination of gold and silver.

None of the proposed changes in the standard was seriously considered by governments. Official inquiries and acts of Parliament were directed at short-run financial stability under the existing gold standard. Two solutions were actively considered: Should the privileged central bank be allowed to continue, and if so, how should it be regulated?

Laissez faire, including free incorporation laws, was making headway in other areas. Privileged companies were under attack. Advocates of free banking argued that competitive banks checked excessive credit expansion by each other.

They pointed to past booms and busts as consequences of the absence of checks on the monopolistic Bank of England (Smith 1936: 71–91; White 1984: 61–76).

On the other side of the perennial argument between those for monopolies which might be directly regulated by the government and those for the discipline of competition, Bank of England Director George Warde Norman asked: 'A single issuer might be easy to deal with, but how are we to deal with five hundred?' (Feavearyear 1931: 245). The London and Westminster Bank's J.W. Gilbart answered that a monopoly bank was the greater threat because it could expand beyond the limits allowed by competition. Testifying before the House of Commons Committee on Banks of Issue, he quoted from a resolution of the association of joint-stock banks:

> the present method of conducting the circulation of the country, by means of numerous issuers, controlled by an effective system of local exchanges, is well adapted to the state of the community, and powerfully promotes the agriculture, trade, mining and general industry of the nation, and that equal advantages could not be obtained by one bank of issue.
> (19 March 1841; Gregory 1929 i: 71)

The government's desire for a rule administered by a dominant authority decided the issue in favor of the Bank, although the rule soon failed. The Bank acquired political support by its assurance to the 1832 committee of inquiry that it had developed a method of maintaining an adequate but not excessive circulation. The Palmer Rule, named for the Bank governor who described it, provided that the Bank hold government securities and gold in a fixed proportion, not forcibly changing the money stock, until it was 'acted upon', that is, passively responding to the public's demand for coin. The Bank would expand or restrict credit as it received or was asked for gold. The dominant paper currency, preferred for its convenience, would behave like gold. Parliament renewed the charter and made Bank notes legal tender (Gregory 1929: i 69–71). Unanswered by the Palmer Rule were decisions of the rate of interest and other loan terms, the whole credit question, in short.

Monetary stability was no better after 1832, and the controversy continued until the structure of the monetary system was settled by a form of currency union established by the Bank Charter Act of 1844. The Bank was given a monopoly of bank notes (the country's currency), secured by its gold. It was separated into an Issue Department, an automatic monetary authority that exchanged notes and gold as the public demanded (a legal enforcement of the Palmer Rule that the Bank had not carried out), and a Banking Department that held Issue Department notes as reserves, and would conduct its business 'like any other Bank' (Bagehot 1873: 43).

This turned out not to be the solution as the next 22 years saw three crises reminiscent of 1825. The Bank of England *did* continue to behave 'like any other Bank' in joining general credit expansions and then running short of reserves when the inevitable contractions ensued. In each case, the government intervened by giving the Bank permission to violate its reserve requirement so that it could assist panic-stricken markets.

Lender of last resort and the time inconsistency of optimal plans

The classic analysis of crises is Bagehot's *Lombard Street* (1873). Bagehot proposed no legal or structural changes, but a policy rule to 'mend and palliate' convulsions by adapting to the system as it was; one in which the 'whole reserve' was kept by 'a single bank' under the Act of 1844 (310). Since the Bank of England was entrusted with the nation's reserve, he argued, it was duty-bound to use that reserve to support the market – and to state its readiness to do so. The Bank was already understood to be the 'lender of last resort' (Baring 1797: 20). Bagehot proposed that it should commit to so behave.

This proposal has to be considered in discussions of the Federal Reserve because it became entrenched in the literature on monetary policy in two ways: historical description and good policy. It is often argued that the improvement in British stability after Bagehot wrote was due to the Bank's acceptance of his advice, and that his advice is as appropriate today as it was in the nineteenth century. The following paragraphs set forth the weaknesses of these assertions and their dangers for monetary policy that have been better understood by central bankers than by economists.

Criticisms of the Fed for not following Bagehot's advice during the Great Depression (Friedman and Schwartz 1963: 395; Meltzer 2003: 282) fail in two realms: history because Bagehot's advice was rejected by the Bank, and theory because, as the Bank understood, it suffers from time-inconsistency (Wood 2003). Bagehot's complaint was not that the Bank failed to assist the market in time of stress – it always came round in the end – but that it did not commit to do so. 'In common opinion there is always great uncertainty as to the conduct of the Bank ...: the Bank has never laid down any clear and sound policy on the subject.... The best palliative to a panic is a confidence in the adequate amount of the Bank reserve, and' a commitment to use it. (196–7).

Soon after Bagehot made this argument in *The Economist*, of which he was editor, in 1866, Thomson Hankey (1867: 25), a director and former governor of the Bank, called it 'the most mischievous doctrine ever broached in the monetary or banking world in this country; viz., that it is the proper function of the Bank of England to keep money available at all times to supply the demands of bankers who have rendered their own assets unavailable'. The moral hazard in Bagehot's commitment was clear: it would promote the difficulties that it wished to avoid. Bagehot repeated his argument in *Lombard Street*, through which Hankey and the Bank's management in general have come down in history as advocates of 'an erroneous policy' because they preferred to see the system that 'ought to be' rather than 'what is' (163, 196).

However, when we examine the implications of alternative policies, Hankey's looks the less dangerous. Reserves are costly, and if we can count on the Bank of England to hold them for us, there need be no limit to our credit.

The issue was not new, and had effectively been settled in the 1840s. It was in the forefront of the debate over the 1844 rule.

Anticipating the modern concept of time-inconsistency (Kydland and Prescott 1977), G.W. Norman told a committee of enquiry that the short-term benefits of Bank interventions were self-defeating in the long term. He admitted that 'the refusal of the Bank to afford accommodation at periods of pressure' might cause 'great inconvenience'. But that was because the 'public have always looked to the Bank for assistance in such cases with too much confidence, and entertained what I consider such exaggerated views as to the means and duties of the Bank' (House of Commons 1840: Q1769). Horsley Palmer responded to a follow-up question:

> Do you conceive that parties have been induced to neglect precautions which they otherwise would have taken in consequence of their reliance upon that assistance? – I have no positive means of knowing; but I should think so.
>
> (Q1770)

The chief architect of the 1844 Act said that unless the rule that tied notes to gold is 'strictly adhered to', it 'becomes a nullity'.

> A general conviction that it will not be suspended on such occasions [of pressure on the money-market] is essential for producing throughout the community that cautious forethought and that healthy tone of self-reliance upon which the safety and utility of the measure must materially depend. Any special provision ... for suspending its application at critical periods must prove mischievous by weakening the conviction that the measure will be adhered to, and thus checking the growth of the feelings and habits which are intimately connected with its success.
>
> (Loyd 1844: 439)

A House of Lords committee of inquiry into the reluctant Bank response to the panic of 1847 raised the issue again, without effect, and the issue was debated into the next century. It supplied the primary theme of T.E. Gregory's *Select Statutes, Documents and Reports Relating to British Banking*. The approach deplored by Bagehot continued along the lines of what has recently been called 'constructive ambiguity'.

> A central banker's willingness to support the financial system in time of potential crisis ... actually causes risks in the system to grow. For this reason, a central bank might be inclined to keep markets guessing about the exact circumstances in which it would be willing to lend. By creating uncertainty in the minds of potential borrowers, such ambiguity might be thought to be constructive because it causes potential borrowers to take on less risk.
>
> (Goodfriend and Lacker 1999)

The position in 1914

Its understanding of the adverse incentives inherent in an unqualified commitment to be lender of last resort meant that the Bank of England also rejected the rest of Bagehot's proposal, namely, a large reserve to enable it to support the market. Contemporaries were troubled by 'the inadequacy of the nation's banking and gold reserves'. However, when the chancellor suggested that the Bank hold more reserves, the governor replied: 'the larger the Bank's own reserves, the less the bankers like to keep *their* money unused' (Clapham 1944 ii: 344–5, 379).

The joint-stock banks had gotten their way, after all. The Bank of England bore much of the burden of reserves without competing aggressively for loans, while the banks were free to compete for the deposits that had become the main banking resource. The Bank, with the help of economic developments, performed its role magnificently. The absence of severe financial crises after 1866, contrasting with their frequency before then, cannot be due to Bagehot's influence. The Bank continued to adhere to Hankey's rejection of the idea of guaranteed bailouts, and refused to increase its reserve. Instead, it used Bank Rate actively, with great effect. The effectiveness of Bank Rate, which increased over time, was due to its credibility. A rise in the rate was a serious signal that a gold loss would be addressed. The 'ultimate answer to Bagehot's problem', R.S. Sayers (1951) wrote, 'was the clear one of a powerful Bank Rate weapon with a "thin film of gold"'. Barrett Whale (1944) wrote: 'the Act of 1844 has worked satisfactorily because it did not work in the way designed'. The intended money rule was subordinate to the discretionary but credible Bank Rate.

The Bank had a lot of help. More than Bagehot's advice or anything the Bank did, improvements in the stability of finance as the century progressed were due to other factors: peace (most crises up to 1797 were instigated by government demands for credit); the consolidation of the banking system (vulnerable small banks had contributed to crises in the latter eighteenth century and were principal causes in the 1820s and 1830s); and in the 1840s, repeal of the corn laws that had protected agriculture and subjected the balance of payments to the vagaries of domestic harvests (Wood 2005: 112–13).

The explicit monetary commitment was finally made in the Currency and Bank Notes Act of 1928, according to which 'the Treasury may authorize the Bank to issue bank notes' beyond the legal limit if the Bank represents 'to the Treasury that it is expedient' to do so, subject to the action subsequently being laid before both Houses of Parliament. Governor Montagu Norman authorized a member of Parliament to say that the Bank was prepared to take advantage of the Act (Gregory 1929 i, ii: lix–lx, 385). A run forced the suspension of convertibility three years later, and we can almost hear Loyd say, 'I told you so.'

The Banks of the United States

> Whereas, it is conceived that the establishment of a Bank for the United States ... will tend to give facility to the obtaining of loans for the use of the

Government in sudden emergencies; and will be productive of considerable advantage to trade and industry in general.

(Preamble to the act to charter the Bank of the United States, 1791 (Krooss 1969: 307–14))

The first Bank (1791–1811)

Secretary of the Treasury Alexander Hamilton proposed a national bank patterned on the Bank of England, including private ownership and limits on credit to the government. The Bank of the United States could lend no more than $100,000 to the United States or $50,000 to any State unless authorized by law. The federal government could not restrict the state banks but the US Bank was empowered to compete with them through branches, and its notes were acceptable in all payments to the United States, a privilege accorded no other bank.

Secretary of State Thomas Jefferson advised the president to veto the Bank Bill. It was not necessary, it infringed on the rights of the States and the people, and was unconstitutional, Jefferson said, because 'The powers not delegated to the United States by the Constitution, nor prohibited by it to the States, are reserved to the States, or to the people' (10th amendment). There was little to be said even for the Bank's convenience, he said, sharing the views of those opposed to the monopoly privileges of the Bank of England.

> [T]he existing banks will, without a doubt, enter into arrangements for lending their agency; and the more favorably, as there will be a competition among them for it; whereas the bill delivers us up bound to the national bank, who are free to refuse all arrangement, but on their own terms.
> (Krooss 1969: 273–7)

Washington took Hamilton's advice and signed the bill.

The United States Banks were one of the main issues separating political parties (Marshall 1807 iv: 244), although there is little reason to believe that banking would have developed differently without them. The constitutionality of the second Bank of the United States was affirmed by the Supreme Court in *McCulloch* v. *Maryland* under 'the doctrine of implied powers', although the federal government established numerous departments and engaged in many activities not mentioned in the *Constitution* without controversy. We must look for the real reasons for the political fights over the Banks in the interests of the groups affected.

The arguments, like the interests, resembled those across the ocean. James Madison, who led the opposition to the Bank in the House of Representatives (2 February 1791), complained that its charter

> did not make so good a bargain for the public as was due to its interests. The charter to the Bank of England had been granted only for eleven years,

94 *Monetary policy*

and was paid for by a loan to the Government on terms better than could be elsewhere got. Every renewal of the charter had, in like manner, been purchased; in some instances at a very high price.

(Krooss 1969: 262–3)

As important to the Jeffersonians/Republicans were the threats to democracy of the government's ability to borrow from the Bank. Easy credit tempted government expansions and war.

Support for the Bank came mainly from commercial interests in the North. Senate proceedings were not published but Table 5.1 shows that in the House the North voted 33–1 for the Bank while the mainly agrarian South voted 18–6 against it. The Bank was generally considered a success, and its life – its charter was for 20 years – was uneventful. Jefferson did not like it and periodically resolved to abolish its 'monopoly' by transferring government deposits to state banks. However, his secretary of the treasury, Albert Gallatin, who found it convenient and 'wisely and skillfully managed', interceded for the Bank and 'ignored Jefferson's request to draw up plans for an independent treasury

Table 5.1 Congressional votes for and against the national banks

	All states	NE[a]	SE[a]	Other slave[b]	NWT[c]	W[d]	
1791	39–19	33–1	6–18				House
							Senate[e]
1811	64–65	44–25	18–34	2–5	0–1		House
	17–17[f]	9–7	7–5	1–3	0–2		Senate
1816	80–71	35–43	34–21	3–2	8–5		House
	22–12	8–7	7–4	6–0	1–1		Senate
1832	107–82	65–28	20–34	12–15	10–5		House
	28–20	14–4	4–8	5–7	5–1		Senate
1841	127–98	61–43	28–31	18–16	20–8		House
	26–23	11–7	7–3	4–9	4–4		Senate
1913	287–85	59–35	39–1	74–11	75–9	40–29	House
	54–34	6–10	10–2	14–2	4–6	20–14	Senate
1927[g]	298–22, yeas and nays not taken.						House
	Accepted with other amendments without separate vote.						Senate

Sources: *Annals of Congress, Congressional Globe, Congressional Record.*

Notes
a Original 13 states and ME and VT, above and below the Mason–Dixon Line.
b KY, TN, LA, MO, MS, AL, AK, FL, TX, and WV.
c Northwest Territory: OH, IN, IL, MI, and WI.
d Others (all west of the Mississippi River).
e Senate proceedings not published.
f Vice-president broke tie vote against the Bank.
g FR charter for 20 years (FR Act, Sec. 4), extended indefinitely in 1927 by McFadden Banking Act, Sec. 18.
Dates of votes (day/month): 1791: H2/8 S2/14. 1811: H1/24 S2/20. 1816 H3/14 S4/13. 1832: H7/3 S6/11. 1841: H8/6 S7/28. 1913: H9/18 S12/19. 1927: H1/24.

system' (Gallatin 1967: 264). Jefferson apologized for the mildness of changes to the hated Federalist system after he became president. 'It mortifies me', he wrote, 'to be strengthening principles which I deem radically vicious, but this vice is entailed on us by the first error.... What is practicable must often control what is pure theory' (Malone 1930: 40). Jefferson liked to talk of sweeping away the machinery of tyranny but he shared Burke's disposition to preserve.

The Bank applied early, in 1808, for a renewal but Gallatin delayed its consideration to avoid Jefferson's veto. Nevertheless, it was narrowly rejected in Congress by a configuration of votes that differed from 1791 (Table 5.1). Many Southerners had come to appreciate the Bank while many Northerners who had wanted finance in 1791 now resented its competition. There were 88 banks in 1811, compared with three in 1791. A Federalist congressman from rural Massachusetts was astonished that representatives 'of the great commercial towns' overwhelmingly voted to kill the Bank. William Crawford, one of Georgia's two senators who supported the Bank, asked rhetorically why certain 'great states' had instructed their members of Congress to vote against the Bank. 'Their avarice', he explained.

> They have erected banks, in many of which they hold stock to a considerable amount, and they wish to compel the United States to use their banks as places of deposit for their public monies, by which they expect to increase their dividends.
>
> (Hammond 1957: 212–16)

These motives were also behind the Constitution's prohibition of State currencies (Article I, Sec. 10). Some who claimed those currencies had been abused were not disinterested. Farley Grubb (2003) wrote that most colonial and State currencies had been carefully regulated and their values maintained. 'Colonial legislatures backed their paper money by linking it not to specie but to future taxes and mortgage payments designed to withdraw it from circulation in a timely fashion.' Prices in these currencies were relatively stable, unlike the Continental Congress's dollar issued during the Revolution. The profits of these currencies were envied by bankers. Dividends of Philadelphia's Bank of North America fell two-thirds in 1785, when the Pennsylvania legislature proposed a new issue of Pennsylvania pounds. 'Unable to compete against state currency in the marketplace, bankers ... constitutionally eliminated their chief paper-money competitor.' This was another shot in the battle for the profits of paper money that had been waged within the colonies and between colonial governments and the authorities in London, and would continue between the states and the federal government under the Constitution.

The second Bank (1816–36)

Gallatin (1830) estimated that the number of banks rose from 88 to 246 between 1811 and 1816, with an increase in their circulations from $23 million to $68 million and a fall in their bullion reserve ratio from 42 to 28 percent. He wrote:

> The creation of the State banks in order to fill the chasm was a natural consequence of the dissolution of the Bank of the United States. And, as is usual under such circumstances, the expectation of great profits gave birth to a much greater number than was wanted.... And, as the salutary regulating power of the Bank of the United States [whose conservative lending policy inhibited expansion by other banks] no longer existed, the issues were accordingly increased much beyond what the ... circumstances ... rendered necessary.

Gallatin supposed that the Bank would have behaved in war as it had in peace, as no central bank has ever behaved. As it was, the War of 1812 was financed by bonds bought with state bank notes. The national debt, which had been reduced from $83 million to $45 million between 1800 and 1811, reached its pre-Civil War peak of $127 million in 1815. The US Treasury and most state banks suspended convertibility after British troops burned Washington in the summer of 1814. As in England, banks continued to operate and their notes circulated at discounts (Nettels 1962: 283–4).

In October 1814, Secretary of the Treasury, A.J. Dallas, proposed a national bank that 'shall loan to the United States $30,000,000 at an interest of six percent at such periods and in such sums as shall be convenient'. This was rejected by Congress as not sufficiently limiting, and Madison vetoed Congress's version. 'The objection of Congress to the original plan', Hammond wrote, 'had been that the Bank had too much of the Government in it. President Madison's objection was that in the Bank proposed by Congress the Government was left out' (Hammond 1957: 232). Responsibility and need had converted Madison to Hamilton's position (Clarke and Hall 1832: 778–80).

In his veto message on 15 January 1815, Madison complained that the capital of Congress's bank – a substantial proportion of which could be subscribed in the form of Government bonds – was insufficient

> to produce, in favor of the public credit, any considerable or lasting elevation of the market price. [Furthermore,] the bank proposed will be free from all legal obligation to co-operate with the public measures; and whatever might be the patriotic disposition of its directors to contribute to the removal of those embarrassments, and to invigorate the prosecution of the war, fidelity to the pecuniary and general interest of the institution, according to their estimate of it, might oblige them to decline a connexion of their operations with those of the national treasury.
> (Krooss 1969: 401–3)

Congress and the president compromised on a bank with capital of $35 million (compared with $10 million for the first Bank and the $50 million originally asked by Madison) and government loans limited to $500,000 (Krooss 1969: 460, 471).

The war was over, however, and government finance was no longer the main issue. The real financial problem had become the chaotic state of the currency caused by the irredeemable paper money issued during the war. 'The erection of a Bank was not so desirable on account of the Government as for the general convenience of the country, Pennsylvania's William Findlay said in the House' (Clarke and Hall 1832: 475). Although hardly necessary to the purpose (except as a political buffer), the second Bank of the United States was adopted primarily to force resumption on the state banks. Their profits were reputed to be large and their specie reserves adequate, but they were not inclined to resume convertibility and their state legislatures were not inclined to compel them.

In shepherding the Bank Bill through the House of Representatives, John Calhoun turned the earlier constitutional objection around. He said the Constitution required Congress to establish an agency for the regulation of the currency. 'No one ... could doubt that' the power (and responsibility) 'to coin money [and] regulate the value thereof' meant 'that the money of the United States was intended to be placed entirely under the control of Congress'. Although not foreseen by the founders, he suggested, money was now mainly paper currency. 'By a sort of under-current' in the form of a

> revolution in the currency..., the power of Congress to regulate the money of the country had caved in, and upon its ruins had sprung up those institutions which now exercised the right of making money for and in the United States.

The states were prohibited from issuing money, but 'In point of fact', added Speaker Henry Clay, 'the regulation of the general currency is in the hands of the state Governments, or, which is the same thing, of the banks created by them.' It was 'incumbent upon Congress to recover ... control', and although direct regulation of the state banks was impracticable, a sound currency might be regained by the restraining influence of a national bank (Clarke and Hall 1832: 672).

Daniel Webster argued that a national bank was unnecessary, that the situation only needed compulsory redemption, and secured a resolution that the government would accept payment only in coin or redeemable bank notes, and keep no deposits in 'any bank which shall not pay its notes, when demanded, in the lawful money of the United States' (Catterall 1902: 23). The resolution was adopted in April 1816, the month the Bank's charter was approved, to become effective the next February.

The Bank was approved, with most of the opposition coming from the northeast, where state banking was strongest. The second Bank had a troubled life. Except for a few years, it reinforced rather than softened financial instability. At the beginning, instead of assisting resumption it participated in a credit boom with the State banks that it was supposed to restrain – much in the manner of the Bank of England. It had 18 branches at the end of 1817, and the head office failed to control them. The notes of any branch were redeemable at all. The Bank was also, for a while, under prodding from Secretary of the Treasury William Crawford, tolerant of State banks' tardiness in redeeming their notes. Gold was leaving the country, however, and the Treasury's resumption was beginning to bite. The government's postwar surplus was paid with bank and Treasury notes that the Treasury converted to gold but was slow to deposit in banks. There was a scramble for liquidity and failures almost included the United States Bank. Its 'grim efforts' to collect its debts aroused a popular hatred of the Bank that 'was never extinguished' (Hammond 1957: 259). 'The Bank was saved and the people were ruined' Andrew Jackson's bank-hating advisor wrote (Gouge 1833 ii: 110).

General resumption was not achieved and the Bank was not out of danger until 1822, so that its conduct as a central bank cannot be judged before that time; nor after the end of the decade, by which time it was embroiled in a political battle for survival. Some have suggested that the Bank under Nicholas Biddle, who became president in 1823, was the first conscious central bank (Catterall 1902: 453–77; Hammond 1957: 286–325). Certainly, he understood the connections between the Bank's portfolio and the money stock. The Bank pursued a conservative lending policy and was a creditor of the state banks so that a Bank restriction acted as a rein on credit. This was good for sound money but not so good for the profits of state banks or the Bank's popularity.

Richard Timberlake (1993: 38–9) suggested that the Bank's maintenance of credit in the face of a gold drain in 1831 was the action of a central bank. There was no stabilization *policy*, however. In 1825, for example, the Bank (like the Bank of England) 'sought self-protection by contracting credit while the country was losing specie' (Meerman 1963). Nor do the data support Jackson's contention that the 'monster' preyed on the state banks. Rather, it tended to move with the state banks, expanding in good times (reducing its reserve ratio) and contracting in hard times. Its conservative tendencies were typical of an industry leader (Highfield *et al.* 1991).

The Bank's charter did not expire until 1836, but Jackson's opponents in Congress made it a campaign issue by voting to renew it in the summer of 1832. New England's strong support of the Bank in 1832, after its opposition in 1816, was a vote against Jackson. The South's opposite move is also seen in Table 5.1. Jackson took the dare and vetoed the bill.

The low marks in economic sophistication that are sometimes given to Jackson are undeserved. First, regardless of whether one agrees with his policies, he understood the structure and operations of the Bank, which is more than can be said of later presidents' understanding of the Federal Reserve. Second, his opposition to the Bank on the grounds, as he stated in his veto message, that legal monopolies and exclusive privileges 'are granted at the expense of the public', was in tune with the contemporary move towards general incorporation laws (Krooss 1969: 817). The Supreme Court's determination in *Charles River Bridge* v. *Warren Bridge* that exclusive privileges are not implicit in corporate charters came in 1837. This was also the high tide of laissez faire, even as it applied to banking. Arguments for competitive banking were strongest, if not overly successful, during this period in Britain and the United States. We saw that some of the exclusive privileges of the Bank of England were taken away and the rest were threatened. Similar forces opposed to the Bank of the United States were stronger.

An important political weakness of both institutions was the passing of the government's need for credit. Henry Clay, who opposed the first Bank's renewal in 1811, had learned by 1816, he recalled on the Senate floor in 15 July 1841, during a debate over another US Bank, 'that war could not be carried on without the aid of banks'. Jackson's supporter, Senator Thomas Benton of Missouri, had declared in 1831: 'The war made the bank; peace will unmake it' (Krooss 1969: 736).

The Whigs, who rode to power on the coattails of war-hero William Henry Harrison in 1840, voted for a third United States Bank with a regional distribution of votes similar to 1832. Harrison died after a month in office, however, and the Democrat John Tyler vetoed the Bank Bill (Holt 1999: 127–35). Another majority was not mustered in favor of a national bank until Woodrow Wilson delivered the Democratic Party to the money-center banks.

The Independent Treasury

Competition for government deposits led to charges of political favoritism, especially for the benefit of democrat 'pet banks', and in 1840, Congress directed the Treasury's coin to be kept 'safely' in its own subtreasuries, independent of banks. Advocates of the Independent Treasury Bill also wished to avoid the risk of failing banks. The *Act* was repealed the next year in preparation for the abortive third bank but was restored in 1846.

Lincoln is not most famous as an economist, but his argument for a national bank showed a concern for the incentives of institutions that was lacking in the next century.

> It is often urged that to say the public money will be more secure in a national bank than in the hands of individuals, as proposed in the subtreasury, is to say that bank directors and bank officers are more honest than sworn officers of the government. Not so. We insist on no such thing. We say that public officers, selected with reference to their capacity and honesty (which, by the way, we deny is the practice in these days), stand an equal chance precisely, of being capable and honest with bank officers selected by the same rule. We further say that with however much care selections may be made, there will be some unfaithful and dishonest in both classes. The experience of the whole world, in all bygone times, proves this to be true.... What we do say is that the interest of the subtreasurer is against his duty, while the interest of the bank is on the side of duty. Take instances: A subtreasurer has in his hands one hundred thousand dollars of public money; his duty says, 'You ought to pay this money over', but his interest says, 'You ought to run away with this sum'.... And who that knows anything of human nature doubts that in many instances interest will prevail over duty...? But how different is it with a bank.... If it proves faithful to the government it continues its business; if unfaithful, it forfeits its charter, breaks up its business, and thereby loses more than it can make up by seizing upon the government funds in its possession. Its interest, therefore,

is on the side of its duty.... It is for this reason, then, that we say a bank is the more secure.

(Speech against the subtreasury and other policies of the Van Buren administration, Springfield, Illinois, 20 December 1839)

Lincoln also worried about the contractionary effects of the subtreasury system on the money stock. These effects turned out to be less than he feared because other incentives, not part of the law, came into play. Much of the history of the Independent Treasury is of breaches of the law by Treasury secretaries concerned for financial stability. The system exposed the monetary base to shocks from federal budgets, seasonal and otherwise. Secretaries sensitive to the financial community supplied liquidity in times of stress by early payments of interest and debt redemptions that had the effect of later open-market purchases (Wood 2005: 141–53). When he was criticized for doing less than the market wanted, Secretary Howell Cobb complained:

There are many persons who seem to think that it is the duty of the Government to provide relief in all cases of trouble and distress ... and their necessities, not their judgments, force them to the conclusion that the Government not only can, but ought to relieve them.

(*Treasury Report, 1857*, pp. 11–12)

Although their actions cannot be called monetary *policy*, in a systematic sense, Congress and the Treasury were concerned with the monetary base. Congress was directly involved in Civil War finance as well as in the resumption of convertibility after the war (Taus 1943: 80–133; Wood 2005: 141–6). The Treasury's gold reserve and the propriety of monetary interventions were frequent subjects of debate, and Friedman and Schwartz (1963: 149) wrote that by the end of the century the Treasury was almost a central bank because its actions 'were being converted from emergency measures to a fairly regular and predictable operating function'. When his actions were criticized as autocratic and in the interests of 'powerful Wall Street speculators', Secretary Leslie Shaw (1902–7) declared: 'It has been the fixed policy of the Treasury Department for more than half a century to anticipate monetary stringencies, and so far as possible prevent panics' (Timberlake 1993: 192). The 1906 *Treasury Report* (49) claimed that if the secretary had more power, 'no panic as distinguished from industrial stagnation could threaten either the United States or Europe that he could not avert'.

Foundations of the Federal Reserve

An act to provide for the establishment of Federal reserve banks, to furnish an elastic currency, to afford means of rediscounting commercial paper, to establish a more effective supervision of banking in the United States, and for other purposes.

(Preamble to the Federal Reserve Act, 1913)

The call for an elastic currency

The foremost monetary issue of the last decades of the nineteenth century was the question of the standard: paper, as the Greenback Party, which opposed resumption, would have it; bimetallism (gold and silver), favored by silver and agricultural debtor interests; and gold, favored by the sound money East that wanted a currency which maintained its value relative to the British pound and the rest of the industrial world that was turning to gold. Paper was defeated in the Resumption Act of 1875, and the victory over the silver interests and William Jennings Bryan in the presidential election of 1896, was solidified by the increases in gold production and the price level beginning that year. The standard was settled (until 1933) in the Gold Standard Act of 1900.

The second monetary issue arose from the frequent financial crises characterized by currency panics and bank failures, followed by industrial depressions. In the *History of Crises under the National Banking System*, O.M.W. Sprague (1910) wrote of major panics in 1873, 1884, 1890, 1893, and 1897. E.W. Kemmerer (1910) counted six major and 15 minor panics between 1890 and 1908.

Panics were laid at the door of the inelasticity of the currency under the National Banking System that had begun as an aid to Civil War finance. The Office of the Controller of the Currency was established by the National Bank Act in 1863 to charter banks that would hold government currency (greenbacks) as reserves and issue a uniform currency (national bank notes) backed by government bonds.

The Act got off to a rocky start. It was too late to help the war effort and few state banks shifted their charters. Most shifted to national charters when Congress eliminated their currencies by a 10-percent per annum tax on them, but returned to state charters as they embraced deposit banking. Small local banks wished to avoid the costly capital and cash reserve requirements of national banks, although national charters were useful to large city banks because, as 'reserve banks', they could be reserve depositories for smaller banks.

The movement for bank reform was strengthened by the crisis of 1890–93, which saw hundreds of bank failures, sharp falls in money and credit, and massive business bankruptcies. 'Almost everyone who wrote or spoke on the subject of banking after 1892 denounced the inelasticity of the currency instituted by the national banking system' (Livingston 1986: 73). National banknotes were restricted, it was said, because of the rigidity of eligible bonds that constituted their backing.[4] Reformers wanted a supply of money that responded to its demand.

Although it was the foremost battle cry, and took pride of place in the Preamble to the Federal Reserve Act, 'elastic currency' was never fully explained. It could not have been a serious proposal without significant qualifications. A money supply that is determined by its demand means an indeterminate price level, certainly a violation of the gold standard that was taken as given by most parties to the debate. The notion that there should always be plenty of money may be attractive but it has been the language of inflationists (Viner 1937: 87–90, 282–9). Chapter 7 ('What they knew in 1914') tells how sound money men saw accommodative money as something to be resisted.

102 Monetary policy

The most prominent monetary reformers, who were bankers and sympathetic to price and financial stability, probably did not mean to be taken literally. They probably meant a currency that would be *somewhat* elastic *sometimes*, depending on the discretion of authorities. Eastern bankers, unlike western populists, did not complain of too little money generally. Although prices fell for three decades after the Civil War, bankers, especially those interested in international finance, preferred the relative stability of the gold standard and the confidence it gave foreign investors. They must have referred to cyclical panics and the seasonal shortages of liquidity, especially at the end of the year when increased currency demand diminished the lending capacities of banks at the time of peak credit demands.

Repeal of the National Bank Act would not have solved these problems, which may be why there was no significant attempt to do so. More to the point, with or without a National Banking System, was the desire for a lender of last resort. Bagehot and the Bank of England were cited as models. Expanding or institutionalizing the clearinghouses, whose certificates amounted to the manufacture of reserves which had been useful in times of stress, were also considered, as were relaxed restrictions on branch banking and terminating the tax on state bank notes (Livingston 1986: 74–80).

Bankers and businessmen came together in Baltimore and Indianapolis in 1894 and 1897 to support the gold standard and propose improvements to monetary stability. They did not obtain legislation immediately, but their advocacy of a currency based on the business loans of banks (commercial paper) instead of government bonds was successful in the long run.

Continental Europe supplied an important reformer when Paul Warburg came from the family firm in Hamburg to Kuhn Loeb in New York at the turn of the century. Warburg envisioned a central bank on the European model, which meant a shift in bank assets from non-marketable loans based on customer relationships to liquid bills eligible for rediscount by the central bank (Livingston 1986: 53–9; Warburg 1910). Warburg deserves credit for key elements of the Federal Reserve Act but reformers decided that it was politically wise to downplay the role of bankers. The National Sound Money League, whose treasurer and general secretary was A. Barton Hepburn of the Chase National Bank of New York, was formed in 1897:

> Fully realizing the prejudice in the popular mind against everything upon the money question which emanated from the vicinity of Wall Street, it was determined to open the main office of the League in Chicago, with a branch in New York.
> (Hepburn 1903: xv–xviii)

The general secretary in New York would issue a monthly bulletin distributed from Chicago.

The political machinations that culminated in the Federal Reserve Act were complex, and the success of reform was often in doubt, but the objectives of the ultimately victorious reformers were settled before the turn of the century. However, the visible sequence of political steps that led to the Federal Reserve System began with the Panic of 1907. Congress responded to this as to no earlier crisis, and speedily adopted the Aldrich-Vreeland Act (1908) that provided for emergency currency secured by commercial paper and a National Monetary Commission to inquire into money and banking problems. It held hearings, commissioned several studies that became famous (such as Sprague 1910, Kemmerer 1910, and Warburg, 1910), and agreed on a plan named for its chairman, Nelson Aldrich, Republican senator from Rhode Island.

Its ideas were not new but the Aldrich Plan 'served notice', for the first time since the Civil War, 'that there were those in positions of importance who had resolved to reform American banking practice' (West 1977: 69). In 1911, Aldrich proposed a bill for a National Reserve Association (NRA) with headquarters in Washington, DC, and 15 branches. The 15 districts would be associations of at least ten banks holding reserves with the NRA. The NRA's notes would replace national bank notes and it would lend to (discount the commercial bills of) member banks. Its note and deposit liabilities would be backed by a 50-percent reserve of gold and US currency.

The NRA's Board of Directors would have 46 members: two chosen by each district, nine more from the districts based on stock ownership, the secretaries of the treasury, commerce and labor, and agriculture, the comptroller of the currency, a governor selected by the president from a list provided by the Board, and two deputy governors selected by the Board. An early version of the Plan gave the president power to remove the governor but this was dropped to secure the support of the Currency Committee of the American Bankers Association (ABA) (Warburg 1930 i: 200–30; West 1977: 75).

Congress did not act on Aldrich's bill because his association with New York bankers inspired opposition and the Democratic Party won control of the House of Representatives in 1910, and would also win the Senate and the presidency in 1912. Democrats publicly distanced themselves from the NRA although the Federal Reserve Act stemmed from the interests and ideas behind Aldrich's proposal. Supporters of the Aldrich Plan had formed the National Citizens' League directed by Laurence Laughlin (1912) of the University of Chicago, and his former student, Parker Willis of Washington and Lee University in Virginia, was an advisor to Virginia Congressman Carter Glass, ranking member of the House Committee of Banking and Currency. Glass hoped to steer banking reform in a more conservative direction than the scandal-filled Pujo investigations of the 'money trust' (US Congress 1913; Kolko 1963: 219–21).

Banking had not been a priority of the Democratic Party or Woodrow Wilson, but its recent notoriety and the attentions of congressmen and industry spokesmen led him to make it an early part of his reform program. Glass approached Wilson shortly after his election to the presidency, and was his congressional liaison for the Federal Reserve Bill that passed in December 1913 (Glass 1927: 73). As Gabriel Kolko pointed out in *The Triumph of Conservatism* that the Progressive Era turned out to be, the confusion over the precise authorship of the Federal Reserve Act [Glass (1927: 238) claimed the entire credit] should not obscure the fact that the major function, inspiration, and direction of the measure was to serve the banking community in general, and large bankers specifically.

(1963: 222)

The most significant difference between the Federal Reserve Act and the Aldrich plan arose from Wilson's demand for more government involvement. The district associations remained (although they became 12 instead of 15) but the president wanted a 'capstone' in the form of a central board composed entirely of presidential appointees: five members with ten-year sequential terms, plus the secretary of the treasury and the comptroller of the currency. 'The power to direct this system of credits', Wilson wrote with satisfaction to the House majority leader, is thus

> put into the hands of a public board of disinterested officers of the Government itself who can make no money out of anything they do in connection with it.... The [Federal Reserve] board can oblige the banks of one region to go to the assistance of the banks of another. The whole resources of the country are mobilized, to be employed where they are most needed. I think we are justified in speaking of this as a democracy of credit.
>
> (*Papers*, 17 October 1914)

Glass told the House:

> no semblance of acquisitiveness prompts [the Federal Reserve Board's] operations; no banking interest is behind, and no financial interest can pervert or control it. It is an altruistic institution, a part of the Government itself, representing the American people, powers such as no man would dare misuse.
>
> (10 September 1913)

When a deputation of bankers requested representatives on the Board, Wilson demanded:

> Will one of you gentlemen tell me in what civilized country of the earth there are important government boards of control on which private interests are represented?

'There was painful silence for the longest single moment I ever spent', Glass recalled, 'and before it was broken' Mr Wilson further inquired:

> Which of you gentlemen thinks the railroads should select members of the Interstate Commerce Commission?
>
> (Glass 1927: 116)

This denial of incentives in public bodies contrasted with earlier periods. Lincoln had doubted and Jackson had scoffed at the notion that citizens might rely on the bank's public spirit. Hamilton (1790) had argued in support of the first US Bank that, like the Bank of England on which it was patterned, its 'careful and prudent administration' would be secured by the 'keen, steady, and, as it were, magnetic sense of the [directors'] interest, ... pointing invariably to its true pole, the prosperity of the institution'.

Returning to Wilson's rhetorical question, the Interstate Commerce Commission represented the railroad industry, as Congress intended, and contained many railroad men. At the time of Wilson's meeting with the bankers, three of five ICC commissioners had strong railroad ties as former employees or lawyers.[5] Similarly, the original Federal Reserve Board of five members included Warburg and W.P.G. Harding, President of the First National Bank of Birmingham, Alabama. The Federal Reserve Act provided that bankers comprise one-third of the Boards of Directors of the Reserve Banks (Sec. 4) and that the Federal Reserve Board be advised by a Federal Advisory Council consisting entirely of bankers (Sec. 12), whose considerable influence has been discussed by Thomas Havrilesky (1993: 251–73). The Reserve Bank heads were bankers. The form of banker representation was a political quibble.

A product of the Progressive Era

The Federal Reserve System was a product of the Progressive Era, which is the name given to the period of expanding government in the early years of the twentieth century. The great rise in incomes and living standards brought by the growing industrial powerhouse had been accompanied by economic and social inequalities that required correction, the historians wrote.

> Science and machinery had outrun social science and political machinery. The practices and principles inherited from an eighteenth-century rural republic were no longer adequate to the exigencies of a twentieth-century urban state. This was true in the political realm, where the fear of government persisted into the period when only government could adequately control the forces that machinery had let loose on society.... The heroes of the day were all reformers

who set out to solve 'the land question, the labor question, the woman question, the money question' (Nevins and Commager 1945: 387).

What they did, we know, was promote monopoly and collusion. Their reforms included the Elkins Act (1903), the Hepburn Act (1906), the Pure Food and Drugs Act (1906), and the creation of the Federal Trade Commission (1914), all designed to limit (prevent 'unfair') competition through new products, advertising, and pricing. The first two acts tightened the Interstate Commerce Act (1887), which had been urged by the railroad companies to 'rationalize' the industry, that is, to limit entry and fix prices. The decline in average railroad rates – by 60 percent since 1870 – ended with the establishment of the Interstate Commerce Commission. The Elkins and Hepburn Acts increased the ICC's powers over rates and lines, which it used with the help of the courts to compel several states to raise their rates in line with others to prevent 'unfair competition'. The Supreme Court declared that a company was 'entitled to ask' for a 'fair return', apparently, Kent Healy (1944) noted, 'almost irrespective of the laws of supply and demand [no] matter what judgment had been used in locating railroads, or what their expenses were'.

The Federal Reserve System was from the same mold. Its goals were the banking industry's, although advertised by politicians as 'in the public interest' and accepted as such by historians. Richard Hofstadter wrote in *The Age of Reform* (1955: 252) that Progressive successes included, in the Hepburn Act, 'the first step toward genuine regulation of the railroads, a thing long overdue', and in the creation of the Federal Reserve System, 'a more satisfactory system of credit subject to public control'.

The Federal Reserve Act tells a different story. Most of its significant features, four of which are developed below, were designed to promote bank profits:

1. *A central bank (supplier of cheap liquidity especially in times of stress) that was not (unlike the Bank of England and the first two Banks of the US) a competitor.*

Chicago banker and ABA chairman George Reynolds had opposed a central bank (presumably on the model of the competitive Bank of England), preferring 'some central overseeing or controlling board.... By which I mean an organization with branches located in various sections of the country, dealing only with banks and the Government.' Legislation to this end could 'count on ... a reasonable measure of cooperation by the American Bankers' Association' (Kolko 1963: 226). 'We cannot afford to overlook the prejudices of the past or the present', Aldrich told an ABA convention in 1911.

> One of the principal objections to the second Bank of the United States was the charge of personal and political favoritism.... We must afford no opportunity for a repetition..., and the new organization must, therefore, do business with the banks alone; it must be their agent, not generally, but for certain specific and well defined purposes ... not in any sense a competitor for the business of existing banks.

The National Citizens League said: 'The reform should not take the form of a dominant central bank.' Nor should the government 'enter the discount and deposit business of banking; but ... should supervise and regulate a cooperative means of assistance ... in the common interest' (Laughlin 1912: iii–iv).

2. *Bankers acceptances.* In addition to making a market for domestic commercial paper in the course of its credit operations (as indicated in the *Act's*

preamble), the Fed was empowered to 'discount acceptances which are based on the importation or exportation of goods and which have a maturity at time of discount of not more than three months, and indorsed by at least one member bank'.

(Sec. 13)

The acceptance privilege, 'one of the most important powers possessed by banks doing foreign business', was denied American banks. The comptroller's rulings that national banks could not have branches or accept drafts or bills of exchange because they were not expressly granted by the National Bank Act had been upheld by the courts (Wilkins 1991; Phelps 1917: 92). International movements of American goods were financed by Europeans. However, Aldrich had a plan, 'or I should more properly say a firm purpose to find a plan, to make the United States the financial center of the world, a position she is entitled to by virtue of her resources, her vast accumulations of wealth, and her surplus capital'. Instead of forcing banks to lend their liquid resources to Wall Street speculators, they should be able to 'safely invest it ... in standard notes or bills of exchange representing the industries or the products of the United States.... And [as Warburg had hoped] they will have in their portfolios commercial paper created for legitimate purposes, which they can take to the District Association and have transformed into cash or a cash credit at any hour of any business day of the year' (Aldrich 1909, 1911).

After serving as a member of the Federal Reserve Board from 1914 to 1918, Warburg was chairman of the International Acceptance Bank from 1921 until his death in 1932, in addition to serving on the Federal Advisory Council from 1921 to 1926.[6] The Fed supported the market by discounting acceptances for banks and buying them in the open market, holding from a third to half of them between 1916 and 1931. When Friedman and Schwartz (1963: 193) suggested that the Fed's 'increases in its holdings of bankers' acceptances while attempting to restrict discounts' betrayed a lack of understanding of these instruments' identical effects on the money stock, they did not consider that a primary purpose of the Fed was to support these markets. Eventually, the Fed decided that the market 'had matured to the point that it could stand on its own', and ended operations in acceptances in 1977, although it continued to discount them for banks (LaRoche 1993).

The Act (Sec. 25) also permitted foreign branches to American banks. The Fed's interest in the profitability of American banks continues. In 1999, Chairman Greenspan complained that their global position was threatened by the archaic legal restrictions under which they had to operate (Calomiris 2000: xv, 338–9). Bankers were finding that anti-competitive protections designed for domestic reasons (limits on branching, pricing, and portfolios) hindered their ability to compete in foreign markets.

3. *Lower reserve requirements.* Federal Reserve member banks were assigned the reserve requirements of national banks, which Table 5.2 shows were substantially reduced by the Federal Reserve Act.

(Sec. 19)

Table 5.2 Selected reserve requirement ratios (%) of national and Federal Reserve member banks (all banks after 1980)

	Demand deposits			Time deposits
	Central reserve city	Reserve city	Country	
1863	25	25	15	Same as demand
1913	18	15	12	5
1917	13	10	7	3
1948	26	22	16	7.5
1970	17.5	17.5	13	5
	Large	Small		
1992	10	3		0

Sources: Federal Reserve Board, *Banking and Monetary Statistics* and *Annual Statistical Digests*.

This was a direct increase in the earnings of national banks, which were required to join the Federal Reserve System. It was an inducement to state banks to join the System, but state requirements remained less than those of national banks and the former overwhelmingly remained outside.

Table 5.2 shows major changes in Federal Reserve member reserve requirements, limited control of which was given to the Fed in the Banking Act of 1935, and taken away in the Depository Institutions Deregulation and Monetary Control Act of 1980. The high requirements imposed in 1936–37 were kept through World War II, after which they were reduced under the pressure of banks as rising interest rates increased their costs (Lown and Wood 2003).

4. *Price fixing*. Adam Smith (1776: 128) wrote:

> People of the same trade seldom meet together, even for merriment and diversion, but the conversation ends in a conspiracy against the public, or in some contrivance to raise prices.

Or reduce costs. In 1884, the New York Clearing House Association resolved 'that no member ... shall pay interest upon or allow compensation for deposits after the 1st January 1885'. Speaking for the resolution, George Coe of the American Exchange National Bank asked:

> How can any honorable gentleman among our number claim the right to selfishly pursue his business in utter disregard of [the] delicate relations by which the association ... is sustained and the business of the nation is safely conducted? We are in a most important sense directly responsible for each other and can not avoid being disturbed by the ignorance, selfishness, or immoral conduct of our most remote members,

particularly 'the eagerness of one bank to draw to itself the business of others by superior inducements' (Sprague 1910: 371–9).

However, Smith (1776: 129) also wrote: 'In a free trade an effectual combination cannot be established but by the unanimous consent of every single trader, and it cannot last longer than every single trader continues of the same mind.' Smith anticipated the Fourth National Bank's O.D. Baldwin, who called Coe's proposal injurious and 'impossible of enforcement' (Sprague 1910: 385–6). New York banks were still trying to collude the next century. Although not directed to do so by the Federal Reserve Act, the Fed did what it could to help. In February 1918, the Board asked the members of the New York Clearing House to tie their deposit rates to the Fed's discount rate. The March *Federal Reserve Bulletin* regretted the aggressive competition for deposits that threatened to 'put the banking system upon an unprofitable basis, thereby weakening our entire banking structure'. The Board wished 'it understood that it does not favor any movement to increase these rates and that it will do all in its powers to discourage it'.

The money stock had risen 11 percent during the past year, and money market rates from 4 to 6 percent, but the Clearing House tried again. The effectiveness of the rates that it adopted in March 1918, is unknown but they were officially given up in 1924 (Cox 1966: 8–11).

The Banking Act of 1933 prohibited interest on demand deposits and authorized the Fed to regulate interest rates on time deposits. The Fed took the Act seriously, and interpreted 'interest' to include all payments and considerations, including credit services, that were designed to attract deposits. However, complaints from their banker constituents persuaded the House and Senate Banking Committees to ask the Fed to back down because their definition violated 'certain banking practices'. Evasions continued although they were not very important during the long period of low interest rates from the 1930s to the early 1960s. The Fed's refusal to allow time deposit rates to reflect market conditions in the 1960s led to 'credit crunches' as depositors shifted to nonbank investments. Increasing evasions of the ceilings persuaded bankers that their main effect was to increase the costs of competition without reducing its intensity, and they were eliminated by the 1980 deregulation act (Wood and Wood 1985: 41, 61–3).

Moving to another cost, Aldrich (1911) looked forward to the 'equality in rates of discount, or rediscount, for all banks, and these rates are to be uniform throughout the country. This, it is believed, will insure steadiness and reasonableness of rates everywhere.' Banks were thus given a reliable source of funds outside the hurly burly of the market place, often on favorable terms. There was always political pressure on the Fed to maintain a low lending rate. This became less important for monetary policy with the development of open-market operations as the main policy instrument, and the discount rate remained a bank subsidy, significantly below the federal funds rate, the market cost of reserves, from the mid-1960s into the next century. It was used in the 1980s to help the Federal Deposit Insurance Corporation prop up failing banks, much as it had in the 1920s (Schwartz 1992). Congress ordered the end of this practice in the Federal Deposit Insurance Corporation Improvement Act of 1992 (Todd 1992). In 2003, the discount rate was raised relative to market rates and the Fed turned to the discount rate as a stand-by facility for creditworthy borrowers at a penalty rate consistent with the Palmer rule of 1832 (Madigan and Nelson 2002). The concluding chapter refers to the departure from these good intentions in 2008.

A fifth item that the large banks would have liked to see in the Act was more liberal branching. This item was notable for its absence from a measure whose professed objective was stability. Most bank failures were of small, local, undiversified banks whose local markets were protected by anti-branching laws (Cottrell *et al.* 1995). However, any rationalization of banking that encroached on these protections was politically impossible. The truth of Aldrich's (1909) statement held for decades:

> Competent authorities base the success of the Canadian system upon their extensive use of branches. Of course, I realize that there are in this country a great many intelligent men who think we ought to have a system of branch banking like the Canadian; but unless I greatly mistake the character of the American people that will not be possible. In my judgment any system which is to be adopted in this country must recognize the rights and independence of the 25,000 separate banks in the United States.

These banks objected to any kind of federal control, and membership in the System was made voluntary to neutralize their opposition (Sec. 9). Branch banking was not liberalized, even as a result of the massive failures of the Great Depression, until the bank depression of the 1980s (Golembe 1960; Kane 1996).

Conclusion

What they got

Banks benefited from the Fed's support of the domestic and international commercial paper markets, as well as cost reductions in the forms of reduced reserve requirements and free payments services, although the last was not directed or implied by law. Private clearinghouses and wire services already functioned, and central bank involvement has not been thought necessary in other countries. The Fed provided these services gratuitously (if inefficiently; large transfers for which speed was desirable were done privately) as another way of attracting membership, at least until 1980, when Congress directed that banks pay for Fed services (Evanoff 1985).

Congressman Henry Reuss described his negotiations with the Fed leading to the 1980 Act:

> We had to placate the small banks and the regional banks and the money-center banks – all of them. [Board staff director] Axilrod would throw new

formulas into the hopper. Volcker ... was always trying to get something more for the banks.

(Greider 1987: 161)

There is no better example than the Federal Reserve of George Stigler's (1971) thesis that, 'as a rule, regulation is acquired by the industry and is designed and operated primarily for its benefit'. The goal of bank stability as an explanation of Fed actions is the primary theme of Chapter 7.

This section ends with two important exercises of the Fed's control of bank reserves. The financial markets are subject to severe seasonal movements. Economic activity and credit demands rise in the fourth quarter while the public's demand for cash erodes bank reserves and the supply of credit. This reinforces other stresses and it was no accident that the fourth quarter had more than its share of panics before 1914.

The Fed saw that it possessed the remedy. Its first *Annual Report* (1914) asked: 'What is the proper place and function of the Federal Reserve Banks in our banking and credit system?' Some say, 'that they are merely emergency banks to be resorted to for assistance only in time of abnormal stress'. On the other hand, the Fed believed that 'Its duty is not to await emergencies but by anticipation, to do what it can to prevent them.'

> So ... if, at any time, commerce, industry or agriculture are, in the opinion of the Federal Reserve Board, burdened unduly with excessive interest charges, it will be the clear and imperative duty of the Reserve Board acting through the discount rate and open market powers, to secure a wider diffusion of credit facilities at reasonable rates.... The more complete adaptation of the credit mechanism and facilities of the country to the needs of industry, commerce, and agriculture – with all their seasonal fluctuations and contingencies – should be the constant aim of a Reserve Bank's management.

Parker Willis, who had become secretary to the Board, wrote that the benefits of the System included the elimination of 'wide fluctuations of interest rates ... from season to season as now exist', and accordingly less 'necessity of emergency measures to safeguard the country from the possible results of financial panic or stringency' (Willis 1915: 75). Seasonality in interest rates virtually disappeared, to be replaced by a strong seasonal in Fed credit (Miron 1986).

Second, Carter Glass argued that by keeping reserves in regional Reserve Banks they would be close to home, away from 'the stock-gambling operations ... of the congested money centers' (Krooss 1969: 2343–6). However, credit continued to flow to its most profitable uses. Country banks still found convenient short-term investments in the money centers. It is ironic that the first large-scale emergency service of Glass's creation was support of New York banks when their stock loans collapsed in 1929.

Before then, in 1927, during 'the high-tide of the Fed', Congress declared its charter 'to have succession until dissolved by Act of Congress or until forfeiture of franchise for violation of law' (Friedman and Schwartz 1963: 240). This renewal of the charter in perpetuity broke with precedent, and was adopted almost without debate as a rider to the McFadden Banking Act that was concerned primarily with branch banking.

What they did not get

There was nothing in the Act about monetary policy. Long-run price movements were governed by the gold standard, and employment and output were not government responsibilities. The Fed's interests in economic fluctuations in the 1920s were part of their concern for financial stability.

Nor did they get a national currency backed by bank assets. Secretary of State William Jennings Bryan and Robert Owen, chairman of the Senate Finance Committee, insisted that Federal Reserve currency be 'obligations of the United States'. As in the case of the Civil War greenbacks, the federal government became the chief issuer of the currency (Laughlin 1933: 152).

The desire to keep it

Banks have been the foremost supporters of the structure and usually of the policies of the Federal Reserve before Congress and elsewhere. This follows from the immediate market benefits described above, and also from the belief that the Fed is inclined towards price stability. Volatile prices produce volatile loan demands and repayment prospects, and bank balance sheets and stock prices are damaged by inflation (Santoni 1986). The recent moves toward central bank independence and low inflation around the world have made the most progress in the countries in which the financial sector is politically most powerful (Posen 1995).

These are important reasons for the Fed's concern for the health (profitability and stability) of banks and the financial markets. Another reason is the Fed's immersion in, with the knowledge and attitudes of a full participant, in these markets. The importance of experience and surroundings as sources of knowledge and conditioners of action are developed in the next chapter.

6 Knowledge, advice, and monetary policy

> All the perceptions of the human mind resolve themselves into two distinct kinds, which I shall call *impressions* and *ideas*. The difference betwixt these consists in the degrees of force and liveliness with which they strike upon the mind and make their way into our thought or consciousness. Those perceptions which enter with most force and violence we name *impressions*, and under this name I comprehend all our sensations, passions, and emotions as they make their first appearance in the soul. By *ideas*, I mean the faint images of these in thinking and reasoning, such as ... the perceptions excited by the present discourse, excepting only those which arise from the sight and touch, and excepting the immediate pleasure or uneasiness it may occasion. I believe it will not be very necessary to employ many words in explaining this distinction. Every one of himself will readily perceive the difference betwixt feeling and thinking.
> (Hume 1739: 1)

There are three steps from theory to policy, the first two being the development of a theory and its translation into a policy model. The first step is one of scientific achievement, or a paradigm shift that provides a new way of looking at and explaining the world. This is what Keynes thought he did in his *General Theory* that undertook to explain what the classical economists saw as anomalies. The second step takes us to the form in which the new theory is accepted, almost certainly with modifications, by those who would apply it to public policy. Economists' resistance to Keynes's ideas was discussed in Chapter 3, and the account of fiscal policy in Chapter 4 showed that their version of the *GT*, with the same old reasons for the same old activist proposals, had little effect on political decisions. The historical/institutional interests described in Chapter 2 dominated the ideas of Chapter 3 in explaining the fiscal practices of Chapter 4.

Is monetary policy different? Fiscal policy is embedded in taxpayers'/voters' interests and realized through the complexities of a representative system that has evolved over centuries. The practical obstacles in the way of the new theory of fiscal policy decreed its dismissal even before its theoretical impotence was fully appreciated. It might appear at first glance that the problems of implementation – the third step in the journey from theory to policy – are less severe for monetary policy. The central bank can conceivably alter its course at any time. It is institutionally freer than Congress to respond to theory and events. This is not sufficient, however. It must also be intellectually free, and minds can be as intractable as institutions.

This is not the place to develop a theory of knowledge, or even, more to the point, a complete theory of the knowledge sufficient for life. It is, however, the place for an analysis of the knowledge that is used in making macroeconomic policy. Our understanding of monetary policy, including its relations with monetary theory, ought to benefit from a study of the reasons for, or philosophies of, the differences between the vocabularies, objects of attention, and policy preferences of economists and policymakers. These two groups are not exceptions to the general tendency of different people to see things differently. Although much knowledge is shared, all is in some degree personal. The lessons and understandings to which every statement or event gives rise depend on two things: the position of the recipient, and the kind of person he is, that is, where he stands and the state of his mind.

Central bankers and economists know – or think they know – different things. The formers' focus on practice to the neglect of theory draws us to philosophies of knowledge as guides to action. The overlapping insights of the British empiricists, American pragmatists, and economic philosophers can tell us much about central bankers, including their distance from the abstract truths of the complete but closed models of economists. The first section below examines the conflict between ideas (theory) and impressions (practice) that interested Hume (see the quotation above). The different views of the world implicit in these alternative paths to knowledge are developed in the next section. The problems of communication between economists with similar languages and backgrounds were discussed in Chapter 3. The obstacles between economists and central bankers are even greater. I try to weave the observations of philosophers, psychologists, and economists who have wondered about the sources of knowledge into a rough understanding of the differences between theorists and practitioners.

The third section examines policymakers' resistance to the limitations (tradeoffs) of economic theory, followed by a look at the bureaucracies that have been erected to promote the prestige and influence of economists, without, as we will see, substantially bridging their intellectual differences with policymakers. Advisors adapt to policymakers more than the other way around, which is not surprising in light of the incentives involved.

The next-to-last section considers whether central bankers' talk is meaningful to themselves or others. Is it possible that the language of 'tone' and 'feel' reflects useful knowledge despite economists' complaints that they are instruments of secrecy and self-deception? Is it possible that the Fed's behavior and language are rationally cautious approaches to complex and politically sensitive tasks in an uncertain environment? Moreover, economists have epistemological problems of their own. We can learn something of both groups by looking over the shoulders of economists as they judge central bankers. The last section considers the capacities of social versus expert knowledge in the conduct of public policy in a democracy. The dominance of the former in our society has resulted in the conservatism that we see in our fiscal and monetary policies.

Sources and limits of knowledge

> *Socrates:* Come now, Protagoras,... how do you stand as regards knowledge?... The opinion of the majority about knowledge is that it is not anything strong which controls and rules; they don't look at it that way at all, but think that often a man who possesses knowledge is ruled not by it but by something else, in one case passion, in another pleasure, in another pain, sometimes lust, very often fear; that just look at knowledge as a slave who gets dragged about by all the rest. Now are you of a similar opinion about knowledge, or do you think that it is something fine and such as to rule man, and that if someone knows what is good and bad, he would never be conquered by anything so as to do other than what knowledge bids him? In fact, that intelligence is a sufficient safeguard for man?
>
> (Plato 1991: Sec. 352)

Protagoras was an 'extreme subjectivist' who held that 'every belief is true for the person who holds it' (Plato 1991: 61). For Plato, on the other hand, true knowledge was general, acquired by reason, and the first of the moderns, Descartes (1637), insisted that nothing should be accepted as true that did not satisfy the demands of reason. He gave two reasons why we are misled if we follow our natural inclination to accept the supposed knowledge of our senses: First, as we all know, our senses deceive us; optical illusions are common and the other senses can be as confusing or misleading. Second, even when the information of our senses is true, it cannot be comprehended, sorted out, by our senses alone. The resort to reason is unavoidable.

The empirical philosophers responded that impressions are as important as reason to knowledge. The former are the events to which reason is applied, and reason itself is conditioned by the senses. To the British empiricists – Locke, Berkeley, and Hume – knowledge consisted

> in determining ... the relation between the human mind and the external world of our sensible experience and what knowledge of reality that relation permits. That is to say, whereas for Plato sense experience was both inferior to and, to a high degree, obstructive of the findings of pure reason and whereas for Descartes the aim was to subordinate sense experience to reason, limiting our knowledge of the external world to what can be made good by reason, for the empiricists sense experience is basic, where we start and what we have to stand on. They do not necessarily maintain that all knowledge is limited to sense experience, nor that experience is infallible; but sense experience is the best that we have available, and such knowledge as is attainable by reason must conform to it.
>
> (Woozley 1957)

It is noteworthy that the empiricist writings were entitled *human* understanding or knowledge (Locke 1690a; Berkeley 1710; Hume 1748). Locke treated knowledge 'as if it were a problem in psychology. He writes as if he were compiling a natural history of the mind'. Neither he nor Hume nor Mill – all economists, we notice – made 'a very clear distinction between philosophy and psychology' (Ayer 1952). They attacked

> the problem of knowledge, not primarily as a theoretical matter involved in a systematic investigation of reality, but as a means of justifying their concentration upon practical concerns by showing the futility of any endeavor to apprehend ultimate truth. Man's knowledge, suited to his place and station, is severely limited in its scope and legitimate pretensions; it is sufficient to guide us toward the fulfillment of duty and the attainment of happiness, but not toward a final comprehension of the vast environment in which our quest for happiness is set.

The empiricists were not anti-intellectual. They

> were as profoundly concerned to establish a constructive philosophy of science as to reach a consistent theory of the competence of knowledge. But the latter naturally imposed rigid limits on the former; there can be no knowledge of an external world, or of mind, hence the only positive task of science is to describe the sequence of human perceptions through the aid of such loose-knit principles of association as empirical inquiry may disclose.
>
> (Burtt 1939)

What could be known had to be empirical. It had to be *sensible*.

That means *personal*. Although there is much that is common in human experiences, particularly in a market economy in which the pursuit of our own ends by satisfying others requires empathy, or sympathy for each others' positions (Smith 1759: pt. I, sec. 1; 1776: bk. I, ch. 2), our experiences are not equal.

It has been said that British empiricism failed because it pushed its premises to their logical fatal conclusions. If all knowledge derives from experience, we are no more than a succession of sensations. Plato believed that 'the position of common sense, that knowledge comes to us from the external world through the senses,... is the lowest type of cognition'. Those 'who believe that nothing is real save what they can grasp with their hands and do not admit that ... anything invisible can count as real' are 'the uninitiated', a 'remarkably crude' sort of people. The initiated, on the other hand, are 'much more refined and subtle'. They 'see that knowledge must be sought above the level of mere sensation or perception, somewhere in the field of that "thinking" or "judging" which has been described as an activity of the mind "by itself"' (Cornford 1935: 29, 46, 109). Neither of these philosophies has to be pursued to the end, however. We only need to accept that the actions of imperfect and imperfectly informed people, central bankers included, who want to know enough 'to get by', are influenced by reason and experience, ideals and interests.

The relations between empiricism and Cartesian rationalism are comparable to those between the limited practical (sensory) knowledge of central bankers and the extensive theories of their more ambitious economist/critics. The latter criticize the former for their rejection of reasoned abstractions (models), and like Plato, tell them that their senses, far from helping them perceive their connections with the economy, are limiting and deceptive, as in 'money market myopia'.

We can imagine Socrates' dialog with a central banker. He 'was always talking of carpenters and cobblers because he was always contrasting the knowledge which men had of their trades with their ignorance of life', in general. They 'know their own craft though they spoil their knowledge by thinking they know many other things of which they are ignorant' (Lindsay 1910: xv). Milton Friedman was thinking like Socrates when he wrote:

> I think it has been an unfortunate thing that we have had a Reserve bank which has been as closely linked to the banking community and to the lending and investment process as it has, not at all because the individuals are trying to feather their own nests ... but because they naturally interpreted the institutions they were dealing with in terms of the environment they knew best and were familiar with.
> (US Congress 1964: 1163)

Friedman's observation is on the mark, unfortunately or perhaps fortunately, but it can be turned on economists. Considerable study in a special environment removed from the hurly-burly of the marketplace, with a set of objectives leading to what is called 'thinking like an economist', is necessary to a successful career in economic theory.

Ideas, experience, and action

Explicit optimization in closed systems versus habit and tacit knowledge in open systems

Let's take a closer look at the different outlooks of central bankers and economists, and ask whether true knowledge of economic relations should be expected to govern policy? Or should we expect policymakers, like Protagoras, to be buffeted by their senses, by their subjective perceptions of events? Not surprisingly, the answer is some of both, although we find, as economists complain, that the latter are stronger. The bearers of theoretically more permanent knowledge, the economists, have gained regular access to central bankers and are in a position to instruct them. Yet the groups remain separated in outlooks, interests, and vocabularies. Their approaches to policy differ in three ways that relate to the precision, spheres, and consciousness of economic knowledge.

Regarding the first, central bankers do not express their models, that is, their understandings of the probable effects of their actions, if they express them at all, as precisely as economists do. Our impression of the vagueness of central bankers' knowledge is based less on the obscure character of their utterances, which might be politically motivated, than on the hesitancy of their actions. Textbook agents continuously and completely revise, or consider revising, optimal prices and quantities, and policymakers similarly maintain the best values of their instruments. They do not *satisfice*, settle into *routines*, or *habitually-react* like the transactions–cost–bound 'cognitive misers' of Herbert Simon (1957) and Richard Nelson and Sidney Winter (1982). They go directly to and maintain their optimum positions.

Economists have long complained that central bankers do not behave like the textbooks, that their too-little, too-late responses to events aggravate economic fluctuations. These failures cannot be blamed on inattention because the assiduousness with which central bankers collect and study information is well known. Rather they reflect monetary policy 'by littles'. This was noticed by economist Alan Blinder (1997a) while a member of the Federal Reserve Board (1994–96), and has often been stated in so many words by officials. It explains such policies as 'interest-rate smoothing' and 'leaning against the wind'.

Second, although there is enough overlap to support the illusion that they are thinking and talking about the same things, central bankers and economists have different conceptions of the world.

> The decision-maker's information about his environment is much less than an approximation to the real environment. The term 'approximation' implies that the subjective world of the decision-maker resembles the external environment closely, but lacks, perhaps, some fineness of detail. In actual fact, the perceived world is fantastically different from the 'real' world. The differences involve both omissions and distortions, and arise in both perception and inference.... Perception is sometimes referred to as a 'filter'.... In fact, the filtering is not merely a passive selection of some part of a presented whole, but an active process involving attention to a very small part of the whole and exclusion, from the outset, of almost all that is not within the scope of attention.
>
> (Simon 1959)

'Selective attention' is more than an instrument of efficiency. It has been necessary to the survival of the species (Coon 1986: 98).

Policymakers and economists not only perceive the environment imperfectly, they experience it from different vantage points. The latter develop simplified general conceptions from which they predict the effects of stimuli for a constant external environment, whereas the former are attentive only to the markets and other institutions with which they are directly involved. Economists construct abstract black-box macro-models in pursuit of empirical regularities. This requires their systems to be 'closed-off from' the effects of the wider, open, complex world (Lawson 1997: 77). Practitioners' knowledge, on the other hand, is microeconomic, and their systems unavoidably open. Decision-makers rely on 'rules' or 'routines' that have 'stood the test of time' during which the environment has remained for practical purposes unchanged. Joseph Schumpeter suggested that a manager's (we may think of a banker or a central banker)

> intentions are never realized with ideal perfection, but ultimately his behavior is molded by the influence on him of the results of his conduct, so as to fit circumstances which do not as a rule change suddenly.... While in the accustomed circular flow [of economic life] every individual can act promptly and rationally because he is sure of his ground and is supported by the conduct, as adjusted to this circular flow, of all other individuals, who in turn expect the accustomed activity from him.... The assumption that conduct is prompt and rational is in all cases a fiction. But it proves to be sufficiently near to reality, if things have time to hammer logic into men. Where this has happened, and within the limits in which it has happened, one may rest content with this fiction and build theories upon it.
> (Schumpeter 1911: 79–80)

Once we step 'outside of these limits', however, 'our fiction loses its closeness to reality'.

> The smallest daily action embodies a huge mental effort. Every schoolboy would have to be a mental giant, if he himself had to create all he knows and uses by his own individual activity. And every man would have to be a giant of wisdom and will, if he had in every case to create anew all the rules by which he guides his everyday conduct.... But precisely the things the performance of which according to this should involve a supreme effort, in general demand no special individual effort at all; those which should be especially difficult are in reality especially easy; what should demand superhuman capacity is accessible to the least gifted, given mental health.
> (Schumpeter 1911: 83–4)

'This is so', Schumpeter (1911: 65) wrote along the same lines as the psychologist/philosopher pragmatists (of whom more below) 'because all knowledge and habit once acquired becomes as firmly rooted in ourselves as a railway embankment in the earth.'

> [O]utside these accustomed channels the individual is without those data for his decisions and those rules of conduct which are usually very accurately known to him within them. Of course he must still foresee and estimate on the basis of his experience. But many things must remain uncertain, still others are ascertainable within wide limits, some can perhaps only be 'guessed'.... Now he must really to some extent do what tradition does for him in everyday life, viz., consciously plan his conduct in every particular.
> (Schumpeter 1911: 84–5)

120 Monetary policy

Furthermore, the old opportunities are no longer applicable. Marginal analysis and maximization have no meaning. It is meaningless to speak of choosing the 'best method' in the sense of 'the most advantageous among the methods which have been empirically tested and become familiar'. Even if the manager recognizes and attempts to adapt to or anticipate change, his plans 'must necessarily be open not only to errors greater in degree, but also to other kinds of errors than those occurring in customary action' (83–5).

An open system is susceptible to unpredictable and even unimaginable influences: to what economists call exogenous shocks. A wait-and-see discretionary approach to decision-making is unavoidable. When Paul Samuelson (1951) was 'unable to isolate any real logical difference, either at the philosophical or pragmatic level', between 'automatic' and 'discretionary' policies, between the 'rules' and 'authorities' of Henry Simons (1936), he was assuming a closed system. So was Allan Meltzer (1993) when he thought central banks had discovered that: 'A rule is nothing more than a systematic decision process that uses information in a consistent and predictable way.' For example, the Federal Reserve behaved between 1987 and 1992 'as if they followed a simple adaptive rule of the type suggested in some recent literature' (the Taylor rule discussed in the next chapter). Such regularities can last a while for central bankers, as for Schumpeter's managers, but in an open system:

> *Time* and *knowledge* belong together.... The impossibility of prediction in economics follows from the facts that economic change is linked to change in knowledge, and future knowledge cannot be gained before its time. As soon as we permit time to elapse we must permit knowledge to change, and knowledge cannot be regarded as a function of anything else.
>
> (Lachmann 1959)

Differences between the roles of time and knowledge in open and closed systems were revealed by the Minutes of the Bank of England's Monetary Policy Committee (MPC) made up of academic economists and career Bank employees, including the governor and deputy-governors, who may be called 'central bankers'. The MPC is a unique forum for policy discussions between members of the two groups on equal terms. For example, in February and May 1998, the staff econometric model implied that the Bank's inflation target required a small increase in its interest-rate instrument. The central bankers were hesitant to raise the rate, 'even if a rise were necessary', however, because of 'near-term uncertainties'. They did not 'feel very confident about the outlook and it would not necessarily be right to draw policy conclusions mechanically from the [staff] projection.... If the downturn proved to be much sharper than currently expected, then an immediate increase in interest rates' might have a severe negative effect on output, and have to be reversed.

> Such a reversal could impair confidence in the economy and damage the credibility of the MPC process ... by creating confusion about monetary

policy.... There was thus a strong case for waiting to get a clearer impression of the extent of the slowdown in the economy before taking policy action.

The economists, on the other hand, held that 'the sheer degree of uncertainty did not represent a proper justification of delay. Uncertainty was a normal state of affairs in economic policy-making and there was no particular reason to believe that uncertainty would be any less in a few months' time.' They argued that 'policy should reflect the latest news and that uncertainty in itself was no reason for delay'. To delay decisions to reduce the risks of reversal was 'irrational'. 'So long as any policy reversals could be properly explained by new developments or improved analysis of the outlook, they need not create confusion about policy.'

The models of Samuelson, Meltzer, and the MPC economists are closed and timeless. Statistical distributions represent known, 'calculated', risks – 'actuarial', Keynes called them – rather than genuine uncertainty. New observations improve predictive ability no more than another toss of a fair coin. In the open, time-dependent systems of central bankers, however, every event carries new information. Uncertainty in time is a problem to be faced rather than assumed away.

Policymakers' view of economic processes was understood by Kenneth Boulding, who in 'The Economics of Knowledge and the Knowledge of Economics' (1966) warned that the

> rationalization of decision-making processes ... through the application of optimizing procedures applied to complex masses of information may have some other costs lurking among the benefits.... For one thing, these elaborate procedures may easily produce a sense of subjective certainty. [T]he principle that 'he who hesitates is saved' is usually very sound.... A little learning may be a dangerous thing.

The reluctance of central bankers to disturb the immediate financial markets at the expense of the uncertain and distant macroeconomy is even more understandable when we realize their personal involvement in the former.

A third difference between the limited knowledge of economic agents and the complete models of economists is, following Michael Polanyi, the *tacit* nature of the former. 'We can know more than we can tell' (1966: 4). Edward Sapir's comment in 'The Unconscious Patterning of Behavior in Society' (1927) that 'it takes an unusually analytical type of mind to define the mere elements of that incredibly subtle linguistic mechanism which is but a plaything in the child's unconscious' may extend to the education of central bankers (also Hayek 1967: ch. 3). 'Decision-making by instinct, gossip, visceral feeling, and political savvy', Boulding wrote, 'may have the virtue of being able to take in very large systems in a crude and vague way, whereas the rationalized processes can only take subsystems in their more exact fashion, and being rational about subsystems may be worse than being not very rational about the system as a whole'. The potentially dangerous effects of central bankers' actions are unlimited, as far as they know, whereas economists' have perfect knowledge of an abstract system that is finite because they have defined it.

Summarizing, what economic agents know differs from economists' models in its inarticulate, tacit incorporation of separate, more institutional, less abstract systems that evolve in unpredictable ways because they are open. Economists see in the failure of central bankers to use the explicit language of constrained optimization the avoidance of responsibility. A good deal of their lack of communication is due to genuinely different views of the economy. The focus of central bankers on financial stability may be less a self-deceiving denial of distant macro-objectives than an affirmation of their 'personal knowledge', to use another Polanyi (1964) term, of a roughly consistent, if incomplete, model.

Blinder complained that the Federal Reserve's approach to policy was 'far too situational'. There was no apparent attempt to agree on a conceptual policy framework. Consensus was sought on a 'meeting-by-meeting' basis instead of through the consistent and complete utility-maximizing framework of economic theory. James Tobin (1977) also urged the adoption of a model that would 'represent the policymakers' beliefs about the way the world works, and it should be explicit. Any policymaker or advisor who thinks he is not using a model is kidding both himself and us.' However, if knowledge is imprecise – founded as much on the senses as reason – and Tobin's models are those of academic economists, his first sentence is infeasible and the second is incorrect.

Central bankers' *images, perceptions, webs of belief,* or *structures of ideas* (using the terms of economic philosophers to avoid the precision suggested by *model*) may be tacit but nonetheless exist. When told that econometric forecasts had failed because of exogenous shifts of what had been postulated as stable money-demand functions, New York Reserve Bank President Paul Volcker (1978) commented that

> portentously pointing to these "shifts" without further explanation seems to me something of a confession of ignorance.... It seems to me the essence of policy making in these circumstances is that judgments must be made in the presence of uncertainty.

Instrumental knowledge: learning, habit, and pragmatism

> After we came out of church, we stood talking for some time together of Bishop Berkeley's ingenious sophistry to prove the non-existence of matter, and that everything in the universe is merely ideal. I observed, that though we are satisfied his doctrine is not true, it is impossible to refute it. I never shall forget the alacrity with which Johnson answered, striking his foot with mighty force against a large stone, till he rebounded from it, 'I refute it thus.'
> (Boswell 1791)[1]

Our quest for enough of a theory of knowledge to comprehend actions brings us to pragmatism, a movement initiated and led in its early years by the American philosophers Charles Peirce (1878), Oliver Wendell Holmes, Jr (1881), William James (1896), and John Dewey (1916). In *Pragmatism, a New Name for Some Old Ways of Thinking*, James (1907) pointed to the philosophy's derivation from the Greek πρᾶγμα, meaning action, from which "practice" and "practical" come. Louis Menand (2001: 369) wrote that 'James took his inspiration from the British empiricists', who 'reduced philosophical concepts like "matter" and "identity" to their "cash value". Pragmatism is an analysis of what people *think* they know. Our 'beliefs are really rules for action', James (1907: 46, 58) wrote, and

> to develop a thought's meaning, we need only determine what conduct it is fitted to produce: that conduct is for us its sole significance. And the tangible fact at the root of all our thought-distinctions, however subtle, is that there is no one of them so fine as to consist in anything but a possible difference of practice.

Truth is what works:

> Any idea upon which we can ride, so to speak; any idea that will carry us prosperously from any one part of our experience to any other part, linking things satisfactorily, working securely, simplifying, saving labor; is ... true *instrumentally*.

To philosophers seeking final principles, James advised:

> if you follow the pragmatic method, you cannot look on any [final] word as closing your quest. You must bring out of each word its practical cash-value, set it at work within the stream of your experience. It appears less as a solution, then, than as a program for more work.... *Theories thus become instruments, not answers to enigmas in which we can rest.*
> (1907: 53)

Similar to the ideas of policymakers in an open economy.

I only know what I have experienced, the 'practical' central banker says. But surely, the economist retorts, knowledge and therefore actions might be improved by reasoning from first principles? Possibly, but this is not how people learn, say the pragmatists: '*ideas (which themselves are but parts of our experience) become true just in so far as they help us to get into satisfactory relation with other parts of our experience*' (James 1907: 58). If central bankers were more articulate, they might, with James, say to their learned advisers:

> A pragmatist turns his back resolutely and once and for all upon a lot of inveterate habits dear to professional philosophers. He turns away from abstraction and insufficiency, from verbal solutions, from bad *a priori* reasons, from fixed principles, closed systems, and pretended absolutes and origins. He turns toward concreteness and adequacy, toward facts, toward

action, and toward power. That means the empiricist temper regnant, and the rationalist temper sincerely given up. It means the open air and possibilities of nature, as against dogma, artificiality and the pretence of finality in truth.

(James 1907: 51)

Israel Scheffler (1974: 97–8) wrote that James

> saw in pragmatism a way of unifying science and religion, since the test of all truth is in experience, and the religious experience of the individual person is surely a phenomenon that needs to be acknowledged as a fact.... Such reflections led him also to *pluralism* in a personal and moral sense, and not only a metaphysical sense.... The test, for pragmatism, of any belief is what difference it makes in life, and on this test, a variety of outlooks pass. Thus, he declares: 'Hands off: neither the whole of truth nor the whole of good is revealed to any single observer, although each observer gains a partial superiority of insight from the peculiar position in which he stands' (James 1901: 264).

This democratic view of the value of everyone's knowledge, like Polanyi's *Personal Knowledge*, contrasts with Plato's reservation of knowledge to the governing few (more on this below).

James taught physiology and psychology before moving to philosophy. His classic *Principles of Psychology* was like Adam Smith's economics, Michael Lawlor (2005) suggested, in its reversions 'to philosophical issues ... surrounding the nature of thought, perception, belief, and truth'. 'I confess', James wrote, 'that during the years which have elapsed since the publication of [*Principles*], I have become more and more convinced of the difficulty of treating psychology without introducing some true and suitable philosophical doctrine' (Perry 1948: 194). Actually, pragmatism was in his psychology from the beginning.

He saw the brain and nervous system as a network of stimulus and response that organizes environmental stimuli into a system of signs to which the brain attaches meaning. In his discussion of the relations between psychology, economics, and knowledge, Lawlor (2005) drew attention to James's understanding of human behavior as the pursuit of self interest. The subjective self ('me', 'I', 'mine') is 'the focus of all action and the subjective perspective through which cognitive interpretation of the world takes place. He dubbed the intensely personal view of the world that conscious thought represents as "the stream of consciousness"'.

> [T]he mind is at every stage a theatre of simultaneous possibilities. Consciousness consists in the comparison of these with each other, the selection of some, and the suppression of the rest by the reinforcing and inhibiting agency of attention.... The mind ... works on the data it receives very much as the sculptor works on his block of stone.

(James 1890 i: 288)

'Carved in stone' might be an apt metaphor for central bankers' knowledge, and economists might agree, although the epithet could be turned on themselves. James's analysis of habit is relevant to our understanding of economic behavior in general.

Habits are learned ways of automatically (without any conscious decision-making or even awareness) dealing with certain combinations of environmental and emotional circumstances. Physiologically, they are due to the plasticity of nervous tissue. Environmentally, they are due to repeated encounters with similar stimuli (James 1890 i: ch. 4; Lawlor 2005). It is not easy to see how they could be replaced by an abstract rule written in a foreign (theorist's) language.

The stabilizing effect of habit is most pronounced when it is developed early, when the nervous tissue is most plastic.

> Could the young but realize how soon they will become mere walking bundles of habits, they would give more heed to their conduct while in the plastic state. We are spinning our own fates, good or evil, and never to be undone.
>
> (James 1890 i: 127)

A co-worker called attention to the

> universally admitted fact that any sequence of mental action which has been frequently repeated tends to perpetuate itself; so that we find ourselves automatically prompted to *think, feel,* or *do* what we have been accustomed to think, feel or do, under like circumstances, without any consciously former *purpose*, or anticipation of results.
>
> (Carpenter 1874; James 1890 i: 112)

James wrote:

> Habit is thus the enormous fly-wheel of society, its most precious conservative agent. It alone is what keeps us all within the bounds of ordinance, and save the children of fortune from the envious uprisings of the poor. It alone prevents the hardest and most repulsive walks of life from being deserted by those brought up to tread therein. It keeps the fisherman and the deck-hand at sea through the winter; it holds the miner in his darkness, and nails the countryman to his log-cabin and his lonely farm through all the months of snow.... It dooms us all to fight out the battle of life upon the lines of our nurture or our early choice, and to make the best of a pursuit that disagrees, because there is no other for which we are fitted, and it is too late to begin again.... Already at the age of twenty-five you see the professional mannerism settling down on the young commercial traveler, on the young doctor, on the young minister, on the young counselor-at-law. You see the little lines of cleavage running through the character, the tricks of thought, the prejudices, the ways of the 'shop', in a word, from which the

man can by-and-by no more escape than his coat-sleeve can suddenly fall into a new set of folds. On the whole, it is best he should not escape. It is well for the world that in most of us, by the age of thirty, the character has set like plaster, and will never soften again.

(1890 i: 121)

Holmes might have said of political economy, as he said of 'the life of the law', that it 'has not been logic; it has been experience'.

The felt necessities of the time, the prevalent moral and political theories, intuitions of public policy, avowed or unconscious, even the prejudices which judges [read central bankers] share with their fellow-men, have a good deal more to do than the syllogism in determining the rules by which men should be governed. The law embodies the story of a nation's development through many centuries, and it cannot be dealt with as if it contained only the axioms and corollaries of a book of mathematics.

(Holmes 1881: 1)

The dependence of the law on the past is clear from precedents but the past is no less important to other systems. 'Bundles of habits' have always been apparent in the financial community, which values appearances such as the seriousness deemed important to trust. Innovation and its roots, brilliance and wit, are frowned on. 'We had a dull dinner at Lady Ashburton's', W.M. Thackeray wrote. 'A party of Barings chiefly' (1945 ii: 647). The banking family might not have been displeased by this, what to some would seem unflattering, description. The financier/diplomat Lord D'Abernon described the Barings as

Strong, sensible, self-reliant men, with a profound belief in themselves, in their family and in their country – eminently just and fair; no trace of hypocrisy or cant; not only solid and square but giving the impression both of solidity and squareness ... not subtle or mentally agile, but endowed with that curious combination of character which lends authority even to doubtful decisions, and makes those who possess it respected in counsel and obeyed as rulers.

(D'Abernon 1931: 14)

In his chapter on 'the development of credit agencies', the historian Thorold Rogers observed that

the theories which the banker listens to patiently never come within the range of his practice. The most voluminous and the most confident writer will not make him turn aside from his traditions. I remember hearing the late Lord Overstone [the banker Samuel Jones Loyd; see ch. 2] say that genius was a dangerous gift to a banker. He ought, the noble lord continued, to be emphatically common-place, to be wedded to a beaten track. There were, he continued, occasional anxieties in a banker's career when he must needs ... oil the machine. But ordinarily it should be automatic.... The mechanism which the directors preside over in Threadneedle Street is the perfection of trained and traditional skill, and the managers are almost as automatic an engine as the Mint is, or as some tell us the pork factories of Chicago are, where a live pig enters at one door and emerges through various machines from another as pickled and packed pork. So I heard at Chicago, though I had not the curiosity to inspect the process.

(Rogers 1909: 66)

An anecdote that illustrates habits in the extreme, useful and perhaps otherwise, is told of T.C. Baring, who had retired in 1888 with no legal obligation for the firm's commitments. Nevertheless, during the crisis that came two years later he withdrew all his cash and securities from the Bank of England and brought them to Barings' offices. One of his bulging bags burst and the contents spilled onto the street as he argued with the cabbie over an alleged overcharge of sixpence (Ziegler 1988: 251).

The operation of these principles of efficiency and stability in the acquisition, use, and retention of knowledge ought to be appreciated by those who reflect on their own experience and behavior. Our learning is costly and time-consuming, and so is our unlearning. Should we expect central bankers to be different? It is not clear, if there is any experiential or physiological basis of knowledge, how macroeconomics, which is an abstraction of causes and effects that does not impinge on us in a clear-cut manner, is learned and used. Admissions of error by macroeconomic policymakers are rare. The consequences of error are too complex and remote. More-or-less plausible arguments that 'things would have been worse if' are always ready. Learning macroeconomics by experience, if it occurs, is from a distance.

An economist's lament: 'What trade-offs?'

A scientific theory by itself is not knowledge. 'Knowledge in the objective sense is knowledge without a knower', Karl Popper (1972: 109) wrote. The impact of a message on one's *image* of the economy, to use Boulding's (1956) term, depends on his existing, experience-dependent image. 'The sender of a message has to rely for its comprehension on the intelligence of the person addressed', Polanyi wrote. 'Unless an assertion of fact is accompanied by some heuristic or pervasive feeling, it is a mere form of words saying nothing' (1958: 21–2; 1964: 254).

The following stories are a small sample of the failures familiar to economic advisors. Martin Feldstein of the president's Council of Economic Advisors recalled:

[O]n one occasion I said to [the president] that, while economic growth at 5 percent a year for five years was 'possible', it was very unlikely and it would not be prudent to base budget policy on such an unlikely event.

> When I reflected on that meeting later that day, I realized that saying that something was 'unlikely' and 'imprudent' was not a way of persuading Ronald Reagan.... Here was a man who had gone from being a local sports announcer to a wealthy movie actor. When his acting career ended, he went on to become governor of the largest state in the nation, having never before held public office. And, after a resounding defeat in seeking the Republican presidential nomination a few years earlier, he won the 1980 nomination and went on to become president. And I was trying to tell him not to believe in something because it was unlikely!
>
> [Budget Director] David Stockman tried a different approach to persuading the president that it would not be possible to cut spending enough to bring the deficit down to an acceptable level without additional tax revenue. Stockman divided the overall budget into dozens of small parts and prepared three sets of options for each part.
>
> I felt that it would not succeed. After all, in each budget area Stockman was showing the president only a small number of possible budget changes. The president continued to believe that there were possibilities that he was not being shown. He kept hoping that there was some general overhaul of the domestic programs that would permit major savings.
>
> (Feldstein 1994)

The president might have relied more on experience – relevant or not, misleading or not – than on economic theory. Successful people are understandably more confident of their prospects than is supported by the 'dismal science' with its tough trade-offs. American 'doers' are fond of inspirational stories such as 'The Little Train That Could' and the sign in a General Motors plant:

> According to the theory of aerodynamics, as may be readily demonstrated through wind tunnel experiments, the bumblebee is unable to fly.... *But the bumblebee, being ignorant of these scientific truths, goes ahead and flies anyway – and makes a little honey every day.*
>
> (Woods 1951: 249–50)

Reagan would have been comfortable with Henry Ford: 'I can't prove it, but I can smell it' (Nevins 1954: 577). Or Justice Holmes: 'It is the merit of the common law that it decides the case first and determines the principle afterwards.'

> Looking at the forms of logic it might be inferred that when you have a minor premise and a conclusion, there must be a major, which you are also prepared then and there to assert. But in fact lawyers, like other men, frequently see well enough how they ought to decide on a given state of facts without being very clear as to the *ratio decidendi*. In cases of first impression Lord Mansfield's often-quoted advice to the business man who was suddenly appointed judge, that he should state his conclusions and not give

his reasons, as his judgment would probably be right and the reasons certainly wrong, is not without its application to more educated courts.
(Holmes 1870)

Herbert Stein observed that presidents 'are not programmed by any economist's model, and it would be unjustifiably conceited for an economist to consider that a fault' (1994: 261). His

> favorite example of a President's attitude comes from Franklin D. Roosevelt. In his 1933 inaugural address he promised an 'adequate and sound currency'. Asked what he meant at a press conference, he replied: 'I am not going to write a book on it.'

An earlier conflict between a young Treasury official and David Lloyd George – chancellor of the exchequer, minister of munitions, and prime minister – was more intense. In 1921, Keynes looked back on the pre-1914 Treasury:

> In some ways I think Treasury control might be compared to conventional morality. There is a great deal of it rather tiresome and absurd once you look into it, yet it is an essential bulwark against overwhelming wickedness. It is because in a way the Treasury is always fighting against odds that it is always necessary that it should have all the weapons proper to its prestige.... And supported by these various elements, it became an institution which came to possess the attributes of institutions like a college or City company, or the Church of England. Indeed, I think it might have been defended on the same grounds which the eighteenth-century sceptics were accustomed to make: 'A defence that would be as a bulwark against too much enthusiasm.'
> (Moggridge 1992: 246)

Keynes was as 'Treasury-minded' as anyone, and when the chancellor of the exchequer told the cabinet that the country could not afford the 70 divisions requested by the military while continuing to finance its allies, he did so on Keynes's advice.

> The battle of finance is being fiercely fought behind the scenes [Keynes wrote to Professor H.S. Foxwell], and the Treasury at least are not behindhand with their warnings. The difficulty is that the consumptionist party [led by Lloyd George], which is beyond measure stupid, regards any counsels for moderation in expenditure as little better than bluff and a sophistry aimed at their particular schemes.
> (Moggridge 1992: 252)

Keynes kept predicting financial collapse. 'I used, four months ago, to think that a crucial point would be reached in May or June', he wrote in March 1916. 'I now think that we shall get through the summer all right' (Moggridge 1992: 265). Lloyd George saw things differently, and complained: 'We are conducting a war as if there is no war' (Gilbert 1992: 152). He urged total war on all fronts, it seemed to Keynes, pushing for an early end and hoping that something would turn up, which it did when the United States entered the war.

After the war, when he wanted low interest rates to finance 'homes for heroes' and was advised by the Treasury that 'capital was not unlimited', Lloyd George responded that his 'wartime experiences refuted the Treasury view' (Skidelsky 1992: 401). His position had substance. He had not just been lucky. By conscription, women in the work force, reform of war materials contracts, negotiations with the United States, and an anti-drink campaign (even suggesting shorter catechisms), he pushed the production frontier beyond the Treasury's assumptions (Grigg 1985: 213). In the next decade, unemployment pulled Keynes to Lloyd George's side, and in their pamphlet for the 1929 election, *Can Lloyd George Do It?*, Keynes and Hubert Henderson defended the Liberal leader's public-works program as a way of expanding employment and output. It was a case of the economist following the politician.

Economists, bureaucracies, and policymakers

Who needs theory? We have a policy

The personal and political difficulties of transmitting ideas are illustrated by Keynes's interactions with his academic and government colleagues. The steps from theory to policy are steep. As we saw in Chapter 3, Keynes's theory was intended as a rationalization of existing interventionist preferences. A good deal of the blame for *The General Theory*'s failure to persuade economists to a new view belongs to Keynes. He was more than tolerant of the young disciples who brought him their interpretations of his message (Skidelsky 1992: 610–15). They shared his ambition to change the way governments approached the economy, and he did not wish to dampen their enthusiasm. 'If the simple basic ideas can become familiar and acceptable, time, experience and the collaboration of a number of minds will discover the best way of expressing them' (Moggridge 1992: 594). He wrote of the Beveridge Report that

> it is better to have got something, even if it is wrong in detail, because I believe the Civil Service has infinite power of making things work once it is clear that it intends to work it. My own feeling is that the first sentence [of the White Paper on *Employment Policy* (1944)] is more valuable than the whole of the rest.
>
> (Moggridge 1992: 709)

The sentence was: 'The Government accept as one of their primary aims and responsibilities the maintenance of a high and stable level of employment after the war.' This corresponded with Keynes's preference for discretion over rules or even a specific model. In a draft proposal for a postwar international clearing union, he wrote:

> Perhaps the most difficult question to determine is how much to decide by rule and how much by discretion. If rule prevails, the liabilities attaching to membership become clear and definite, whilst the responsibilities of the central management are reduced to a minimum.... If discretion prevails, we have to decide how far the ultimate decision can be left to the individual members and how much to the central management.... If rule prevails, the scheme can be made more water-tight theoretically. If discretion prevails it may work better in practice.
>
> (Moggridge 1992: 677)

Of course decision-makers should comprehend the 'basic ideas'. When a Treasury official complained of Keynes's ideas of demand management that they were 'a voyage into the stratosphere for most of us', Keynes shot back:

> Very sorry, but it does seem to me quite essential that all of you should become accustomed to the stratosphere – if that is really what it is! For, if the argument which I have tried to bring into the open in my paper is not understood by those responsible, they are understanding nothing whatever....
>
> And after all, it is very easily understood! There is scarcely an undergraduate of the modern generation from whom these truths are hidden. And, once they have been digested and entered into the apparatus of the mind, it is possible for most people to move fairly safely over a terrain otherwise most dangerous.
>
> (Moggridge 1992: 711)

Even for Keynes, *The General Theory* was mostly decoration, like the family *Bible*, prominently displayed but unread.

Interactions/misunderstandings

Whatever is left of an idea after being filtered through the scientific community, the task of applying it to policy remains. Even the certainty-equivalent, unKeynesian–Keynesian model accepted by economists was resisted by policy-makers. Anyone who has witnessed a congressional hearing will sympathize with Keynes's frustrations during a visit to the United States to negotiate postwar financial arrangements:

> There was never at any time an opportunity for continuous or coherent oral exposition to the right audience. A Washington meeting has to be experienced to be believed. At the Main Committee any continuous argument or indeed more than a dozen sentences were always out of place. At the technical and other Sub-Committees there would be twenty-five or more

persons present at any one time, but their composition would be continually changing as they floated in and out of the room to attend to telephone calls or other business, so we were seldom addressing the same audience for more than ten minutes together. One would suddenly discover that even the chairman had disappeared without explanation to return half an hour later, and the actual spokesman on the American side would break off his remarks at any moment to answer a call from without. Indeed in Washington the Ancient Mariner would have found it necessary to use a telephone to detain the wedding guest. For it is only on the telephone that one can obtain undivided attention. If you seek an interview, your American friend will spend half the time talking on the telephone to all quarters of the compass, until in despair you return to your own office and you yourself ring him up, when you can expect to secure his concentrated mind for as long as you like, while someone else wastes his time keeping a date with him in the chair you have so wisely vacated.

(Keynes *Collected Writings* xxiv: 195–6)

Keynes described the last days of the preparation of the Bretton Woods report:

It is not easy to keep track of it because none of us are seeing it as a whole, but in bits and pieces....

[I]f we are hasty we shall find that there are a number of points which will be raised later, just logical errors and inconsistencies, and so forth, which will be very tiresome, and I think it will be dangerous to our project if there are too many opportunities for re-opening this at later stages....

There are ... certain final technical matters we haven't considered at all, what the lawyers call the final act, which embodies the results of this Conference. No attempt has yet been made to draft that, and it hasn't been considered by any body.

The conference was extended a few days, but

We, all of us, had to sign of course, before we had a chance of reading through a clean and consecutive copy of the document.... Our only excuse is the knowledge that our hosts had made arrangements to throw us out of the hotel ... in a few hours.

(Moggridge 1992: 747)

I have dwelt on Keynes because the information is available. He was active in public life and recorded his activities and impressions, but his problems with persuasion were not unusual. As a member of 'the establishment' – the intellectual middle class with access to the highest reaches of government – Eton scholar, son of a Cambridge don and one himself, civil servant, and friend of prime ministers, he was better placed than most sellers of ideas. Physical access is not enough, however. Federal Reserve Board Chairman Marriner Eccles would have understood Keynes's comment that Treasury Secretary Henry Morgenthau 'has easier access to [President Roosevelt's] presence than to his mind' (Moggridge 1992: 779).

The reorganized Federal Reserve Board (under the Banking Act of 1935) was to assume its duties on 1 February 1936, and in the third week of January the majority of its members had not been nominated. Eccles managed to get a meeting with the president on a Saturday afternoon to 'prod him into action'. The hopeful advisor arrived punctually and was ushered into a room where Roosevelt, his mother, and two secretaries were seated around a radio. The president put a finger to his lips and pointed the visitor to a seat.

> I had come to him [Eccles recalled] brimming over with banking matters. But it turned out instead that I was his very unwilling guest at the opera. The radio was turned to the Metropolitan's performance of one of Wagner's works.... [M]y indifference to Wagner turned into deep resentment that his music had got in the way of an immediate consideration of matters vital to American banking.
>
> (Eccles 1951: 71)

Eccles fidgeted through three acts of opera and intermissions filled with Roosevelt's recollections of boyhood holidays in Germany learning to love Wagner. After the radio program, Eccles was given enough time to get Roosevelt's approval of part of his agenda. The president might have managed their time together for political as much as for cultural ends, limiting Eccles to items that Roosevelt, beleaguered by conflicting claims, wished to consider. In fact the list of appointments recommended by Eccles and accepted by the president was altered a few days later to accommodate the vice-president's request for a political favor.

It might be supposed that some of the obstacles encountered by Keynes and Eccles are overcome by the institutionalization of advice in the form of resident staffs. However, these can hinder as much as help. Bureaucracy has costs, one of which is its tendency to limit the range of ideas considered. In their pursuit of security and influence, advisory groups typically impose consistency of opinion – party lines – on their members. A unified front is seen as essential to an effective agency. Conflict is considered the enemy of credibility. To call a view 'controversial' is to damn it – as if in economics it could be anything else. Only the most prestigious ideas are admitted, and in the realm of macroeconomic policy that means the classical/Keynesian model supplemented by econometrics, that is, with statistical estimates of the relationships 'filled in'.

The strong card of economists seeking influence is the scientific status of their advice.

> There is by now a long and fairly imposing line of economists from Adam Smith to the present who have sought to show that a decentralized economy motivated by self-interest and guided by price signals would be compatible with a coherent disposition of economic resources that could be regarded, in

a well-defined sense, as superior to a large class of possible alternative dispositions. Moreover, the price signals would operate in a way to establish this degree of coherence. It is important to understand how surprising this claim must be to anyone not exposed to this tradition. The immediate 'common sense' answer to the question 'What will an economy motivated by individual greed and controlled by a very large number of different agents look like?' is probably: 'There will be chaos.' That quite a different answer has long been claimed true and has indeed permeated the economic thinking of a large number of people who are in no way economists is itself sufficient grounds for investigating it seriously.

(Arrow and Hahn 1971: vi–vii)

Bringing order out of the apparently chaotic market economy is a wonderful achievement. Even the finest machine requires adjustments, however, and this is where policy activists come in. They receive scientific status from the classical model, always in the background, like modern medicine, conferring the authority to adapt it to circumstances. We have already discussed this practice. It is what Keynes observed in the classical economists, although he saw 'departures' instead of 'adjustments'. In rejecting the *GT*, 'Keynesian' activists recognized that their influence depended on precise, econometric, predictions. They understood that policymakers would no more accept Keynes's uncertainty than a patient would prefer a medicine-man's elixir over a university-certified doctor's government-approved prescription.

Contrasting views of the value of 'scientific' precision are shown by the following exchange between an outsider and an insider. Paul Davidson, a 'post' (professedly 'true') Keynesian in the complicated nomenclature of modern macroeconomics, told Arrow that 'the trouble is that neoclassical economists confuse risk with uncertainty. Uncertainty means non-probabilistic.' Arrow replied:

Quite true, you're quite correct that Keynes is much more fruitful, but the trouble with *The General Theory* is, those things that were fruitful couldn't be developed into a nice precise analytical statement, and those things that could were retrogressions from Keynes but could be developed into a nice precise analytical statement. That's why mainstream economics went that route.

(King 1995: 21)

The mainstream 'general equilibrium' journey described above in Chapter 3 picked up speed as Keynes proposed a different path. The 'first rigorous analysis of the problem of equilibrium was by Abraham Wald in 1935–36', who proved that all markets (now and forever) could be cleared at non-negative prices, Gerard Debreu wrote in his Nobel-prize-winning contribution to the theory of a perfect-information, zero-transactions-cost economy without uncertainty (1959: ix). Wald's work was refined over the next half-century by mathematical proofs of the stability, existence and other properties of general equilibria that occupy the highest status of economic scholarship.

I do not mean that Davidson is a medicine-man, only that officials prefer Arrow even though his activist prescriptions (as opposed to the implications of his theories) are like Davidson's and his model has been 'conclusively falsified', according to his collaborator, Hahn (1984),

> because in capitalist economies there is a medium of exchange and generally a market in the claims to profits of firms. Neither of these phenomena could arise in a pure Arrow-Debreu world [the most sophisticated expression of general equilibrium theory] where all transactions occur at a single initial date.... [T]he theory describes a world in which no Keynesian problems could arise.

My point is not to defend one model of economic advice over another. Model comparisons would be difficult even if criteria were agreed. In any case, such comparisons are not part of the purpose of the present study, which is to *understand* policymaking. There is something to be said for the easy approach preferred by economists before and since Keynes, which uses the perfect-information, zero-transactions-cost neo-classical model as the basic framework, to be relaxed as necessary. However, this is not how monetary policy is made. Of models of capitalist economies, economic advisers use the one that is most removed from their clients' perceptions.

Keynes tried to deal with the open world of time, uncertainty, and costly choices in which central bankers find themselves. Their advisors, on the other hand, apply the model that Keynes attacked. '[S]ober economists gravely upholding a faith in the calculability of human affairs could not bring themselves to acknowledge that this could be his purpose', G.L.S. Shackle (1962) wrote: 'They sought to interpret *The General Theory* as just one more manual of political arithmetic.'

Another illustration of the communication problems caused by these differences, and of the difficulties of changing one's professional mannerisms and outlook, was the little tempest stirred up by economist Alan Blinder, just appointed to the Federal Reserve Board to serve the remaining 18 months of an unexpired term. The occasion was a conference of economists, central bankers, and other officials staged by the Federal Reserve Bank of Kansas City. Blinder (1994) reminded the group that the Federal Reserve, unlike the central banks that had shifted to the single goal of low inflation, was statutorily responsible for '*both* maximum employment *and* stable prices'. He gave the standard classroom lecture on the inflation-unemployment trade-off in the Phillips Curve, which he saw as stable. 'There has been barely any change in econometric estimates of the Phillips curve for twenty years.' The implications for 'Central Banking in a Democracy', which was the title of a subsequent speech in which he expressed surprise at the publicity attracted by his speech, were 'profound'. The Fed has to be ready to raise interest rates when inflation is too high, but not so far as to depress employment.

So monetary policy is forced to strike a delicate balance between the two goals. It is an excruciatingly difficult decision, with a great deal at stake.... That's why they pay them the big bucks!

Blinder was taken aback by the furor that followed in the financial press, which interpreted his speech as a public clash with Chairman Greenspan (Woodward 2000: 130–3). After all, he had only said what every economist knows, and 'was fully consistent with the practices of central banks all over the world, regardless of what they preach'. It showed, Blinder said, 'what can happen when a Federal Reserve governor publicly endorses the view that the Federal Reserve should be serving the national interest rather than just the parochial interests of the bond market. He rejected the notion that he had crossed his colleagues. Greenspan had been present at the speech and 'never indicated that I had said anything unusual'.

Blinder was unaware that lecturing one's associates in public – talking down to them, telling them 'what everybody (else?) knows' – is unusual outside the classroom. Reputedly with aspirations to succeed Greenspan as chairman, he was not reappointed to the Board. The Board's previous academic New Economist, Sherman Maisel (1973: 78–9), had a similar experience. He found, like the economists on the Bank of England's Monetary Policy Committee, that after the staff had presented their large-scale econometric model his fellow central-bankers' conversation turned to money market conditions (barely evident in the model) using words whose meanings and implications for monetary policy he thought ambiguous. Neither Blinder nor Maisel admitted, perhaps even to themselves, that the miscommunications with their colleagues of different backgrounds could not be resolved by persuasion, even of people with foreign tongues.

Accommodations

Most economists with aspirations to influence are politically more sensitive than Blinder. They know there must be accommodations between the classical/Keynesian models of advisors and the open systems of their employers. Not surprisingly, the accommodations are overwhelmingly in one direction. 'Experienced government economists have learnt that if they are to be effective [employed?] they must accept the facts of economic life', A.W. Coats observed in a discussion of 'Economics as a Profession' (1993). Robert Nelson wrote in 'The Economics Profession and the Making of Public Policy' (1987):

> In practice, economists involved with government must also tailor their advocacy of market methods, efficient resource use, and other economic approaches to the political environment in which they work. They modify proposals to make them attractive in terms of equity or to avoid infringing on real or perceived 'rights'. Economists in government agencies also recognize that they are members of an organization with its own history and traditions to which they must conform to some degree. In short, economists who apply economic methods in government develop and exercise skills in

bureaucratic and political tactics, which are necessarily interwoven with their exercise of economic expertise.

This is another way of saying, in Henry Kissinger's (1959) words about another field of action: 'all too often what the policymaker wants from the intellectual is not ideas but endorsement'. Edwin Nourse, the first chairman of the President's Council of Economic Advisors, learned this lesson the hard way. He thought of himself as an apolitical advisor whose job was to lay out a range of economic possibilities from which the administration would choose. President Truman did not want alternatives, however. He wanted the same contributions from his economic advisors as from the rest of his team: straightforward support of the administration's goals. Nothing was apolitical. Everyone in the administration, experts as well as political appointees, were expected to be involved in the development and defense of a complete package (Hargrove and Morley 1984: 55). Nourse would not publicly defend specific policies, although his associate, Leon Keyserling, thought (in Nourse's words) 'that we could always phrase our analysis and recommendations in such a way that there would not appear to be any conflict between our views and those of the President' (Nourse 1953: 217).

Truman (1956: 207–8) seized on the Council's hum-drum mid-year 1948 report as a revelation of crisis that called for a special session of the Republican Congress. His challenge to implement the platform of the recent Republican convention was part of the president's election campaign. Nourse complained publicly of the political use of the Council, and left soon after, to be succeeded as chairman by Keyserling.

It is argued that the advisor can be a propagandist of values, such as for free trade or stabilization (Kaysen 1968). The Kennedy–Johnson Council of Economic Advisors believed that the 1964 tax cut was the result of their campaign for fiscal activism, even though it was implemented during an economic expansion (Camp 1977: 21–45; Heller 1966: 69–73). An explanation more consistent with the data is that the Council was used by the politically attuned Kennedy to prepare the electorate, including fiscal conservatives, for the tax cut that was planned for non-Keynesian reasons. The 1964 tax cut fit the downward drift that followed World War II. Voters were as pleased with this as with the later Reagan tax cuts under another banner.

Who's crazy?

Tone and feel

We need people who feel the pulse of the market.

(Sproul 1980: 178)

Central bankers speak a different language than economists. Robert Rouse, manager of the securities Desk for the Federal Open Market Committee, explained his job to a congressional committee:

hour-by-hour developments, particularly those in the Federal funds market, in the Governmental securities market, in the progress of Government securities dealers in finding the financing required to carry their portfolios of Government securities, provide the manager of the account with information which gives him an informed judgment of the degree or tightness in the market – sometimes referred to as the 'feel of the market'.

(Joint Economic Committee, Hearings, June 1961: 5)

President Alfred Hayes of the New York Reserve Bank responded to a follow-up question:

Senator Pell – One final question: I notice that in one of your reports you say you take more into account the tone of the market than actual statistics. I was wondering if you could enlarge on that thought.
Mr. Hayes – Well, the tone of the market is a very difficult thing to describe unless you are actually sitting at this trading desk, which is the nerve center of the System for keeping in touch with credit and banking and money market developments.

But I would say that it is a compound of all kinds of impressions you get from the volume of trading, the speed of trading, what is happening to prices, what the Bank's position is, whether the dealers are hard up for financing or have plenty of financing, whether funds are well distributed throughout the country or not well distributed.

It is such a combination of a great many things to which we refer rather briefly and not particularly usefully as the tone of the market, but we do not have a better term.

Karl Brunner and Allan Meltzer deplored the Fed's unscientific language:

Can the FOMC guide the Manager of the System open market account in deciding the degree of ease or restraint...? Reference to 'tone' or 'feel' without any clear indication of the meaning attached to these words cannot serve as a guide. The Manager must make a judgment about what the Committee member had in mind if he is to follow [their] advice....

The position of the [members] is that the Manager knows what they mean because he has participated in the discussion, heard their remarks, and understood the interpretations. Moreover, the argument runs, the reference to 'tone' and 'feel' occurs in the context of a particular set of events....

The inherent obscurity of the entities denoted by 'tone' and 'feel' renders any judgment about [them] dubious.... Even the consensus of a group of 'experienced men' adds little if Congress and the public cannot appraise the validity of the consensus.

(1964a: 15)

Researchers have tried to make sense of the Fed, with little success. They have found some 'operational' meaning, that is, correlations between the frequency of 'tone' and 'feel' in FOMC discussions of money market conditions. Leonall Andersen (1969) found that since 'the Desk Manager's qualitative assessment of money market conditions such as bank borrowings tended to be supported by market data,... there is validity to the concept of "tone and feel of the market"'.

However, he found no correlation between money market pressures and intermediate policy guides – bank reserves, the money stock, and long-term interest rates – through which Fed actions were supposed to influence its ultimate goals of employment and inflation. Labeling the money market approach 'naïve', Anderson called for the conduct of policy within 'a general equilibrium framework [with] variables other than those strictly from financial markets'. That is, the Fed should exchange its view of the world for that of their advisors.

Cognitive dissonance

The Fed's obscure language has been called worse than useless. Denials and excuses seem human and harmless enough, but Thomas Mayer (1990) complained that they are self-generating because they lessen the urgency to develop better policies that would reduce the need to minimize regret. The Fed's focus on simple and immediate financial-market conditions minimizes the chances of error, and the imprecise, qualitative, nature of decisions reduces the chances of being found out, by themselves or others.

Social psychologist Elliot Aronson defined cognitive dissonance as 'a state of tension that occurs whenever an individual simultaneously holds two cognitions (ideas, attitudes, beliefs, opinions) that are psychologically inconsistent'. Referring to experiments in which subjects had been induced to lie, the cognition '"I have said something I don't believe and it could have bad consequences for people" is dissonant with my self-concept; that is,... with my cognition that "I am a decent, reasonable, truthful person"' (1980: 102–3, 125). This is the basis of the hypothesis 'that people act so as to avoid having to realize that they have made mistakes' (Mayer 1990).

Cognitive dissonance might apply to policymakers who value their reputations and self-esteem. The Fed has incentives to emphasize data which suggest that conditions are not as bad as they seem, or would have been in their absence, and to project the blame for undeniably bad outcomes onto irresistible (political, foreign, or monopoly) forces, while taking credit for favorable events. We might think of these as conscious measures to promote the status and effectiveness of the institution. In his analysis of FOMC behavior as cognitive dissonance, however, Mayer interprets them as irrational and ultimately dangerous props of self-esteem in the face of error. Policymakers reduce cognitive dissonance by avoiding responsibility, he wrote,

> either by adhering to a theory dogmatically or, at the other extreme, by an atheoretical pragmatism. The Fed has clearly chosen the latter. It makes

policy by intuitive feel and pays little attention to more formal economic reasoning; from reading the FOMC minutes, one would hardly know that many of the participants are professional economists.

(Mayer 1990)

Mayer found cognitive dissonance in the use of advisors more for support than enlightenment:

> The Fed has a large and excellent staff, but if rumors and general impressions can be trusted, that staff seems to have disappointingly little influence on policy. Much of its work consists of sophisticated and often esoteric analyses that are not likely to have much effect on day-to-day policy. Moreover, at least until recently, if rumors can be believed, the staff's work was channeled through a filter that made its results seem more unanimous, and in accord with the FOMC's current policy, than was justified.
>
> (Mayer 1990)

Junior members of the staff described their place in the policy process to an interviewer:

> The Monday briefings are tightly orchestrated by the senior staff to ensure that none of the more junior economists, who are present to make reports or answer questions, are likely to disagree with one another – or with their superiors.... There is only one acceptable point of view and it is usually that of staff director Steve Axilrod.
>
> (Cobb 1986)

The proof of the pudding is in the eating, and Mayer found the Fed lacking.

> The FOMC has also shown a strong tendency to stick with its policies. Thus, in the 1970s it persisted in trying to stabilize the funds rate, even though that policy both caused inflation and resulted in a pro-cyclical growth rate for the money supply. That policy cannot be explained by saying that targeting interest rates was a reasonable policy, with much support among academic economists, because the Fed was not *targeting* interest rates in the sense of selecting the appropriate funds rate – usually it was stabilizing the funds rate around whatever level it happened to occupy.
>
> The FOMC's response to the lag of monetary policy also seems like an attempt to reduce cognitive dissonance. Estimates of the lag diverge widely, with small models usually showing short lags, whereas big econometric models – including the Fed's own model – generally show long lags. If these models are right, then the Fed needs to forecast far ahead.
>
> (Mayer 1990)

This was not done, according to a staff econometrician:

It is difficult if not impossible to produce judgmental forecasts with a horizon much beyond a year.... As a result, only the model was available. Some senior staff and many FOMC members had a great distrust of models. As a result, longer-run forecasts were viewed as highly untrustworthy [and] not treated seriously by the policy-makers.

(Pierce 1980)

Mayer saw the Fed's focus on the financial markets as a way of hiding from the most significant effects of its actions.

Has the Fed allowed its choices of target variables to be influenced by its wish to avoid cognitive dissonance? It probably has. In selecting its targets, the Fed has usually preferred interest rates to the growth rate of some monetary aggregate. One reason may be that interest-rate targets are easier to attain than monetary-growth-rate targets. The Fed can set the funds rate precisely, but not the monetary growth rate. Hence, the Fed can avoid some apparent failures by using an interest-rate target rather than an aggregates target.

(Mayer 1990)

Some of Mayer's criticisms were supported by Governor Maisel's recollections of FOMC meetings. Degrees of emphasis on a variety of objectives and methods differed between individuals and from meeting to meeting. Regional and sectoral conditions, interest rates, the balance of payments, Government deficits, political pressures, and many other items entered the discussions. 'Having observed them in many meetings, I could rank the participants according to their views on how restrictive or accommodative monetary policy should be.' These preferences were correlated with members' forecasts. 'One who favored a low [money] growth rate almost always saw a booming economy.... Conversely, those who favored greater expansion usually estimated the growth that would occur without monetary ease as very slight.'

Although the value system of each member came into play during discussion, the actual goals and objectives being sought were rarely discussed. Frequently I played the devil's advocate by urging a more open discussion of objectives and proposed trade-offs, but I never succeeded in focusing the debate in this manner. Each member remained free to vote his own value judgments and prejudices without ever having to state or defend his objectives.

(Maisel 1973: 48–9)

Mayer's descriptions of behavior were accurate. At least they agreed with the recollections of FOMC members and staff. However, his explanation of that behavior is not the only one possible. It is just as easily explained as rational. Mayer, Maisel, and Blinder expect too much or their criticisms are in the interests of agenda that are not themselves free of cognitive dissonance. A view from the standpoint of the FOMC suggests an alternative, eyes-wide-open, perception of policy. It is true that they focus on the financial markets in which they are immersed while minimizing the wider effects of their policies, and make such verbal concessions as seem politically necessary – such as adherence to the Phillips Curve during periods of unemployment (see below).

Should we expect anything else? Central bankers' actions are governed by their experience and environment, which provide the corpus of their knowledge. What are the alternatives? Even supposing that, somehow, by blotting out experience and surroundings, they could operate within the closed and certain system of economic theory, they would still have to choose from the many models pressed on them. Mayer believed that the FOMC's preference for an interest rate target over his preferred monetarist prescription of money growth was a pathological desire to avoid criticism by aiming at an easy target. After condemning the FOMC's interest target as not 'a reasonable policy, with much support among academic economists', he concluded:

> Another way in which avoiding cognitive dissonance may bias the Fed toward favoring an interest-rate target over a money-stock target is that the current money-stock data available at FOMC meetings are subsequently revised substantially. [They are based on samples and their seasonal factors are highly variable.] Suppose that the FOMC is told that money growth is exceeding its target, and it therefore adopts a more restrictive policy. Afterward, when the money data are revised, the FOMC might realize that its restrictive policy and the costs it inflicted on the economy were unnecessary. Interest-rate targeting presents no such danger.
>
> (Mayer 1990)

This might be thought careful behavior deserving of some praise, but many, perhaps most, economists, like those on the Bank of England's Monetary Policy Committee, prefer that the FOMC base its decisions unreservedly on statistical expectations in the certainty-equivalent manner of economic theory.

Something can be said in defense of central bankers, if not of their brilliance at least of their rational ignorance that may not always produce worse results than the more fearless economists. Although accusations of an excessively narrow outlook, of 'money market myopia', are not without merit, central bankers' views are broader in some respects than those of economists. Their open system recognizes uncertainty and the possibility of learning. Economists might be as cognitively dissonant as policymakers. Their models are claimed to be testable but refutation is never admitted. Failures are blamed on shocks from outside their closed systems – of which they think they are innocent, Volcker complained – and there is no confession of mistaken 'approaches'.

Talk about cognitive dissonance! 'I don't think it's quite fair to condemn a whole program because of a single slip', General Turgidson told the president in *Dr. Strangelove*.

Mayer's criticism in large part amounted to a defense of his own preferred (monetarist) theory over the interest instrument that central banks traditionally used, and is now (again) generally accepted by economists. Because of technological changes and problems of measurement, the monetarist rule was never feasible. In addition, logically most telling, monetarists never settled on a *definition* of money, as opposed to *identifying* various types (M1, M2,...) whose compositions changed frequently – as they must if officials try to keep a lid on them.

It is possible that Fed officials understand each other and what they are doing without being able to explain themselves. It may be necessary, if not satisfying, to treat the Fed's assurances as generously as Louis Armstrong's, who when asked to define jazz, said: 'Man, if you gotta ask, you'll never know.'

It may seem odd to compare Satchmo with J.P. Morgan, but the two artists had much in common. Morgan was 'in his element' in the foreign exchange market (Strouse 1999: 351).

> Ever since his first trip abroad at age fifteen, he had been fascinated with the prices of money in different markets. Clerks at his Wall Street office brought him hourly reports of currency quotations, and at home over breakfast he got the figures from London by wire or phone. He monitored exchange markets the way a doctor takes a pulse.

A congressional committee asked why he had insisted on exclusive control of a US bond issue in Europe.

> *Senator Vest* – If the gold was abroad, I take it for granted that anybody could get hold of it who had the means to do so. If you were actuated by the desire to prevent a panic, why were you not willing that other people should do it, if they wanted to?
> *Morgan* – They could not do it.

President Grover Cleveland recalled that he had asked Morgan how he had known he could 'command the cooperation of the great financial interests of Europe'. 'I simply told them that this was necessary for the maintenance of the public credit and the promotion of industrial peace', Morgan replied, 'and they did it.' The reticence of central bankers is seen as political evasiveness, but it is present in the financial markets even among those without official positions. Central banks are institutions with origins in the financial system, whose functions, experience, and knowledge exist relative to that system. Contending that '[t]he main need is for a general understanding and acceptance of an appropriate rule to take all but low-level discretion out of money' (Yeager 1962: 17) asks people to act independently of their environment and experience.

Fed-speak may be no more self-serving, no less rational, than the language of other accountable bodies. Of course the Fed takes credit for good times, rejects blame for the bad, and extols its actions as in the general interest. Responding to criticisms that the Fed was overly solicitous of the big banks, Governor Andrew Brimmer (1989) defended bail-outs of large banks by saying that the Fed 'has a major responsibility in the containment of those types of risks which threaten to disrupt the fabric of the financial system which is so vital to the economy at large'. 'If the model is sufficiently vague', Mayer wrote, 'any action can be justified.' What did he expect? The Fed was created by and for the money-center banks.

The Fed's fluctuating Phillips-curve rhetoric also has a reasonable, if not theoretically rigorous, explanation. As the prosperity of the 1990s progressed, officials became increasingly vocal about the importance of what had apparently become the Fed's unique goal of price stability. Chairman Alan Greenspan (1994a) told an audience of economists and central bankers: 'Monetary policy basically is a single tool and you can only implement one goal consistently.' His predecessor told the same group that 'price stability ... is to be treasured and enshrined as the prime policy priority'. It is an 'inextricable part of a broader concern about the basic stability of the financial and economic system' (Volcker 1994). The record showed that the goal was not price stability but low inflation. In any case, it seemed that the Fed had unilaterally repealed the Employment Act of 1946, which specified the goals of 'maximum employment, production, and purchasing power'. The new policy might be reconciled with the 1946 Act since, according to Chairman Greenspan's statement on 20 July 2000 while delivering the semiannual report on Monetary Policy: 'Maximum sustainable growth, as history so amply demonstrates, requires price stability. Irrespective of the complexities of economic change, our primary goal is to find those policies that best contribute to a non-inflationary environment and hence to growth.' This repealed at least the model underlying the 1946 Act, which recognized trade-offs.

A few months later, however, the FOMC reacted to reports of an economic slowdown (and a new president) by considering 'the potential desirability of moving from a statement of risk weighted toward rising inflation to one that indicated a balanced view'. As the slowdown continued, a 'balanced view' was revealed to mean the promotion of 'a more satisfactory economic expansion', in place of the single-minded focus on price stability (Wood 2001).

The Fed had also temporarily rediscovered the Phillips curve in the previous (1990–91) recession (*Federal Reserve Bulletin*, March 1991), and would do so again in 2008, when Chairman Ben Bernanke (who had supported the single, inflation, target; see the next chapter) publicly supported a fiscal stimulus package (*New York Times*, 17 January 2008) and the FOMC indicated its intention 'to promote sustainable economic growth and price stability' (Federal Reserve Board press release, 30 April 2008).

Shifts to and from Phillips-curve rhetoric can be interpreted in at least two ways. The Fed's apparent submissions to immediate pressures are consistent with model uncertainty, but also with a firm belief that the Phillips Curve does not exist in combination with political awareness. We should not expect Fed spokesmen, especially before their congressional overseers, to show insensitivity or impotence towards the unemployed.

The next chapter presents a consistent model, with political qualifications, of Federal Reserve policy. It will not satisfy those who would like a complete quantitative model of a closed system but it will portray the Fed as rational in its

Policymakers and the public

Knowledge, language, and the possibility of democratic policy

The Fed's image of its surroundings is implicit and inconstant. Its actions are less a policy than reactions to an open and changing economy. This does not mean that its actions are without order. However, any expectation that it will issue an explicit model, complete with estimated parameters and precise forecasts, is doomed to disappointment. The problem – if it is a problem – is not unique to central bankers. Human actions are seldom accompanied by statements of principle. Not much would get done if they were. Buyers and sellers are content with mutually beneficial trades. Underlying principles may be guessed at, and we appeal to what we believe are the interests of others. Adam Smith saw in the principle of sympathy, meaning the tendency to imagine ourselves in the other fellow's shoes, a mainspring of exchange. Traders seldom discuss principles before agreeing terms, however. Efforts to go beyond what is necessary for the business at hand risk rejection and are avoided. If different views have 'the same practical import', John Dewey (1927: 91) asked, 'What is logic between friends?'

Governor Maisel might have understood his colleagues if he had studied Dewey. 'I've told you my vote. You want a reason, too?' He was no doubt as much in the dark about the minds of others in faculty meetings at his university. Why should the Fed be any different?

These principles of exchange, and of life generally, are unavoidable and have even been praised. In his pragmatic analysis of learning and choices in democracies, Dewey wrote:

> The strongest point to be made on behalf of even such rudimentary political forms as democracy has already attained, popular voting, majority rule and so on, is that to some extent they involve a consultation and discussion which uncover social needs and troubles. This fact is the great asset on the side of the political ledger. De Tocqueville wrote it down almost a century ago in his survey of the prospects of democracy in the United States. Accusing a democracy of a tendency to prefer mediocrity in its elected rulers, and admitting its exposure to gusts of passion and its openness to folly, he pointed out in effect that popular government is educative as other modes of political regulation are not. It forces a recognition that there are common interests, even though the recognition of *what* they are is confused; and the need it enforces of discussion and publicity brings about some clarification of what they are. The man who wears the shoe knows best that it pinches and where it pinches, even if the expert shoemaker is the best judge of how the trouble is to be remedied.
> (Dewey 1927: 206–7)

To be effective, therefore, Dewey continued with a thought that applies to central banks and other expert bodies, they must be guided by the public.

> It is impossible for high-brows to secure a monopoly of such knowledge as must be used for the regulation of common affairs.... A class of experts is inevitably so removed from common interests as to become a class with private interests and private knowledge, which in social matters is not knowledge at all.... No government by experts in which the masses do not have the chance to inform the experts as to their needs can be anything but an oligarchy managed in the interests of the few. And the enlightenment must proceed in ways which force the administrative specialists to take account of the needs.
>
> (206)

The philosopher/educator was concerned with how that enlightenment would proceed, which he saw as '*the* problem of the public'.

> The ballot is, as often said, a substitute for bullets. But what is more significant is that counting of heads compels prior recourse to methods of discussion, consultation and persuasion, while the essence of appeal to force is to cut short resort to such methods. Majority, just as majority rule, is as foolish as its critics charge it with being. But it never is *merely* majority rule. As a practical politician, Samuel J. Tilden, said a long time ago: 'The means by which a majority comes to a majority is the more important thing': antecedent debates, modification of views.
>
> (207–8)

Dewey hoped that this process would become more enlightened with education. Since individuals learn by trial and error, or 'experimentalism', fundamentally as in the laboratory, the population would learn to apply the scientific method to social and political questions. Alexis de Tocqueville, noticing the absence of scientific procedures in the American population's decision-making, was less optimistic. He contrasted, in the words of Harvey Mansfield and Delba Winthrop, the 'democratic eagerness to get practical applications of science' as opposed 'to the "ardent, haughty, and disinterested love of the true" characteristic of a few' (Tocqueville 1840: xxxii). He was persuaded that 'Equality develops the desire in each man to judge everything by himself; it gives him in all things a taste for the tangible and real.' Such people

> distrust systems, they like to hold themselves very close to the facts and to study them by themselves; as they do not allow themselves to be easily filled with respect for the name of anyone like themselves, they are never disposed to swear by the word of the master.... Scientific traditions hold little dominion over them; they never stop for long at the subtleties of a school and they are not easily fobbed off with big words.
>
> (Tocqueville 1840: 433)

Tocqueville was interested in the practical consequences of the politics of a particular country, but his observations apply to social transactions everywhere.

> [T]he habits of mind suited to action are not always suited to thought. The man who acts is often reduced to contenting himself with what is nearly so because he would never arrive at the end of his design if he wished to perfect every detail. He must constantly rely on ideas that he has not had the leisure to fathom, for it is much more the timeliness of the idea he makes use of than its rigorousness that helps him; and all in all, there is less risk for him in making use of some false principles than in wasting his time in establishing the truth of all his principles. It is not by long and learned demonstrations that the world is led. There, the quick look at a particular fact, the daily study of the changing passions of the crowd, the chance of the moment and the skill to seize it decide all affairs.
> (Tocqueville 1840: 435)

These ordinary decision-makers are not entirely at sea. They are guided by the experiences of themselves and their institutions. Economists concede that individuals seldom apply scientific methods, but argue that in pursuing their interests they behave according to economic principles and produce the efficient outcomes of theory, after all. This seems unacceptable for policymakers, whom economists expect to understand and apply the theory of the day.

Economists are not alone in setting this standard. Dewey believed that the success of democracy ultimately depended on the application of scientific methods by voters and their elected representatives. He hoped that 'deliberative' democracy would be able, through rational debate and the sifting of evidence, to solve social problems by scientific procedures. The success of this effort hinged on the reform of education to make people think like scientists about political questions – disinterestedly, intelligently, empirically. Not surprisingly, Richard Posner (2003) observed, Dewey was pessimistic about the future of American democracy.

Posner's analysis of the futility of Dewey's aspiration to make the political process scientific also invoked Tocqueville. 'The history of the United States in the half century since Dewey's death suggests [to Posner] that his pessimism was misplaced, that he had succumbed to the intellectual's typical mistake of exaggerating the importance of intellect.' There is little evidence that Americans have become better informed about political issues, and even less that they devote more time and effort to their analysis. They are interested in politics, but their interest is in results rather than in principles or the application of scientific methods to political decisions.

> The role of the people at large in the governance of a large democratic nation is altogether more passive than its role in the concept of deliberative democracy. People know when things are going well or going badly and will vote accordingly, but that is about it. And the relevant 'well' or 'badly' is well or

> badly *for them*. They vote their interests. Voting is rarely disinterested. The political parties know this, and so their campaigns appeal to interests, rather than to the Good.
>
> (Posner 2003)

In going Dewey one better, Posner suggests that the philosopher underestimated the epistemic strength of democracy, which

> enables public opinion to be reliably determined, thus providing vital feedback for the policy initiatives of political leaders and other officials. Nondemocratic regimes find it difficult to gauge public opinion, and as a result sometimes adopt, as it were inadvertently, policies so radically unpopular as to kill the regime.
>
> (Posner 2003)

This is as true of economic as political decisions. Central bankers, like voters, make decisions according to their narrow interests and limited knowledge. Not always for the worse. The superior performance of the Independent Treasury under the direction of Congress in the nineteenth century compared with the expert but remote Federal Reserve Board during the Great Depression is an example of the importance of general discussion and of genuine as opposed to nominal accountability.

Could the Fed have done better? If we tried harder, if the minds of the best and the brightest were applied in a concerted fashion to monetary (and other social) questions, wouldn't we have better policy? Maybe. Maybe not. The question whether authoritative policies are the best way to use the knowledge of society remains. The following discussion considers some of the opposing views of philosophers. The dispute bears directly on our inquiry into the stability of macroeconomic policy in the next chapter.

Constrained and unconstrained visions

Reliance on democracy is confidence in the constrained visions of the electorate, meaning the open systems, personal knowledge, tacit dimensions, empiricism, pragmatism, and experience discussed above. The competing full-information approach to public policy is preferred by those whose understandings, or visions, of the world are unconstrained. Thomas Sowell (1987: 43) compared them in the context of the eighteenth century but the debate continues. A 'vision' is one's 'sense of how the world works'. A person's vision is 'constrained' if he knows that he understands only part of the workings of the world. His vision is 'unconstrained' if he believes that he knows the causal relations of the wider world sufficiently to be able to manage them for the general welfare. A person with constrained vision thinks himself fortunate if he is able to deal satisfactorily with his immediate surroundings. Adam Smith's great contribution was to show that substantial social benefits are realized by a society of selfish people with constrained visions. William Godwin's *Enquiry Concerning Political Justice* (1798), on the other hand, represented the confidence and virtue of the 'age of reason' in which 'the liberally educated and reflecting members' of society should, as in Plato, be 'guides and instructors' to the people.

Voltaire looked to absolute rulers – he compared the governments of Western Europe unfavorably to Catherine the Great's Russia – for rational states. 'It is most advantageous for the prince and the state when there are many philosophers. The philosophers having no particular interest to defend, can only speak up in favor of reason and the public interest' (Sowell 1987: 46). In the next century John Stuart Mill wrote that much could be accomplished if 'the most cultivated intellects' and 'superior spirits would but join with each other', and the universities sent forth 'a succession of minds, not the creatures of their age, but capable of being its improvers and regenerators' (1989 xviii: 86, 129; xv: 631).

Godwin believed that experience was overrated – 'unreasonably magnified' – compared with 'the general power of a cultivated mind. [W]e must bring everything to the standard of reason' (1798 ii: 172).

> Nothing must be sustained because it is ancient, because we have been accustomed to regard it as sacred, or because it has been unusual to bring its validity into question.
>
> (Godwin 1798 i: 185)

The opposite view is associated with conservatives for whom knowledge is social. Edmund Burke wrote:

> We are afraid to put men to live and trade each on his own private stock of reason; because we suspect that this stock in each man is small, and that the individuals would do better to avail themselves of the general bank and capital of nations and of ages.
>
> (Burke 1790: 182)

A constrained vision does not doom society to stagnation, however, because experience is an effective as well as a dear teacher.

> The growth of knowledge and the growth of civilization are the same only if we interpret knowledge to include all human adaptations to environment in which past experience has been incorporated. Not all knowledge in this sense is part of our intellect, nor is our intellect the whole of our knowledge. Our habits and skills, our emotional attitudes, our tools, and our institutions – all are in this sense adaptations to past experience which have grown up by selective elimination of less suitable conduct. They are as much an indispensable foundation of successful action as is our conscious knowledge.
>
> (Hayek 1960: 26)

Man 'is better served by custom than understanding', Hayek (1979: 157) wrote, because he has 'learnt to do the right thing without comprehending why it was the right thing'. There is 'more "intelligence" incorporated in the system of rules of conduct than in man's thoughts about his surroundings'.

This accords with Holmes's argument that it is a 'fallacy' to conceive of the law as purely articulated logic, for while 'in the broadest sense it is true that the law is a logical development', it is not 'worked out like mathematics from some general axioms of conduct'.

> The development of our law has gone on for nearly a thousand years, like the development of a plant, each generation taking the inevitable next step, mind, like matter, simply obeying a law of spontaneous growth.
> (Holmes 1897)

This does not mean that intelligent public policy is impossible, but we should be careful.

> Rage and phrenzy will pull down more in half an hour than prudence, deliberation, and foresight can build up in a hundred years. The errors and defects of old establishments are visible and palpable. It calls for little ability to point them out; and where absolute power is given, it requires but a word wholly to abolish the vice and establishment together.... To make every thing the reverse of what they have seen is ... easy.... No difficulties occur in what has never been tried. Criticism is almost baffled in discovering the defects of what has not existed....
>
> At once to preserve and to reform is quite another thing. When the useful parts of an old establishment are kept, and what is superadded is to be fitted to what is retained, a vigorous mind, steady persevering attention, various powers of comparison and combination, and the resources of an understanding fruitful in expedients are to be exercised; they are to be exercised in a continued conflict with the combined force of opposite vices; with the obstinacy that rejects all improvement, and the levity that is fatigued and disgusted with every thing of which it is not in possession. But you may object – 'A process of this kind is slow. It is not fit for an assembly which glorifies in performing in a few months the work of ages. Such a mode of reforming possibly might take up many years.' Without question it might; and it ought. It is one of the excellencies of a method in which time is among the assistants, that its operation is slow and in some cases almost imperceptible.
> (Burke 1790: 274–5)

A theme of this book is not that conservatism in monetary and fiscal policies is good or bad – that question is left open – but that it is unavoidable in a democratic society of enduring interests.

Monetary mystique: pathological or creative?

> We see only one explanation for the Fed's insistence on secrecy. Over the whole of its history, two things have been constant: the Fed's desire to avoid accountability and its efforts to maintain a favorable public image. They explain both its secrecy and its consistent opposition to every attempt to establish clear criteria for judging its performance.
>
> (Friedman 1993)

This chapter closes with an effort to make sense of the Fed's communications with the financial markets. Contrary to the common superficial suggestion, the Fed's actions are not secret. Its actions are immediately and widely known. It is stingy with explanations, however, and does not commit to the future. What are secret about the Fed are its model and future behavior – like nearly all practitioners. The Fed's tendency to play its cards close to its vest – despite economists' protests that a clearly stated objective would contribute to economic efficiency and be more easily attained as investors anticipated announced targets – may be more than a self-serving avoidance of criticism. It may be an essential part of a rational monetary policy with which even economists might be content.

The central bank is a securities dealer, and dealers do not make unqualified commitments. They must adapt to market conditions. Bids and offers are for limited times and amounts. This is where rational expectations criticisms of interest rules were misplaced. Their proof of infinitely large changes in money and the price level is derived from the assumption of unlimited buy and sell commitments (McCallum 1981).

Central banks are different from private dealers in being responsible public bodies, and as such are expected to reveal their intentions. They are unable to do this except in terms that are so qualified as to appear evasive – which in fact they are. An open commitment by a securities firm risks failure. A public central bank cannot go bankrupt but a long-term commitment risks unknown effects in an open system (Goodfriend and Lacker 1999).

Instructive case studies of calculated obfuscation were presented in Fred Greenstein's account of Dwight Eisenhower's *Hidden-Hand Presidency* (1994: 68–9). Ike was a master of the strategy of silence, if possible, and of the appearance of ignorance, if necessary, to defuse explosive situations. In the briefing before his 31 July 1957 press conference, he was reminded that Egyptian President Nasser had been trying to provoke an official reaction by anti-American speeches. Ike said that if the subject came up, he would say that he had not read Nasser's speeches.

He learned before another press conference that the previous day Secretary of State John Foster Dulles had 'wandered' into a public discussion of the disposition of American missiles in Europe. After phoning Dulles to learn exactly what he had said, Ike told his staff that if the question came up at his own conference, he would 'be evasive'. 'It did and he was.' A reporter said that Dulles had 'disclosed that consideration is being given to a plan for establishing nuclear stockpiles of weapons and fissionable materials for NATO powers', and asked how the president stood on the matter. 'Now I don't know what he told you about a plan', Ike said. 'What we have just been doing is studying means and methods of making NATO effective as a defensive organization.... Now that is all there is to that.'

On another occasion, his press secretary worried about appropriate responses to questions concerning American willingness to use tactical nuclear weapons in a limited war. 'Don't worry Jim, if that question comes up', the president said, 'I'll just confuse them.' When a reporter asked if he 'conceived' of the use of atomic weapons in a conflict with the Chinese, Ike responded:

> Well, Mr. Harsch, I must confess I cannot answer that question in advance. The only thing I know about war are two things: the most unpredictable factor in war is human nature in its day-to-day manifestation; but the only unchanging factor in war is human nature. And the next thing is that every war is going to astonish you in the way it occurred, and the way it is carried out. So that for a man to predict, particularly if he has the responsibility for making the decision, to predict what he is going to use, how he is going to do it, would I think exhibit his ignorance of war; that is what I believe. So I think you just have to wait; and that is the kind of prayerful decision that may some day face a president.

Ike thus conveyed an ambiguous warning to the Chinese while sidestepping politically divisive encounters with right-wing China Firsters and congressional doves. This was hardly pathological; it was not self-deception. Fed officials may also know what they say. The Fed's evasiveness was defended by Volcker in a letter to the House Subcommittee on Domestic Monetary Policy:

> The heart of the problem, as I see it, is that markets constantly are trying to anticipate what *might* happen in the future. They would like the Federal Reserve to in effect 'tell' them. But, by the nature of things, we cannot. Our own operations in the market from day to day are dependent upon future events – some technical, some not – that we cannot reliably forecast with accuracy. Our danger in immediate release of the directive is that certain assumptions might be made that we are committed to certain operations that are, in fact, dependent on future events, and these interpretations and expectations would tend to diminish our needed operational flexibility.
>
> (Goodfriend 1986)

We can learn more about the Fed by listening to its language positively as an expression of a 'wait and see' position in an open system than negatively as an evasion of the closed system preferred by theorists. The FOMC has increased the disclosure of its decisions. Since 1994, it has announced fed funds target changes immediately upon making them, and has made fewer changes between meetings. An asymmetric Directive also hints at its leanings, but traders must still take their chances (Thornton 2001; Thornton and Wheelock 2000).

7 The stability of monetary policy
The Federal Reserve, 1914–2007

[W]hy is it that during the pre-1979 period the Federal Reserve followed a rule that was clearly inferior? [W]hy is it that the Fed maintained persistently low short-term real rates in the face of high or rising inflation. One possibility ... is that the Fed thought the natural rate of unemployment at this time was much lower than it really was..., although it is not clear why the Fed should have held this view over such a long period of time.

[A] related possibility is that ... neither the Fed nor the economics profession understood the dynamics of inflation very well. Indeed, it was not until the mid- to-late 1970s that intermediate textbooks began emphasizing the absence of a long-run trade-off between inflation and output. The ideas that expectations may matter in generating inflation and that credibility is important in policy-making were simply not well established during that era. What all this suggests is that in understanding historical economic behavior, it is important to take into account the state of policy-maker's knowledge of the economy and how it may have evolved over time. Analyzing policy-making from this perspective, we think, would be a highly useful undertaking.

(Clarida *et al.* 2000)

The Fed's variable reputation

There is a widespread view among economists that the Fed has only recently begun to focus on price stability and take account of expectations. A review of Michael Woodford's (2003) widely noticed contribution to the theory of monetary policy noted that 'During the past two decades,... central bankers [have come to] agree that price stability is an important goal and that "credibility" of policy and "transparency" of its implementation are crucial to accomplishing that goal' (Green 2005). Woodford stated at the outset that 'paradoxically' the recent period 'of improved macroeconomic stability has coincided with a *reduction* ... in the ambition of central banks' efforts at macroeconomic stabilization'. They

> have committed themselves ... to the control of inflation, and have found when they do so that not only is it easier to control inflation than previous experience might have suggested, but that price stability creates a sound basis for real economic performance as well.

> What appears to be developing, then, at the turn of another century, is a new consensus in favor of a monetary policy that is disciplined by clear rules intended to ensure a stable standard of value, rather than one that is determined on a purely discretionary basis to serve whatever ends may seem most pressing at any given time.
>
> (Woodford 2003: 2)

This new respect for the Fed, approaching its 'high tide' of the 1920s (Friedman and Schwartz 1963: ch. 6), contrasts with its nearly universal condemnation by economists during the first three or four decades following World War II, when they agreed that monetary policy suffered from a defective policy framework. Where they disagreed was in the nature of those defects. Keynesians complained that monetary policy was not more responsive to events, particularly unemployment. 'No one but Mr. Martin knows', James Tobin (1958) wrote, 'how much slack the Federal Reserve is willing to force upon the economy in the effort to stop inflation.' Monetarists, on the other hand, believed that active policies such as 'leaning against the wind' exacerbated economic fluctuations (Friedman 1959: 93). All 20 academics testifying to Congressman Wright Patman's subcommittee on *The Federal Reserve after Fifty Years* opposed the Fed's independence. Paul Samuelson testified: 'A central bank that is not responsible is irresponsible, rather than independent', by which he meant that it should be responsible to the administration. Most economists advocated the subordination of monetary policy to a coordinated (and discretionary) macroeconomic policy. John Gurley said that Fed 'independence ... is like having two managers for the same baseball team.... That we have a separate manager for monetary policy gives rise to unreasonable situations.' The monetarist minority (Milton Friedman, Allan Meltzer, and Karl Brunner) advised that discretion be taken away from the Fed by means of a monetary rule (US Congress 1964: 1105, 1309, 1134, 937).

Although they differed about the solution, critics agreed on a major source of the problem: the Fed's obsession with the stability of the money markets at the expense of the larger economy. Meltzer told Patman's committee that the Fed's

> knowledge of the policy process is woefully inadequate,... dominated by extremely short-run week-to-week, day-to-day, or hour-to-hour events in the money and credit markets. [T]heir viewpoint is frequently that of a banker rather than that of a regulating authority for the monetary system and the economy.

Friedman observed that the Fed 'naturally interpreted' the world in terms of its immediate environment (US Congress 1964: 927, 1163). Keynesian populizer Alvin Hansen (1955) thought the Fed's fear of upsetting the market 'one of the most curious arguments I have ever encountered', and Sidney Weintraub (1955) suggested that the Fed should be interested less in financial stability and more with 'broader conceptions of economic policy'.

Many of these criticisms were on the mark, particularly those directed at the Fed's focus on the financial markets. However, they overlooked its attention to expectations even though the two were inseparable. Stable price expectations have always been thought by the monetary authorities, and usually by economists (the Keynesian era excepted), to be indispensable to financial and general economic stability. The discussion in the next section shows that, contrary to Green, Woodford, and Clarida *et al.*, monetary policymakers' understanding of the economy, with its emphasis on credibility and the role of expectations in generating price fluctuations, has been stable since the founding of the Fed, and indeed long before then. Economists have followed the Fed in recent years rather than the other way around. Another difference between the knowledge of economists and monetary policymakers is the greater stability of the latter – consistent with the opening epigraph from Hume and fiscal policy as shown in Chapter 4. Economists gyrated from classical to Keynesian to New Classical theories while the Fed continues to see the world today much as it did in the 1920s.

The vital roles of the price level and its expectations in the Fed's model of monetary policy are described in the following section. The Fed's actions are governed by its interests subject to its knowledge. Conveniently for the Fed, both point to financial stability, which includes price stability because credit is governed by expectations. Booms and busts are bad for everyone, including banks, in whose interests the Fed was founded, and has continued to be their main political support. Only the bankers defended the Fed to Patman (US Congress 1964: 1231, 1876, 1882).

The three periods of low inflation seen in Figure 7.1 – the 1920s, the 1950s and 1960s, and since the early 1980s – correspond to the three periods of greatest Fed independence, and are the most prominent indications that its behavior and probably its views of economic relations – its model – have been stable. 'Independence' here means primarily free of Executive direction, which is usually for deficit finance but sometimes for macro-political objectives such as employment. Independence is seldom all or nothing, however, and the fourth section considers political and institutional limits on the Fed's freedom of action. The last three sections report estimates of a simple model that can be inferred from Fed statements and behavior, compare that model with recent theory (the Taylor rule), and offer a brief conclusion.

What they knew in 1914

What did the new central bankers bring to their job? Not monetary theory, because policymakers do not look at the world that way, a point developed in Chapter 6. Nor was the Federal Reserve System's formal structure derived from existing institutions such as clearinghouses or the Independent Treasury. Customs are not as easily suppressed, however, and it was a beneficiary of a firm financial tradition.

The Fed's intellectual background was exemplified by William McChesney Martin, Jr, chairman of the Federal Reserve Board from 1951 to 1970. His grandfather was a partner in a grain storage company that borrowed heavily as grain prices rose, and then failed after the panic of 1893, when its loans were called in the midst of falling prices. Martin Sr was the first chairman of the Federal Reserve Bank of St Louis. In his teenage years junior often accompanied his father and a local banker 'down dusty, rutted roads to visit individual farms. Bill saw his father sweating in the blistering sun and often heard him ... expressing his concern about excessive borrowing by overly optimistic farmers' (Bremner 2004: 8, 13). A fifth of the district's banks failed in the 1920s, after farm values rose with farm prices during and after World War I and then collapsed.

These sequences – the rapid ascents and collapses of prices – were already an old story, and so was their popular interpretation that consisted of two parts: the latter is an effect of the former and people never learn (Schumpeter 1954: 743–7). Some of these experiences/lessons are described below.

The crisis of 1819 impressed monetary histories (if not the memories of market participants), including William Graham Sumner's (1874). He quoted from reports of the Pennsylvania legislature, which attributed the distress to the expansion of banking during the War of 1812.

> In consequence..., the inclination of a large part of the people, created by past prosperity, to live by speculation and not by labor, was greatly increased. A spirit in all respects akin to gambling prevailed. A fictitious value was given to all kinds of property. Specie was driven from circulation as if by common consent, and all efforts to restore society to its natural condition were treated with undisguised contempt.
> (Sumner 1874: 79–80)

'Land in Pennsylvania', he wrote, 'was worth on average, in 1809, $38 per acre; in 1815, $150; in 1819, $35. The note circulation of the country in 1812 was about $45,000,000; in 1817, $100,000,000; in 1819, $45,000,000.' Depression was followed by recovery and another boom that collapsed in its turn in 1825.

A similar pattern was seen in England. The 1825 crash is particularly important in monetary history because it began Bagehot's history of central banking, and has been called 'the principal historical case on which he built his argument' that the Bank of England 'should stand as a lender of last resort in time of crisis' (Fetter 1967). The boom was initiated by 'easier credit' and 'the recovery of commodity prices' following depression, A.E. Feavearyear (1931: 218) wrote, on the basis of which 'the public began to speculate.... Many of the projects were of the usual "bubble" type, and yet people of substance and of established reputation went into them.'

'The crash did not come upon people unawares. [Prime Minister Lord] Liverpool warned the speculators of the inevitable collapse, and told them that when it came they must not look to the Government as on former occasions ... to relieve the situation' (Feavearyear 1931: 219–20). The panic of 1825 was the occasion on which, Bagehot (1873: 190) wrote, '[T]he Bank of England at first acted as unwisely as it was possible to act. By every means it tried to restrict its advances. The reserve being very small, it endeavoured to protect its reserve by lending as little as possible.'

The Bank eventually supplied credit and the crisis passed, indicating to Bagehot that it should have so committed from the beginning. We saw in Chapter 5 that the Bank rejected this advice, nor was it respected by the American banking students discussed below. The Bank Act of 1844 was designed to prevent speculative increases in credit. Its architect, Samuel Jones Loyd (1844: 424–5) wrote: 'The revulsion of 1837 was the consequence of a long preceding period of prosperity, which had generated excessive credit, over-trading, and over-banking.' This course would have been checked at an early stage if the gold reserve had been permitted to limit the paper circulation. 'But under our present more "convenient and accommodating" system, the aggregate paper circulation was kept at its full amount during a heavy drain of bullion from September 1833 till 1837.... The result was the crisis of 1837.' Banker and economic historian Thomas Tooke stressed the importance of price expectations to a parliamentary committee of inquiry (House of Commons 1832: Questions 3882–3; Loyd 1844: 424).

> Do you conceive that a sudden fall of prices is productive of less distress ... than a gradual fall? – I know ... many instances in which persons have been ruined by a gradual fall of prices, who would have been safe if it had been a sudden one; nothing is more injurious to parties who continue to hold than a long protracted fall ... ; there never is, in any particular article of trade, a sound state till the impression has become perfectly general and confident in all classes of consumers that the price has seen its lowest; every body knows, who has any experience in trade, that the moment such impression prevails there is an end of distress among the persons concerned in that particular article.

The issue of credibility had been raised by banker Francis Baring in 1797, following the Bank's suspension of convertibility. After the panic leading to the suspension passed, the question of when the Bank should resume was asked. A critic of the Bank admitted that the government had been 'bound to intervene'. However, the

> really objectionable part of their conduct consisted in their continuing the suspension after the alarms of invasion which had occasioned the panic had completely subsided; when the confidence of the public in the stability of the Bank stood higher than ever; and there was no longer any thing to fear from a return to cash payments.
>
> (Anonymous 1797)

Baring disagreed.

> My chief reason is, that credit ought never to be subject to convulsions; a change even from good to better ought not to be made until there is almost a

certainty of maintaining and preserving it in that position; for a retrograde motion in public credit is productive of consequences which are incalculable. With this principle in view, I am averse to the Bank re-assuming their payments generally during the war whilst there is a possibility of their being obliged to suspend them again.

(Baring 1797: 69)

Real bills were no protection against price speculation, but rather tended to magnify the problem. *Bankers' Magazine* (1878: 917–21; Anderson and Cottrell 1974: 311–12) wrote of the failure of the City of Glasgow Bank in 1878, that a 'bank should never, to any large amount, make such advances as do not turn into cash without long delay', especially when its borrowers are 'carrying on a speculative and risky trade'.

> We know that there are some who consider that it is a legitimate thing for a bank to accept bills largely against produce, and that when sufficient securities are held against liabilities of this nature, no very great amount of risk is incurred. To a moderate extent this may be the case. But we do not think it consistent with the prudent conduct of business for a bank unless it holds very large sums indeed in reserve, at call and short notices, ... as the City of Glasgow Bank appears to have done.... For the securities held by a bank against acceptances are not, it must be remembered, securities which mature at a given date like [Treasury] bills, they are securities which it takes time to turn into cash, securities which are more or less at the command of the market.

Like Loyd in the 1840s and the New York Fed's Benjamin Strong in the 1920s, and as experienced by Martin's grandfather, the financial press of 1878 realized that the security of real bills varied with prices.

Gold discoveries carried costs as well as benefits. Economist Charles Dunbar (1904: 269–74) reported that the gold coming from California after 1849 'was a spur to enterprise and a new incentive to the anticipation of gains likely to accrue in the future'. By 1857,

> nearly every branch of domestic business was driven to the extreme point to which the competition of a singularly active and pushing class of men could force it, and this process was accompanied by an extension of mercantile credits in length as well as in amount ... managed by the aid of a great number of banks established upon unlike and often insecure systems, acting upon no common principle, and with no important guaranty for the faithful and prudent discharge of their functions. Nevertheless people agreed that 'the country never was so rich'.

'This was the way gentlemen had [also] talked in 1837', Bray Hammond (1957: 709–10) noted.

Banker James Gibbons wrote shortly after the panic of 1857 that the diminishing reserves of banks should have been a warning. Their overextended positions were

> astounding. If such a departure from equilibrium does not foreshadow the suspension of specie payments as inevitable, it lessens our surprise that it should have occurred (to borrow the words of the [New York] Bank-Superintendent) 'with overflowing granaries, exemption from pestilence, neither internal insurrection nor foreign invasion, and our country at peace with every nation on earth'.

Yet, the 'market is uneasy with high loans and low specie', although each hoped to be among the first to jump. When the crisis came – all it needed was a spark, in this case the suspension of the New York office of the Ohio Life Insurance and Trust Company – banks demonstrated 'unusual sensitiveness and want of self-possession', and tried to save themselves at the expense of their borrowers as prices dropped and values disappeared (Gibbons 1859: 343–4, 365–8; Hammond 1957: 710–15).

Indiana banker, Comptroller of the Currency, Secretary of the Treasury, and financier Hugh McCulloch compared 1837 and 1857 in his first (1866) annual *Treasury Report*:

> The great expansion of 1835 and 1836, ending with the terrible financial collapse of 1837, from the effects of which the country did not rally for years, was the consequence of excessive bank circulation and discounts ... under the wild spirit of speculation which invaded the country....
>
> The [1857] financial crisis was the result of similar cause, namely, the unhealthy extension of the various forms of credit.

He also wrote of the Maine lumber industry in 1832 and the panic of 1873 as examples of 'financial troubles' that 'invariably followed imprudent speculation' based on 'the improper use of individual credit' (214).

Writing in 1909 about *Forty Years of American Finance*, journalist Alexander Noyes observed that the

> panic of 1873, in its outbreak and in its culmination, followed the several successive steps familiar to all such episodes. One or two powerful corporations, which had been leading in the general plunge into debt ... marked by the rashest sort of speculation ... had kept in the race for debt up to the moment of ... ruin.

When the 'bubble of inflated credit' was 'punctured ... general liquidation was started'. Each crisis was preceded by a general feeling that the repetition of history was 'impossible' (188, 312, 329).

He felt alone again in the 1920s, when he warned that 'reckless' speculation would lead to a day of reckoning.

> The speculative mania seemed by 1929 to have neither geographical nor social bounds.... There were occasions, even in social conversation, when expression of disapproval or skepticism would provoke the same resentment as if the controversy had to do with politics or religion. It was not in all respects an agreeable task to point out in the *Times* what seemed to me the very visible signs of danger. As in the similar circumstances of the short-lived speculative mania of 1901, expression of such judgment had to meet the denunciatory comment that the writer was trying to discredit or stop American prosperity.
>
> (Noyes 1938: 323–4)

Some things never change.

R.G. Hawtrey (1932: 41–2) wrote of the similarity of the 'great American financial crises, such as those of 1873, 1893, and 1907', each of which 'came at the climax of several years of growing credit inflation. Expanding credit meant expanding demand for commodities of all kinds. Expanding demand meant first increasing productive activity, and then rising commodity prices.' Profits rose more than in proportion to commodity prices because of lags in wages and overhead expenses.

> The price of a share depends upon the profits or dividends anticipated from it. A credit expansion which increases the profits increases the price. If the increase in profits is due to an ephemeral cause it ought not to produce a proportional increase in price.... But people often base their expectations of future yield upon present yield without taking sufficient account of exceptional circumstances. [W]hen the expansion came to an end and was succeeded by a credit contraction, the reaction in the Stock Market was equally exaggerated.

'The peculiarity ... of an up-grade movement which rests on modern credit facilities', Edwin Seligman (1908) wrote of the crisis of 1907, 'is that we wear magnifying glasses or look at the future in too roseate a light.'

> It is a natural tendency of human nature to capitalize one's hopes and expectations too liberally. If this is done on a continually larger scale, the capitalization becomes so great that actual earnings do not come up to our anticipations or the fear of a discrepancy between actual and anticipated earnings begins to obsess us.... If the ... necessity [of readjustment] is sudden, we have a crisis or panic.

Irving Fisher (1922: 66) also attributed a good part of financial fluctuations to slowly adjusting interest rates. Expansions are characterized by rising credit, commodity prices, and profits, and end with the 'loss of confidence' that 'is the essential fact of every crisis' and 'is a consequence of a belated adjustment in the interest rate'. 'The economic history of the last century', he wrote, 'has been characterized by a succession of crises.'

> Juglar [1893] in his description of the conditions preceding crises mentions the signs of great prosperity, the enterprise and the speculation of all kinds, the rising prices, the demand for labor, the rising wages, the ambition to become at once rich, the increasing luxury, and the excessive expenditure.
> A crisis is, as Juglar in fact defines it, an arrest of the rise of prices. At higher prices than those already reached purchasers cannot be found. Those who had purchased, hoping to sell again for profit, cannot dispose of their goods.
> (Fisher 1922: 265–6)

Dennis Robertson pointed to

> the numerous errors of judgment and forecast which mark the course of a trade boom – these things are evils in themselves and bring evils more spectacular in their train. We have a right to ask that our monetary system should be so managed as to restrain and not to promote them....
> Central Banks can up to a point check the expansion of the money-supply; and ... while we cannot be sure that their power to do so is in all circumstances complete, there is good reason to believe that if it were used earlier and more resolutely than it has sometimes been in the past, many of the evil excrescences of a trade boom could be lopped away.
> (Robertson 1928: 159, 163)

Those who wanted an elastic currency and lender of last resort were powerfully criticized in Wilbur Aldrich's *Money and Credit* (1903: 96–7). It was futile, he argued (like the Bank of England's Thomson Hankey), to try to ameliorate panics without addressing their causes. It was impossible

> to find a way by which ... over-speculation and conversion of liquid capital into fixed capital can be made to go on forever, by legislation or intervention of government.... When over-production and inflation of credit have brought on a crisis, no currency juggle can prevent losses.... Any permanent plan of extending credit in face of crises would simply be discounted and used up before the pinch of the succeeding crisis.... The true time for banks to begin to prepare for a panic and provide for their reserves, is before a careless extension of credit in the mad industrial race which invariably precedes a panic.

Economists are correct, in some respects, to point to the Fed's learning, but when it comes to price expectations and their dependence on the credibility of monetary policy, economists have the most to learn. From 1936 into the 1970s, during one of the greatest inflations in history (Brown 1955), macroeconomic theory was dominated by fixed-price models while the primary concern of Martin and others at the Fed was inflation.

The Fed's model

> The economy grew continuously ... from late 1982 through mid-1990, [and] unrealistic expectations of what the economy could deliver seem to have developed. In addition, households and businesses apparently were skeptical that inflation would continue to decline and, based on their experience during the 1970s, may even have expected it to rebound. As a consequence, many may have shaped their investment decisions importantly on expectations of inflation-induced appreciation of asset prices, rather than on more fundamental economic considerations. In the commercial real estate sector, assessments of profit potential ... went too far, leading to an unavoidable period of retrenchment.
>
> (Greenspan 1993)

Overview

Greenspan's analysis of events leading to the 1990–91 recession would not have been out of place earlier, as he realized: 'It is not that this process was unforeseeable in the latter ... 1980s.... The sharp increase in debt and the unprecedented liquidation of corporate equity clearly were unsustainable and would require a period of adjustment', which he compared to the 'classic busts ... that seemed invariably to follow speculative booms in pre-World War II economic history' (Greenspan 1992). In July 1994, during another expansion, he regretted that 'market participants in designing their investment strategies [particularly the accumulation of inventories] seemed to give little weight to the possibility that interest rates would rise' (Greenspan 1994b). Out of the nineteenth century!

Greenspan wanted price stability but did not want to be tied to a target. His 2002 warning that 'a specific numerical [inflation] target would represent an unhelpful and false precision' echoed Benjamin Strong. 'Rather', Greenspan said, 'price stability is best thought of as an environment in which inflation is so low and stable over time that it does not materially enter into the decisions of households and firms.' Strong (1930) had said that

> It should be the policy of the Federal Reserve System ... to maintain the volume of credit and currency in this country at such a level so that, to the extent that the volume has any influence upon prices, it cannot possibly become the means for either promoting speculative advances in prices, or of a depression of prices.
>
> (Speech to Farm Bureau Convention, December 1922)

Chairman Paul Volcker said in 1983:

> A workable definition of reasonable 'price stability' would seem to me to be a situation in which expectations of generally rising (or falling) prices over a considerable period are not a pervasive influence on economic and financial

behavior. Stated more positively, 'stability' would imply that decision-making should be able to proceed on the basis that 'real' and 'nominal' values are substantially the same over the planning horizon – and that planning horizons should be suitably long.

(Orphanides 2006)

The declarations by Fed officials in the 1990s (discussed in Chapter 6) that monetary policy is a single tool with the single goal of price stability, which is 'inextricably part of a broader concern about the basic stability of the financial and economic system' (Volcker 1994; Greenspan 1994a), were anticipated by an embattled Martin who regretted that the Fed had been 'too easy' during the 1954–57 expansion. He told the Joint Economic Committee:

If we had the whole period to go through again, I think I would be inclined toward having a little more restriction in monetary policy from the latter part of 1954 to date. If we had been more restrictive, we would have had more influence, not that monetary and credit policy is the only thing, but it would have been a more stabilizing force in the economy.

(US Congress 1957: 1304–5)

The continuity of public statements was, when the Fed was able, matched by its behavior. The similarity of the views of Fed chairmen expressed through a history that is approaching a century reflects the stability of their understanding of the economy and the role of the central bank. The remainder of this section is a chronological account of these expressions and accompanying actions. Although decisions are made by committees, it is helpful to organize the story around leading personalities: Benjamin Strong, head of the Federal Reserve Bank of New York, 1914–28, and the longest-serving and most-influential chairmen of the Board of Governors of the Federal Reserve System, Marriner Eccles, 1934–48, William M. Martin, Jr, 1951–70, Arthur Burns, 1970–78, Paul Volcker, 1979–87, Alan Greenspan, 1987–2006, and Ben Bernanke, 2006–. Strong was the leader in the Fed's early years because of his personality, the financial importance of New York, and the focus of the Fed's operations on the financial markets. Power was centralized by the Banking Act of 1935. Until then, the chief policymaking group was the open-market committee of Reserve Banks, led by New York. The Reserve Banks also decided their discount rates, although changes were subject to the Board's approval. The 1935 Act formalized the Federal Open Market Committee, with the chair of the Board of Governors in Washington also chair of the FOMC: which has 12 members, the seven members of the Board, the President of the Federal Reserve Bank of New York, and the remaining four rotated among the other Reserve Bank presidents.

We will see that the 1935 power shift from New York to Washington was cosmetic, with the attention given to the financial markets – New York – largely unchanged. The most space in the account of the Fed's model is given to its earliest, most complete, and still enduring expression that came out of New York.

1922–32[1]

We begin after the Treasury released the Fed from its support of government bond prices. Although that release came at the end of 1919, postwar price fluctuations did not settle enough to permit a 'normal' monetary policy until the beginning of 1922. The stability of the model that was developed in these years was verified by successive observers. From the 1920s through the 1960s, it was termed the 'Strong' or 'free-reserves' rule. Elmus Wicker (1969a) wrote that the 'period between 1922 and 1933 reveals a record of fundamental consistency and harmony with no sharp breaks in either the logic or interpretation of monetary policy'.[2] He saw that consistency in the rule outlined by Strong at a Governors' Conference in April 1926:

> As a guide to the timing and extent of any [open-market] purchases which might appear desirable, one of the best guides would be the amount of borrowing by member banks in principal centers.... Our experience has shown that when New York City banks are borrowing in the neighborhood of $100 million or more, there is then some real pressure for reducing loans, and money rates tend to be markedly higher than the discount rate. On the other hand, when borrowings of these banks are negligible, as in 1924, the money situation tends to be less elastic and if gold imports take place, there is liable to be some credit inflation.... In the event of business liquidation now appearing it would seem advisable to keep the New York City banks out of debt beyond something in the neighborhood of $50 million. It would probably be well if some similar rule could be applied to the Chicago banks, although the amount would, of course, be smaller and the difficulties greater because of the influence of the New York market.
> (Chandler 1958: 240)

The Strong rule was applied in 1924, 1927, and 1930 (see Figure 7.2, where bank free reserves are inversely related to their borrowing from the Fed, explained in the *1951–69* subsection), and also explains the increase in reserve requirements to mop up the excess reserves that accumulated in the mid-1930s. The Fed's inactivity during the Great Depression has been attributed to Strong's death but his successors were faithful to his legacy. The Fed assisted the money market in the wake of the October 1929 crash, and when assistance was no longer required, that is, when the New York and Chicago banks were out of debt to the Fed, it was ended. The Fed's disregard of the waves of bank failures during the Great Depression was not a failure to assist the money markets. The bank failures of the Great Depression were regional insolvencies that did not impinge on money-center liquidity. When that liquidity was threatened by the international crisis of September 1931, the Fed stepped in to offset the loss of gold.

The Board's 1923 *Annual Report* remains the most complete official statement of its model. (The later large-scale econometric models of the Board's scholars, interesting though they might have been regarding the workings of the economy, were not, as we saw in Chapter 6, guides to policy). The first step in the development of its model was the recognition that the gold standard constraint taken for granted by the Federal Reserve Act was inoperative in the 1920s. The international monetary system had been transformed by the Great War and its aftermath. Gold came to the United States in great quantities for war materials and safety. The nation's monetary gold stock (in billions) rose from about $1.5 at the end of 1914, to $2.9 at the end of 1918, and $4.0 in early 1924, from which it changed little until revaluation in 1934 (Federal Reserve Board 1943: 536–7). Gold's restraint had been loosened but the Fed was determined to prevent its large stock from fueling excessive credit.

The Fed resisted the efforts of members of Congress to impose an explicit policy rule based on inflation (or anything else) (Chandler 1958: 202–3). The 1923 *Report* noted that

> price fluctuations proceed from a great variety of causes, most of which lie outside the range of influence of [Federal Reserve] credit.... No credit system could undertake to perform the function of regulating credit by reference to prices without failing in the endeavor.

Furthermore, since the 'price index records an accomplished fact', a policy based on it would lack timeliness and predictions would be unreliable.

However, having limited its responsibility, further discussion brings us to prices as an important goal or guide, after all. We begin with the determinants of credit.

> No statistical mechanism alone, however carefully contrived, can furnish an adequate guide to credit administration. Credit is an intensely human institution and as such reflects the moods and impulses of the community – its hopes, its fears, its expectations. The business and credit situation at any particular time is weighted and charged with these invisible factors. They are elusive and can not be fitted into any mechanical formula, but the fact that they are refractory to methods of the statistical laboratory makes them neither nonexistent nor unimportant. They are factors which must always patiently and skillfully be evaluated as best they may and dealt with in any banking administration that is animated by a desire to secure to the community the results of an efficient credit system. In its ultimate analysis credit administration is not a matter of mechanical rules, but is and must be a matter of judgment – of judgment concerning each specific credit situation at the particular moment of time when it has arisen or is developing.

Fortunately, there were 'among these factors a sufficient number which are determinable in their character, and also measurable, to relieve the problem of credit administration of much of its indefiniteness, and therefore give to it a substantial foundation of ascertainable fact'. Those factors were 'in large part recognized in the Federal reserve act, [which] therefore, itself goes far toward indicating standards by which the adequacy or inadequacy of the amount of credit provided by the Federal reserve banks may be tested'. The Act had

> laid down as the broad principle for the guidance of the Federal reserve banks and of the Federal Reserve Board in the discharge of their functions with respect to the administration of the credit facilities of the Federal reserve banks the principle of 'accommodating commerce and business'.

How do we know when commerce and business, as opposed to 'speculation', are accommodated? The Act included a further guide to Fed credit by limiting its discounts to real bills, but that was insufficient. There were

> no automatic devices or detectors for determining, when credit is granted by a Federal reserve bank in response to a rediscount demand, whether the occasion of the rediscount was an extension of credit by the member bank for nonproductive use. Paper offered by a member bank when it rediscounts with a Federal reserve bank may disclose the purpose for which the loan evidenced by that paper was made, but it does not disclose what use is to be made of the proceeds of the rediscount.

The problem of determining when credit is excessive or deficient relative to production and trade remains. We are given an insight into this determination by the Board's expression of concern for prices and speculation. Although

> the interrelationship of prices and credit is too complex to admit of any simple statement, still less of a formula of invariable application, [they may] be regarded as the outcome of common causes that work in the economic and business situation. The same conditions which predispose to a rise of prices also predispose to an increased demand for credit.

We come back to prices in the end.

1933–51

The president and Treasury largely controlled monetary policy from the coming of the New Deal in 1933 until 1951. The inflation of the late 1930s was made possible by the devaluation of the dollar in terms of gold and the gold inflows that followed. The 1941–45 war effort was financed by Fed credit, over which the Fed did not regain control until nearly six years after the war's end.

An exception to the Fed's loss of control in the 1930s was its new power over reserve requirements. Legal reserve ratios were fixed by the Federal Reserve Act of 1913 until the Banking Act of 1935 gave the Federal Reserve Board authority to change them. Conditions inviting the new instrument's use soon appeared. Excess reserves were large, and a potential for inflationary finance if banks decided to lend them. They needed to be 'mopped up'. Raising discount rates would be useless because banks had no reason to borrow from the Fed. Nor would security sales do the job because excess reserves exceeded the Fed's portfolio. The only course seemed to be an increase in reserve requirements (Federal Reserve Board *Annual Report* 1935: 231–2; Anderson 1968: 78–9).

Required-reserve ratios were doubled between 1936 and 1937, reducing excess reserves from $3.2 (in billions) to $0.9. However, by October 1938, they had regained their 1936 level as bank loans were cut 10 percent during the severe economic decline that lasted from May 1937 to June 1938 (Federal Reserve Board 1943: 400–1). Excess reserves had been large because of the lack of profitable investments and fears of deposit losses. Banks wanted their excess reserves. They were 'excess' only in the legal sense that reserves exceeded official requirements. The Fed's actions have been called 'inexcusable' (Timberlake 1993: 295), but they were not inexplicable. They were a straightforward application of the Strong rule.

1951–69

The Strong rule, now called the 'free-reserves guide', resumed and was observed into the 1960s and beyond (Brunner and Meltzer 1964b; Andersen 1969; Calomiris and Wheelock 1998). Free reserves are bank excess reserves less borrowing from the Fed: $R_f = R_e - R_b$. Excess reserves were small in the 1920s but grew in the 1930s and remained substantial for several years. This is why, as seen in Figures 7.2–7.5, free reserves were continuously negative in the 1920s but often positive thereafter. High bank borrowing from the Fed normally corresponds with low excess reserves. The Fed's independence was constrained much of this period, but the experience is instructive because it was made to fight for, and enunciate, its model.

The 1952 *Report* of the Ad hoc Subcommittee of the Federal Open Market Committee (FOMC) on the *Government Securities Market* was a technical statement of the best method of achieving the Fed's objectives in its new environment. After 18 years under the direction of the Treasury, primarily pegging government securities prices, the Fed had regained its independence in the Treasury–Federal Reserve Accord of March 1951. The Fed was given the freedom 'to minimize monetization of the public debt', and an FOMC subcommittee was formed to study how to use that freedom most effectively. The Fed's belief system was indicated by the declaration of the *Report* (which the FOMC accepted) that the

> maintenance of a relatively fixed pattern of prices and yields in the market for securities was inconsistent with its primary monetary and credit responsibilities ... – that a freer market ... would lessen inflationary pressures and better promote the proper accommodation of commerce, industry, and agriculture. [A] securities market, in which market forces of supply and demand and of savings and investment were permitted to express themselves in market prices and market yields, was indispensable to the effective execution of monetary policies directed toward financial equilibrium and

economic stability at a high level of activity without detriment to the long-run purchasing power of the dollar.

(FOMC 1952: 259)

Free markets are 'least likely to be seriously disturbed' by open market operations if they are in 'very short-term Government securities' (mainly Treasury bills), the *Report* (267) stated. It was in effect concerned with the technicalities of achieving the goals of 1923.

Economists objected that the Fed was giving up one of its most powerful instruments in order to protect securities firms from risk. They contended that its responsibilities for economic stability required the Fed to be ready to enforce significant changes in long-term rates (Hansen 1955; Ahearn 1963: 65–9). Sidney Weintraub (1955) complained that 'Economic stabilization would suffer a sharp setback if the view took root that the central banking mechanism was designed to protect bondholders from changes in capital values rather than reserved for broader conceptions of economic policy.'

Keynesians were farther than the Fed from Keynes's belief that credible interest rates promoted stability. The always-ready revision of interest rates implied by Keynesian policy models violated Keynes's (1936: 203–4) warning, discussed in Chapter 3 above, that 'a monetary policy which strikes public opinion as being experimental in character' is less likely to succeed than one 'rooted in strong conviction'.

Nothing was given up, the subcommittee's *Report* stated, because open market operations 'initiated in the short-term sector [would spread] to other sectors of the market' through the arbitrage activities of investors 'who are constantly balancing their investments to take advantage of shifts in prices and yields between the different sectors of the market' (267). The force of arbitrage had been demonstrated during the Fed's pegs of long and short yields at 2.5 and 0.375 percent during World War II. The elimination of the risk of long terms that justified the spread under free conditions resulted in the Fed's ownership of 0.2 percent of the former and 92 percent of the latter as the public chose the higher risk-free yield (Wicker 1969b).

When Chairman Martin told the Senate Banking and Currency Committee (US Congress 1956b: 5), 'Our policy is to lean against the winds of deflation or inflation, whichever way they are blowing', he was consistent with the Strong-free-reserves rule. He also wanted to lean in a way that did not disrupt the financial markets – small movements in short-rates in the tradition of central banking, like the Fed in the 1920s and the Bank of England before 1914 (Hawtrey 1938). Friedman (1959: 93) might have been right when he criticized this policy as destabilizing because the effects of leaning against today's wind may not be realized until the wind has turned. However the constant-money-growth rule that he (and Mayer in Chapter 6 above) proposed in place of discretionary interest rates had no precedent in the thinking or behavior of central bankers.

A further, political, reason for 'bills only' might have been independence from government pressure to depress long rates. If so, it lasted until 1961, when the new administration pressured the Fed to 'twist' the yield curve in the direction of low long rates (to encourage fixed investment) and high short rates (to attract short-term foreign capital) by buying long terms and selling short terms. 'Operation twist' was ineffective, although the Fed did not try very hard to thwart the arbitrage that was bound to defeat it (Wood 2005: 256–61).

Fed actions in the 1960s were outcomes of conflicts between its preferences and administration pressures for monetary expansion. Martin found himself at the head of an FOMC divided between sound-money conservatives and easy-money members whose number was increased by Kennedy and Johnson appointees (Maisel 1973: 69–70). The battle over monetary policy became more intense with the pressures of Vietnam. The discount rate was raised in 1965, over Johnson's opposition, as free reserves became negative. Inflation was not slowed as the federal deficit continued to rise, and the Fed capitulated in the face of the 'credit crunch' of late 1966. Rising interest rates threatened the solvency of institutions making long-term loans, and inspired disintermediation as market rates rose above legal ceiling rates on deposits. 'The squeeze on banks' forced them to unload 'a heavy volume of securities that had nowhere to go even at distress prices', New York Reserve Bank President Alfred Hayes (1970) observed, and the Fed increased its open-market purchases.

The next time, in 1969, Martin resolved to stay the course, and quarreled with a president, Richard Nixon, who did not wish to bear the political costs of ending the inflation that he inherited. Chairman Paul McCracken of his Council of Economic Advisors hoped that inflation could be slowed without causing unemployment through a policy of 'gradualism', which in another time of decision Paul Volcker dismissed as a 'comforting word meaning that nothing very drastic is going to happen' (Neikirk 1987: 98). As quietly as possible – 'no announcement effect' – Governors Daane, Robertson, and Maisel urged (Maisel 1973: 75–6). However, Martin realized in 1969, like Volcker in 1979, Strong in the 1920s, and the Bank of England in the nineteenth century, that the markets needed to be convinced that something *was* going to happen. Worried about the administration's commitment and the market's expectations, the Fed raised the discount rate in December 1968, before Nixon took office. In February 1969, Martin apologized to the Joint Economic Committee for past errors and promised they would not be repeated. The Fed had been 'overly optimistic in anticipating immediate benefits from fiscal restraint' (US Congress 1969: 648–51):

> We must deal with a heritage of cost and price increases that is continuing to generate further cost and price increases, and – importantly – has become deeply embedded in business and consumer expectation. After several years of rapidly rising prices, it is only natural that many spending decisions are motivated now by the fear that prices will be even higher next year, or by the conviction that inflation will bail out even the most marginal speculation.

Despite the temporary income tax surcharge, Martin observed, 'consumers continued to increase their outlays at a rapid rate, drawing on their savings and borrowing heavily to finance both higher taxes and higher spending'. The futility of temporary measures was general.

> Expectations of inflation are deeply embedded,... and speculative fervor is still strong. A slowing in expansion that is widely expected to be temporary is not likely to be enough to eradicate such expectations. [W]e have had quite a credibility gap as to whether we meant business at the Federal Reserve.

The Fed had succumbed to Bagehot's temptation, indicating, 'perhaps unwisely', after the 1966 credit crunch that 'we don't want a recurrence'. '[I]f you don't take some risk in policy you never get any result', Martin said. He addressed the lack of resolve by the administration, which 'has raised the ghost of overkill at the first sign of a few clouds in the sky' (US Congress 1969: 668–9). The *New York Times* reported: 'Martin strongly implied that this will not happen again and that restraint will persist even when there are clear signs the economy is slowing and in the face of some increase in unemployment' (Bremner 2004: 253). He wanted 'market expectations' to understand that 'the Board is unanimous today in meaning business' (US Congress 1969: 668–9, 680).

Money growth slowed and unemployment rose, but inflation remained above 6 percent, and in April 1966, the Fed raised the discount rate. '[T]here is no gadgetry in monetary mechanisms and no device that will save us from our sins', Martin told an audience of bankers in June. 'We're going to have a good deal of pain and suffering before we can solve these things' (Matusow 1998: 25). The Fed kept its nerve until February 1970, when in Arthur Burns's first meeting as Martin's successor, after what Maisel (1973: 25) described as 'the most bitter debate I experienced in my entire service on the FOMC', monetary policy changed direction.

1970–79

'Eisenhower liked to talk about the independence of the Federal Reserve', Burns said at a meeting of the president's economic advisors in February 1969. 'Let's not make that mistake and talk about the independence of the Fed again.' In October, invited to Nixon's office for 'a little chat' shortly before his nomination to the Fed's leadership, Burns was told: 'You see to it – no recession.' Martin is 'six months too late', Burns replied: 'I don't like to be late' (Matusow 1998: 20, 31).

Figure 7.1 shows the steady rise in inflation from 1 to 5 percent per annum in the 1960s, and then the rapid rise to 9 percent in 1973–74. Average inflation in the 1970s was 6.4 percent, compared with 2.3 percent in the 1960s. The rise in inflation was clearly caused by the Fed's expansionary policy, whether measured by the increases in money or the low interest rates relative to inflation. A much discussed question is 'Why did the Fed behave as it did?'

One answer is that the Fed under Burns acted from political motives, first engaging in monetary ease to support Nixon's reelection campaign in 1972, and

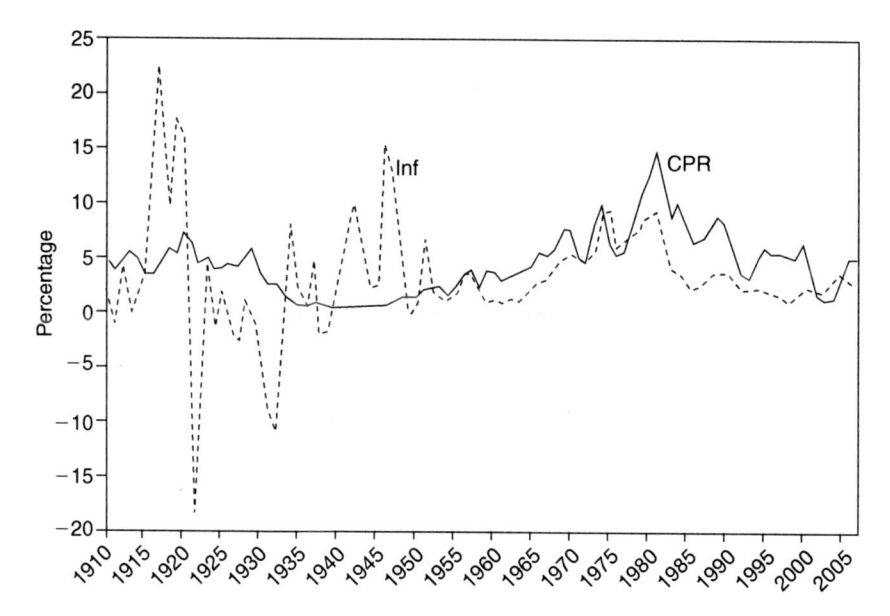

Figure 7.1 Commercial paper rate and inflation, 1910–2007.

then preventing interest rates from rising to reflect inflationary expectations for fear of the short-term costs of disinflation (DeLong 1997). Another answer is that the Fed was pursuing a Phillips-curve policy but the natural rate of output had fallen because of a productivity slowdown. As a result the Fed overestimated full-employment output and the potential benefits of inflation, as suggested in the chapter's opening quotation (Clarida *et al.* 2000). These explanations of the 1970s inflation have been characterized as the difference between poor play (policy) and poor hand (bad luck) (Velde 2004).

A third explanation that differs from the first two in not being driven by the optimizing policy models of economists is that the Fed continued to be guided by the Strong-free-reserves rule, but the relation between free reserves and the economy changed. This might also help explain the Fed's behavior in the Great Depression, and is examined in connection with the estimates reported below.

1979–present

The Fed's escape from the administration's pressures in October 1979 resembled 1951. The public was tired of inflation, Congress resented the president's apparent domination of the Fed, and he was politically weak. In the earlier case, the Korean War had bogged down and President Truman's popularity also suffered from his quarrel with the legendary General Douglas MacArthur. In 1979,

172 *Monetary policy*

President Carter was afflicted by unemployment as well as inflation (stagflation) and threats to his renomination. The Fed's decision to allow interest rates to reflect inflationary expectations and the long-period of high real rates because the market was slow to believe in the new anti-inflationary policy are indicated in Figure 7.1. Its announcement of a monetarist conversion was a political maneuver to enable the Fed to allow interest rates to rise sufficiently to stop inflation. 'Don't look at us; we're just controlling money' (Volcker and Gyohten 1992: 166–9). The Fed has to be careful even when the president is weak: by waiting until the next administration before making the 1951 Accord effective (Figure 7.1 shows that interest rates did not rise significantly until after the 1953–54 recession), and by distancing itself from the unpopular rise in interest rates in 1979.

Low inflation continued under succeeding chairmen: Greenspan (1987–2006) and Ben Bernanke. The latter's first *Monetary Policy Report* to Congress, in February 2006, stated:

> Inflation prospects are important, not just because price stability is in itself desirable and part of the Federal Reserve's mandate from the Congress, but also because price stability is essential for strong and stable growth of output and employment. Stable prices promote long-term economic growth by allowing households and firms to make economic decisions and undertake productive activities with fewer concerns about large or unanticipated changes in the price level and their attendant financial consequences. Experience shows that low and stable inflation and inflation expectations are also associated with greater short-term stability in output and employment, perhaps in part because they give the central bank greater latitude to counter transitory disturbances to the economy.

The Fed's fears of 'too roseate' expectations and 'irrational exuberance' (Greenspan 1996) continue, and a third of its *Monetary Policy Reports* to Congress deals with the financial markets.

Qualifications

Politics

The central hypothesis of this discussion is that the Fed has been guided by its (narrow and persistent financial) interests and information subject to political pressures that emanate from more general concerns of the body politic. Although the Fed is legally a creature of Congress, for much of its existence it has been controlled by the Executive. Monetary policy was directed by the Treasury during and for a year after World War I and from March 1933 to March 1951. As indicated above, some say it was subservient to the Executive, or at least to political motives, from February 1970 to October 1979. Depending on whether the last period should be counted, the Fed lacked independence 20 to 30 of its first 66 years.

The Executive has also sought influence over monetary policy on other occasions – by appointments, meetings, and signals such as public statements and press leaks. So do congressmen. Both are usually on the side of ease, although exceptions have been important (Havrilesky 1993: ch. 2, 4, 9). Congress intervened on the side of price stability by coming to the defense of the Fed's independence of the Executive on four occasions. In 1922, the Fed asked to defend itself before Congress after being attacked for its role in the deflation/recession of 1920–21, which succeeded the inflation of 1918–20. The Senate complied with a resolution to consider all complaints against the Fed, referring them to a previously established Commission of Agricultural Inquiry. The Commission's report was generally favorable to the Fed, but criticized its lack of resistance to the Treasury's pressures to support government finance. With more resistance, 'much of the expansion, speculation, and extravagance which characterized the postwar period could have been avoided' (Elliott 1960; US Congress 1922: 219–23, 296–305). This support of the Fed's independence helped it weather attacks during the Great Depression. The administration was unhappy with the Fed – 'a weak reed to lean on in time of trouble', President Hoover (1952 ii: 212) called it – and the House of Representatives passed several bills that would have required the Fed to counter the deflation, but neither the administration nor the Senate would infringe the Fed's independence (Krooss 1969: 2661–2).

The building resistance of the Fed to the Treasury's bond support program after World War II, with growing congressional support as inflation persisted, was noted above. The Fed's decision to free interest rates in 1979 followed a succession of congressional actions to monitor monetary policy. The 'barrage' of legislation, as Havrilesky (1993: 111) called it, directed at the Fed in the 1970s was partly inspired by Congress's resentment of its subservience to the president, who had used it to bring the monetary expansion during the 1972 election campaign that foreshadowed the 1973–75 recession. Congress directed the Fed to announce targets and testify biannually to the House and Senate Banking Committees (Carlson 1979). The Fed might have counted on Congress's protection in 1979, as in 1951, when it turned from the easy money preferred by the administration.

A fourth instance of substantial congressional support – perhaps more than the Fed wanted – was in the late 1980s, when Stephen Neal, chairman of the House Subcommittee on Domestic Monetary Policy, proposed a 'joint resolution directing the Federal Open Market Committee of the Federal Reserve System to adopt and pursue monetary policies leading to, and maintaining, zero inflation' (*Congressional Record*, 101st Congress, 1st session, 1 August 1989: H4845). This may be seen as a reaction to the record peacetime deficits of the Reagan administration (1981–89), the Fed's backsliding of 1984–86, when its credit rose faster than at any other time since World War II, and the succeeding restriction. Volcker's retirement (in 1987) was probably hastened by Treasury pressures and easy-money appointees to the Federal Reserve Board. Neal criticized the Fed's pursuit of a 'wide array of goals and objectives, many of which are in conflict with each other, or are simply beyond the reach of monetary policy'.

If the Fed is presumed to be ... coresponsible for helping attain virtually all things economic desired by any administration or Congress, how can it hold out, consistently, against political pressures to bend policy this way or that, to provide temporary relief for whatever current problems dominate the political landscape? The best defense against these pressures would be a clear definition of the single objective – zero inflation – which monetary policy can and should achieve, over a reasonable period of time, and which must not be compromised for any other purpose.

The resolution was more limiting than the Fed traditionally preferred. Price stability was important to them, but Strong and Martin had wanted the flexibility to respond to special problems. On the other hand, the support that Chairman Greenspan and several Reserve Bank presidents gave the Neal resolution might be understood as a willingness to yield some of that flexibility (to the extent that they would have to make a case for it when it was needed) in return for the independence to pursue price stability; and who is to choose the price index and the period over which it (or part of it) is to be stable? Central banks with government-assigned inflation targets have considerable discretion (Bernanke et al. 1999). The Fed's confidence in its strength vis à vis the Executive was strikingly revealed in 1988, when Greenspan publicly 'objected quite strongly' to a letter from the Treasury's chief economist urging it to speed up the economy (Havrilesky 1993: 37).

In several countries, the government (through the finance minister) sets an inflation target for which the central bank is responsible. This procedure is not available in the United States because of the constitutional separation of the powers of the executive and legislature (Wood 2007). Congress is normally (excepting crises) as unwilling to delegate its control of monetary policy as the budget. Its practice has been to enact general rules regarding 'employment, production, and purchasing power', and loosely monitor the Fed. Congress has established no body with the authority to be more specific. It is up to the Fed to try to influence, but in the end accommodate the sense of Congress.

We saw in Chapter 4 that the end of the Cold War and the onset of the War on Terror were accompanied respectively by a fall and rise in the federal deficit. It is reasonable to wonder why the Fed has not monetized the post-2001 deficit. An answer suggested by the above discussion is that Congress's resumption of its close watch on monetary policy (begun in the 1970s) is here to stay, reinforced at present by criticisms of the president and the war in Iraq. On the other hand, this episode may not be a real test of the Fed's independence of the Executive because the deficit is not primarily due to the war or other fiscal emergency. Table 4.1 shows that the effect of the current war on the deficit is unusual in three respects: a smaller increase in war spending (as a percentage of GDP), the increase in war spending is exceeded by that in civilian spending, and there has been a reduction in revenues (due to the 2001 tax cut) as a percentage of GDP (20.8 to 18.8). The former percentage would have produced a $110 billion surplus in fiscal 2007. The independence of the Fed has not been tested by the War on Terror.

The monetary standard

Although the dollar was not completely severed from gold until 1971, its devaluation by act of Congress in 1934 effectively removed the gold standard's restraint on monetary policy. The country remained on the gold standard officially, but there could have been little faith in its constraint. The elimination of gold reserve requirements on Federal Reserve liabilities when they threatened to bind in the 1960s preceded the final suspension of the standard in the 1970s (Federal Reserve Board 1975: 896).

Federal Reserve rhetoric in the 1950s was not much different from the 1920s. It continued to worry about inflation and inflationary expectations. An explanation of the post-1933 inflation which fits our financial markets framework is that in combating speculative movements the Fed could soften credit restrictions. This imparted an expansionary bias to Fed credit. Stopping inflation has long-term benefits and short-term costs, and freedom from the gold constraint permits the Fed to lessen the latter. Bankers' and central bankers' aversion to price changes used to be symmetric, even with a little more aversion to inflation. The end of the gold constraint reversed the bias. In 1962, as on other occasions, Chairman Martin assured a congressional committee that monetary policy had not been too tight in recent years. 'We just have not erred that way. The errors have been the other way and that is what has caused us so much trouble' (US Congress 1962: 634).

Estimates

The Strong-free-reserves rule is evident in Figures 7.2–7.5, which show the inverse relation between free reserves and interest rates, both the Fed discount rate, i_d, and the federal funds rate, i_f. The fed funds rate has been the chief monetary-policy instrument most of the post-World War II period. It was not reported regularly until 1953, so another low-risk short-term rate – on bankers acceptances – is used in place of i_f until then. The discount rate was the principal instrument until the 1930s, and has been used since in a supporting role.

The periods chosen are those in which the Fed's independence was greatest, although 1970–78 and parts of the others are questionable. Some of the periods are adjusted for estimation because, in the first, the Fed had to wait through 1920–21 to allow the economy to settle down sufficiently to be amenable to a systematic policy. In the second, the Fed's independence under the Accord was not applied until 1953. In the last, several years – possibly to 1987 – were required for the public's inflationary expectations to adjust to the new regime, that is, for the Fed's credibility to be established. The high real rates in the meantime are seen in Figure 7.1.

Estimates of the rule are reported in Table 7.1, which reveals that the Strong-free-reserves relation has been significant throughout the Fed's history when it was free to target interest rates. Specifically, the left-hand side of the table shows that the change in the New York Reserve Bank's discount rate, i_d (the

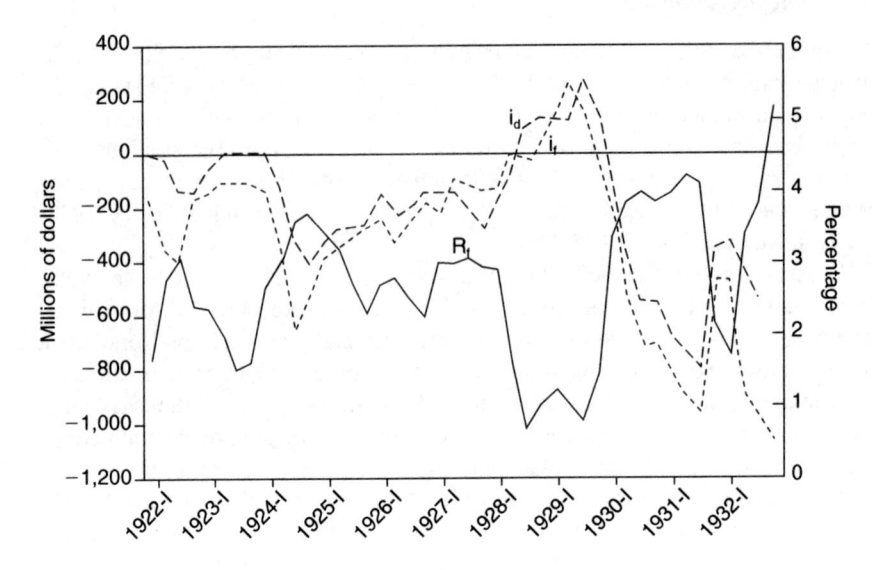

Figure 7.2 Fed discount rate (i_d), short-term market rate (i_f), and free reserves (R_f) (quarterly averages, 1922–32).

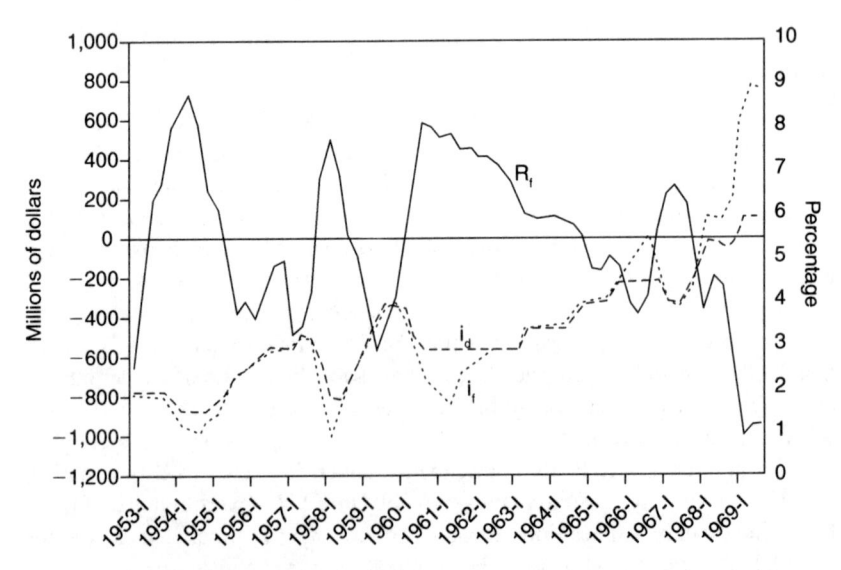

Figure 7.3 Fed discount rate (i_d), Fed funds rate (i_f), and free reserves (R_f) (quarterly averages, 1953–69).

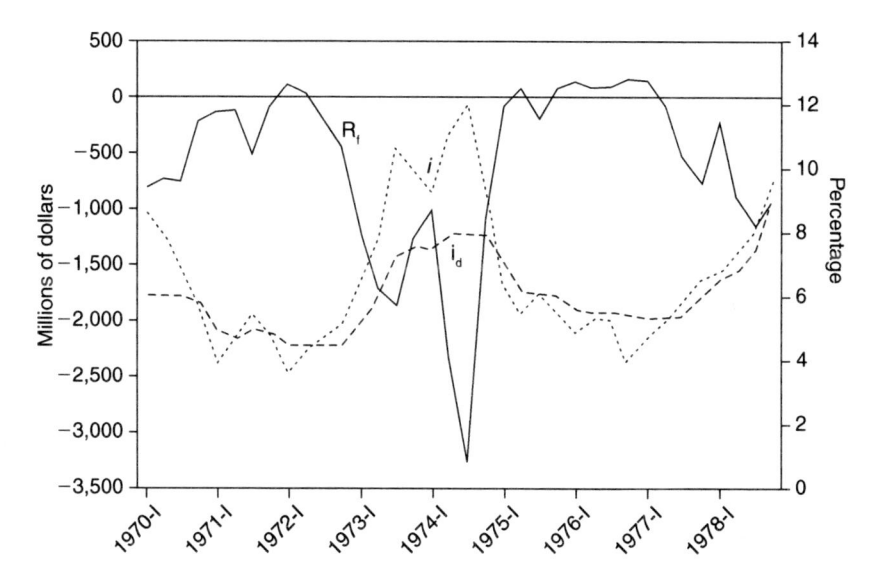

Figure 7.4 Fed discount rate (i_d), Fed funds rate (i_f), and free reserves (R_f) (quarterly averages, 1970–78).

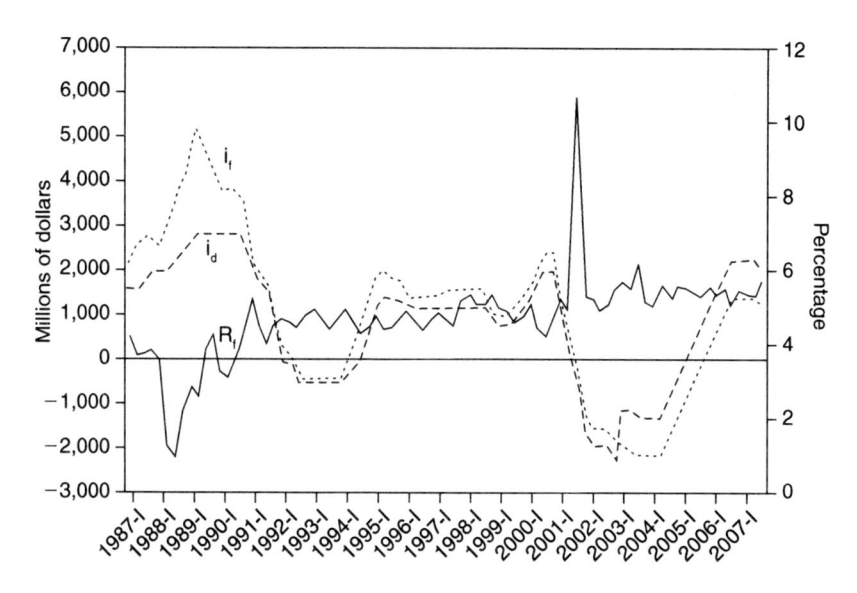

Figure 7.5 Fed discount rate (i_d), Fed funds rate (i_f), and free reserves (R_f) (quarterly averages, 1987–2007).

Table 7.1 Fed discount (i_d) and Fed funds (i_f) rate responses to free reserves (R_f) (changes in quarterly averages)

	Dependent variable di_d					Dependent variable di_f				
	Constant	dR_f	di_{d-1}	R^2/h	b	Constant	dR_f	di_{f-1}	R^2/h	b
1922.1–	0.00	−1.38[a]	0.13	0.38	—	0.019	−2.11[a]	0.01	0.49	−2.13
1932.4	(0.07)	(4.77)	(1.11)	−1.31		(0.29)	(6.16)	(0.08)	0.60	
1953.1–	0.04	−0.73[a]	0.38[a]	0.49	1.59	0.060	−1.53[a]	0.38[a]	0.61	−2.46
1969.4	(1.55)	(6.28)	(4.33)	2.17		(1.81)	(9.19)	(5.29)	0.60	
1970.1–	0.02	−0.32[a]	0.63[a]	0.47	1.18	−0.014	−1.54[a]	0.25[a]	0.62	−2.05
1978.1	(0.39)	(3.23)	(4.77)	2.39		(0.10)	(6.68)	(2.23)	2.43	
1987.1–	0.01	−0.11	0.60[a]	0.35	0.86	0.001	−0.36[a]	0.75[a]	0.58	−1.44
2007.3	(0.13)	(1.27)	(6.72)	1.39	−0.28	(0.05)	(4.47)	(10.38)	−0.31	

Sources: Federal Reserve Board (1943, 1945) and releases.

Notes
i_d = Federal Reserve Bank of NY discount rate.
i_f = bankers acceptances through 1952, then fed funds rate (%).
R_f = free reserves in $000s. Absolute values of t statistics in parentheses. R^2 adjusted for degrees of freedom. Durbin's h does not reject the hypothesis of no serial correlation.
a Indicates significantly different from zero at the 5% level.
Data adjustments:
R_f is for Fed and member commercial banks to 1979 (estimated before 1929, when excess reserves were not reported, by assuming excess as a proportion of total reserves constant at the 1929 ratio; R_f depended principally on R_b) then for all depository institutions. The 9/11/01 spike in R_f was smoothed for the regressions.

discount rates of the other 11 Reserve Banks are closely attuned), responded negatively to the change in the free reserves, R_f. The right-hand side does the same for i_f. Free reserves were not much discussed after the 1960s although they continued to be considered (Thornton 2006), and the Fed funds rate has remained consistent with the Strong-free-reserves rule.

The lagged interest rate is used as an independent variable to account for smoothly changing interest rates. It has long been observed that the interest-rate decisions of central banks respond slowly to economic changes (Wicksell 1898: ch. 11; Fisher 1930: ch. 19; Hawtrey 1938: 313–14). Arguments for why the Fed might engage in interest smoothing include: (i) forward-looking expectations in which agents expect interest changes to continue, so that the Fed moves cautiously to avoid excessive market responses; (ii) uncertainty about data and the transmission mechanism, which are subject to revision; and (iii), consistent with the Fed as bankers' patron, interest smoothing supplies them with information and risk-reducing services (Sack and Wieland 2000; Skaggs 1984; Goodfriend 1993). Lagged interest rates are statistically significant every period except under the gold standard, when the serial correlations of inflation and interest rates were low. Expectations of a quick reversal of deviations from normal rates were strong, and the central bank's freedom to control those movements was limited.

The interest-smoothing model may be written as follows. The first equation states that the preferred interest rate responds negatively to free reserves.

$$i_t^* = a - bR_t \tag{7.1}$$

but adjusts partially such that

$$i_t = i_{t-1} + c(i_t^* - i_{t-1}) \text{ where } 0 \leq c \leq 1 \tag{7.2}$$

Adjustment to the interest target is zero or complete as c is 0 or 1. Substituting (7.2) into (7.1) gives

$$i_t = ac - bcR_t + (1-c)i_{t-1} \tag{7.3}$$

Implied estimates of b are indicated in Table 7.1. Those for i_f are larger than for i_d because the former has been more variable (responsive).

The Strong-free-reserves rule captured a good part of Fed behavior in every period, even in 1970–78, when the response of i_f to R_f was nearly the same as in 1953–69. (The response of i_d relative to i_f declined throughout.) These results, in combination with the great price changes of the Great Depression and the 1970s, indicate that the Fed's model was at times an insufficient guide to price stability. Commercial bank borrowing from the Fed fell relative to aggregate output during 1930–32. The low borrowing led the Fed to believe that its policy was easy despite the great falls in money and prices. 'Fed officials believed that their policies were as responsive to changes in economic activity as they had been during the 1920s' (Wheelock 1990). In fact, they were more responsive to R_f, with the absolute value of the coefficient rising from − 1.52 during 1922–29 to − 2.58 during 1930–32 (compared with the − 2.11 shown in Table 7.1 for 1922–32) Didn't they know what was happening to the economy at large? Perhaps, but the focus of their actions was the financial markets. Although the rhetoric differed in the 1970s, when aggregates were much discussed, the problem may have been of the same kind but in the opposite direction – with R_f understating rather than overstating inflation. Implications of these failures for revisions in the conduct of monetary policy are considered in the conclusion of this chapter.

The smaller estimated responses in the last period may be due to deviations from that rule by Fed lending to distressed banks and responding to other financial crises (although the 9/11/01 spike was smoothed for the regressions); or perhaps to improved credibility such that a given change in the rate induced a more serious response. This is consistent with the greater variance of R_f (note the spread of ±2,200, which exceeds other periods) relative to that of i_f during 1987–2007 than other periods.

This simple model of the Fed's behavior over the long term is only a beginning, and we should not exclude the possibility of other influences on monetary policy, such as gold and the stock-market before and during the Great Depression (Hamilton 1987; Eichengreen 1992; Siklos 2008). However, although they might have had indirect effects through bank reserves, gold and stock-market variables do not improve the explanations of i_d and i_f in Table 7.1 (Wood 2008b). Simple though it is, the model presented here captures a considerable degree of stability in the Fed's behavior when its interest-rate instruments were available. It must be mentioned, however, that our estimates stop short of the great increase in Fed lending in response to the subprime mortgage crisis of 2008.

A new theory

The focus of the Strong-free-reserves rule on banking and the financial markets has little appeal for economists, who prefer to explain monetary policy within their own aggregate framework. The most popular model among economists in recent years has been the Taylor rule, the name given to the following equation, which according to John Taylor (1993) explained monetary policy during 1987–92.

$$i_{ft}=p_t+r^*+0.5(p_t-p_t^*)+0.5Y_{gt}=a+bp_t+cY_{gt} \qquad (7.4)$$

where p_t is inflation over the past year, i_f is the Fed funds rate, p_t^* is desired inflation, r^* is the equilibrium real Fed funds rate, Y_{gt} is the output gap, and the data are quarterly averages. The constant term in the second equation is made up of the desired values, and b and c are free to be estimated instead of using Taylor's fixed values.

Taylor's equation does not fit well outside his original period (or even then when the variables are differenced to reduce autocorrelation) without substantial econometric massaging (Hetzel 2008: 278–9). It also bears a strong resemblance to the Phillips Curve that often traced the data but was impotent for policy. However, because the Taylor rule has become the standard way that economists look at monetary policy (Asso *et al.* 2007), it is worthwhile to compare it with the Strong-free-reserves rule.

The left-hand side of Table 7.2 shows estimates of the Taylor rule as stated in the second equation of (7.4); the right-hand side of the table adds the Taylor equation to free reserves. Both expressions include the lagged interest rate. Comparing the left side of Table 7.1 with the right side of Table 7.2, we see that the Taylor rule underperforms the Strong-free-reserves rule in all four periods, although not by much in the last period. Official references to inflation and the income gap are cited as evidence of the use of the Taylor rule (Orphanides 2003), but these variables are often correlated with free reserves. Changing i in light of output and inflation may be difficult to distinguish from responses to free reserves. Strong and his colleagues believed that free reserves signaled loan demands which varied with the strength of the economy and inflation. The models might be distinguished somewhat by examining whether inflation and the output gap enhance the explanatory power of the Strong-free-reserves rule. The right sides of Tables 7.1 and 7.2 indicate 'not much'.

The frequent significance of Y_g in both models in Table 7.2 suggests that the Fed was attentive to economic activity beyond its effect on free reserves. *GNP* was not reported before the 1940s, but it may be the best summary of the wide range of activities reported in government and private sources, and discussed by policymakers.

Conclusion

Federal Reserve monetary policy has been more stable than is generally appreciated. When not being used to monetize the deficit, it has pursued financial stability. It is true, as the chapter's opening quotation suggested, that to understand monetary policy we must account for policymakers' knowledge of the economy. That knowledge was explored in this chapter, and was found to be firmly grounded in a long and coherent history of banking practices in which expectations have been a paramount concern. Bankers and central bankers have been ahead of economists in this regard. Difficulties arise when we try to explain stable monetary policy by variable economic theory.

Its stability does not mean that monetary policy has always been appropriate. The concentration on the financial markets might avoid some errors but neglect of the wider economy opens the door to others. Congress and the electorate distanced themselves from monetary control when they delegated policy to an expert body. The Fed can be compared to Schumpeter's managers, accustomed to familiar grooves, and James's habitual pragmatists in its failures to adapt to changed connections between finance and the economy. Congress punished the Fed for its failures to address the deflation of the Great Depression and the inflation of the 1970s. Monetary policy was transferred to the Treasury in 1933 and

Table 7.2 Taylor and Strong-free-reserves rules compared: dependent variable di_f

	Taylor rule					Strong-free-reserves and Taylor rules combined					
	Constant	dYg	dp	di_{f-1}	R^2/h	Constant	dR_f	dYg	dp	di_{f-1}	R^2/h
1922.1–	−0.02	0.06	0.01	0.20	0.08	−0.02	−2.18*	0.68*	−0.01	−0.01	0.55
1932.4	(0.16)	(1.66)	(0.47)	(1.32)	1.70	(0.34)	(6.56)	(2.73)	(1.00)	(0.09)	−0.17
1953.1–	−0.08	0.19*	0.067	0.44*	0.42	0.02	−1.40*	0.045	0.02	0.37*	0.66
1969.4	(0.89)	(4.62)	(1.78)	(4.42)	0.72	(0.23)	(6.93)	(1.18)	(0.73)	(4.90)	0.70
1970.1–	0.96	0.07	−0.16	0.28	0.0	0.279	−1.54*	0.096	−0.05	0.23	0.60
1978.1	(1.19)	(0.31)	(1.26)	(1.63)	1.54	(0.49)	(6.09)	(0.64)	(0.55)	(1.98)	−1.46
1987.1–	−0.06	0.22*	0.02	0.66*	0.53	−0.05	−0.32*	0.169*	0.02	0.72	0.60
2007.3	(0.46)	(3.02)	(0.43)	(8.51)	−0.77	(0.46)	(3.98)	(2.41)	(0.49)	(9.85)	−1.34

Sources and definitions: From Tables 4.5 and 7.1. Durbin's h does not reject the hypothesis of no serial correlation in the residuals.

the terms of existing Board members were ended in 1936. Monetary policy was not returned to the Fed until 1951, after Congress decided that it was being abused by the president. The damage was less in the 1970s, but Congress's monitoring increased. Whether more public oversight would have improved general economic stability is uncertain. Nevertheless, serious congressional oversight should compensate for the Fed's neglect of the economy.

A fourth approach (after monetary policy by an independent Fed, by the Executive, or by the Fed monitored by Congress) is policy by an academic rule. This is unlikely because it is unsupported by interests. It would also be unsatisfactory for similar reasons – insensitivity to finance and the electorate.

Part III
Conclusion

8 It's interests after all

> He wanted to know the history of the country. He had a college textbook, a big thick one. [H]e prodded it with his finger, and said, 'I durn near memorized every durn word in it. I could name you every date.' Then he prodded it again, this time contemptuously, and said, 'And the fellow who wrote it didn't know a God-damned thing. About how things were. He didn't know a thing. I bet things were just as they are now. A lot of folks wrassling around.'
>
> (Warren 1946: 72)

The success of an idea for public policy – its acceptance and implementation – requires the cooperation or at least the submission of the interests affected. That is asking a lot, as the previous chapters tried to show. Economists, whose profession is defined by the study of the utility-improving choices of individuals, should be the last to be surprised that taxpayers and the financial community resist the intrusions of outsiders into the monetary and fiscal policies affecting them.

More is at stake in taxing and spending than the details of government budgets. Mechanisms of control, as much as amounts, have been fought over as long as governments have existed, and the resolutions of these conflicts have determined our form of government. We should not expect these controls to be given to independent experts with their own agenda.

New financial procedures are also resisted. Although the government may prescribe a change in the monetary framework, its implementation is necessarily conditioned by the existing financial culture with its considerable interests and traditions.

Of course there is always the possibility of persuasion. The Keynesians promised higher and more stable employment if they were given control of part of the budget. Their goals were noble, they were offered at a time of need, and a great deal of homage was paid to their plan. But that was all. Keynes's ideas floundered on the rocks of communications, interests (at two levels), and logic. His difficult general model of uncertainty in a monetary economy with the possibility of persistent disequilibrium was rejected by economists with interests of their own. His disciples accepted Keynes's interventionist policies while retaining the more tractable classical equilibrium model free of transaction (including

Conclusion

information) costs. Even the simplified 'Keynesian' model found no place in practice (as opposed to rhetoric), running up against economic and political interests even before its intellectual collapse under the illogicality of systematically deceiving informed agents.

It is difficult to conceive of the application of one of these (Keynes's or Keynesian) models – even if the intellectual problems were solved – without threatening Congress's fiscal control. Considerable flexibility, and therefore discretion, would be required. It is notable that no formal arrangement to straddle these difficulties was attempted. Congress is not interested, and even the textbooks that extol active employment policies are content with shifting the appropriate curves. Those who think of government debt as an instrument of macro-management have not thought it necessary to pay attention to the problems of efficiency or control. The last may be insuperable in our democracy. The descendants of the English barons and backcountry American farmers live on in the determination of Congress (for whom much of politics is still local) to maintain control of the government's taxing and spending powers. Significant executive discretion is as distant as when Congress took it from Alexander Hamilton.

At a glance, monetary policy looks more susceptible to expert influence. Monetary institutions have undergone considerable legal changes, including the monetary standard (from bimetallic to gold to fiat money), the banking structure (based on state and national regulations, which are sensitive to the regulated), and monetary authorities (from the Banks of the US to the Independent Treasury System to the Federal Reserve). Economists have been involved in, or at least on the scene of, some of these changes.

However, when we come to the day-to-day management of the monetary authority, we must account for the characteristics of the managers, and these have changed little over time. Institutional frameworks have changed, but the kind of people in them have not. Central bankers have always been bankers and/or people operating in a bankers' milieu. That means considerable continuity because institutional assignments – goals and methods – have been broad and subject to a good deal of judgment. The bankers exercising these judgments inherit common and deeply felt interests, experiences, perceptions of the world, and their place in it. Simply put, they see their overriding objective as the health and stability of their immediate environment. There is nothing more that they can do for the economy and society than provide sound money and finance, which fortunately are in their own interests, as well.

Bankers have always appreciated that financial stability requires an environment of price stability. It is economists who have sometimes not been so sure. In the 1950s and 1960s, the majority of economists advocated monetary shocks, the more surprising the better, to make the Phillips Curve work, while central bankers continued to argue that the credibility of monetary policy was essential to financial and general economic stability. Substantial fluctuations in money and prices have been due to government pressures for cheap finance, but when central banks have been allowed to be independent of government budgets, they have been consistent in their methods and objectives – in the case of the Federal

It's interests after all 189

Reserve, from Benjamin Strong to William McChesney Martin, Jr, Paul Volcker, Alan Greenspan, and Ben Bernanke.

The different ambitions of central bankers and economists are reflected in their views of the economy. There is no better example of the divergence between advisors and actors than economists' criticisms of the money-market myopia of central bankers. Instead of selecting the unique instrument values that maximize expected utilities within clear-cut and complete certainty-equivalent models, like economists in the classroom, central bankers prize caution above action.

Economists criticize central bankers' refusal to articulate reasons for – the model underlying – their actions and inactions. This refusal ('inability' is a better word) is honest and inevitable if the world is uncertain and much of their knowledge of it is tacit and personal, but appears irresponsible and undemocratically secretive to economists confident in their own models. On the other hand, central bankers' reluctance to do anything that threatens to harm themselves or the interests they serve is consistent with what might be regarded as one of the strengths of democracy. Tying authorities to interests gives up the possibilities of the perfection that might be attained by an authoritative regime, but avoids some of its dangers.

I will go a step further by saying that central bankers' pursuit of the interests of their immediate financial clients may deliver substantial benefits to the wider public. Those who see the recent pursuit of financial stability as the consequence of advances in economic theory are looking in a rear-view mirror. However, the purpose of this book is not about what ought to be, but what is. I do not know whether we would be better off if economic theory had more influence on monetary and fiscal policy. What I think I do know is that it is unlikely to happen to any significant extent. For good or ill, interests have their way, with theories performing as cheerleaders on the sidelines.

It might be argued that the substitution of fiat for commodity money requires more direction from central bankers because the former is less market-driven. There is no technical limit to price changes. The skeptical reply to this point has two elements: the gold standard was not automatic, and it was suspended when it interfered with other government goals, particularly war finance. The central bank's role in the delivery of financial stability was important even under the gold standard. We saw that it was much discussed in the formation of the Federal Reserve, which took its assignment seriously. The gold standard did not interfere with the Fed's commitment to financial stability under Strong and Martin any more than the fiat standard under Volcker, Greenspan, and Bernanke.

Some things change, such as government appetites for finance, but any serious model of monetary policy must account for the people in the central bank who are affected in recognizably persistent ways by the knowledge and interests arising from their circumstances in the financial markets. The force of this environment was dramatically illustrated in 2008, when the FOMC, which included a record four of ten academic economists (most of its life it had one or less) came to the assistance of the financial markets in ways that were unprecedented in size and scope (Wood 2008a).[1]

We considered wider public interests in fiscal policy and should not forget them in monetary policy. The period since the mid-to-late 1970s is unique in the combination of the Fed's independence of the Executive and congressional oversight. The Fed was a backward step from the Independent Treasury System (1846–1914) in the public's influence on monetary policy. For example, when the Treasury began to retire greenbacks at a rapid pace after the Civil War, it was slowed by congressmen who had heard from their constituents (Wood 2005: 142). A similar interest by the majority of Congress in 1930–32 might have made a difference, but the insertion of another – 'expert' – body, although a 'creature of Congress', diminished the latter's sense of responsibility, so that its oversight of monetary policy was slight and periodic.

Financial stability has its benefits, but when its connections with the wider economy shift, as during the Great Depression, while those who feel the pain have been disenfranchised, disaster results. Closer congressional oversight is not free of errors, but the chances of great error are reduced. This may be the greatest advantage of democracy – the realization of interests in government policies.

Notes

2 Interests: a history of tax conflicts

1 When Johnson was criticized for accepting £300 a year, he said: 'I wish my pension were twice as large, that they might make twice the noise.' Boswell, *Life of Johnson*, 14 July 1763.
2 To William Shirley in December 1754, published in the *London Chronicle*, 8 February 1766, while the repeal of the *Stamp Act* was being debated in the House of Commons.
3 This passage seems to be due to Brougham (1839: 57–8). Pitt's 'allusion to the maxim of English law that every man's house is his castle' is cited in *Parliamentary History*, March 1763, but the quotation may be more Brougham than Pitt.
4 The grandson of a participant wrote a history of the conflict that emphasizes the peaceable behavior of the resistors and their mistreatment by the authorities (Brackenridge 1859).
5 Effects of the Louisiana Purchase are not seen between the presidential terms in Table 2.1 because of the speed with which the loan was repaid; $11,250,000 of the $15,000,000 purchase price was financed by bonds payable in four installments after 15 years, the rest from the budget surplus. Debt at the ends of 1803–06 (in millions) was $77.0, $86.4, $82.3, and $75.7 (Dewey 1928: 121–6).
6 The first assertions of the right of nullification were the Kentucky and Virginia resolutions of 1798–99, respectively, by Jefferson and Madison, protesting the Alien and Sedition Acts of Congress. Several states have prevented the execution of federal laws, but South Carolina's action against the federal tariff laws was the 'only example in which theory and practice coincided' (Fleming 1957).
7 For example, 'EU threatens WTO action over U.S. ban on Internet gambling', *International Herald Tribune*, 10 March 2008.

3 Ideas: the theory of stabilization policy

1 The footnote at the beginning of the *GT* states that 'the classical economists' was a name invented by Marx to cover Ricardo, James Mill and their *predecessors*.
   I have become accustomed ... to include in "the classical school" the *followers* of Ricardo, those, that is to say, who adopted and perfected the theory of the Ricardian economics, including (for example) J.S. Mill, Marshall, Edgeworth and Prof. Pigou.
2 William Wordsworth, Prelude, XI, 1.108, celebrating the French Revolution.
3 Friedman (1997) pointed out that the journalist's omission of the second half of his statement – 'no one is any longer a Keynesian' – altered its meaning, which was: 'We all use Keynesian terminology [and] many of the analytical details [and] at least a large part of the changed agenda [of] the *General Theory*'.
4 See Pigou's (1936) complaints and Hicks' (1936) statement that the ideas which Keynes attributed to 'the ordinary economist [leaves him] quite bewildered'.

192 Notes

5 The distinction between *uncertainty* in this sense and calculable *risk* is sometimes attributed to Knight (1921: ch. 7), although LeRoy and Singell (1982) pointed out that Knight, unlike Keynes, saw agents as having at least subjective probabilities.

4 Practice: the stability of Federal government deficits

1 *Gross Domestic Product* is the market value of production in a country; *Gross National Product* is the value of production by a country's residents no matter where they live.
2 The sum of corporate and personal income taxes as a percentage of GDP fell from 16.5 in the fiscal year 1944 to 11 in 1959, and has varied between 8.5 and 12.5 since then. The top personal income tax bracket fell from 94 percent in 1944 to 28 percent in 1988, and has been in the thirties since 1991. Social insurance and retirement taxes as a percentage of GDP rose from 1.6 percent in 1945 to 6.9 percent in 2001, before falling slightly (US Treasury, *The Budget for Fiscal Year 2008*, Historical tables).
3 The estimated relation (with t-statistics in parentheses) for 1877–2007 is $\Delta c = 0.001(1.6) - 0.108(5.7)\Delta w$, $R^2 = 0.20$.

5 The interests and institutions of monetary policy

1 The Whig Party was not organized until 1833 (Holt 1999: ix).
2 Tallies were claims on government revenues payable in the order they were collected, named for the notched sticks used in Norman times. Tontine payments went to surviving investors.
3 See Capie (1993 vi) for the charter.
4 In fact, eligible US bonds did not limit national bank notes, never being more than 30-percent utilized (James 1976).
5 Chairman Judson Clements had been president of the Rome and Northern Railway, lawyer Charles Prouty had represented railroads, and Edgar Clark had been head of the Order of Railway Conductors (*Dictionary of American Biography*; *Who's Who in America*; Kolko 1965).
6 In order that the terms of Board members expire sequentially, initial appointments were for two, four, ..., ten years. Warburg was appointed for four years and not reappointed.

6 Knowledge, advice, and monetary policy

1 Johnson's 'common sense' refutation has been criticized on the grounds that Berkeley's idealism does not disregard the senses (Berkeley 1710: ix). The first sentence of his *Principles of Human Knowledge* states that the objects of human knowledge are *ideas* imprinted on or perceived by the senses.

7 The stability of monetary policy: the Federal Reserve, 1914–2007

1 This discussion of the Fed's model follows Wood (2005: 181–210).
2 Wicker agreed with Brunner and Meltzer (1968) except for their claim that the 'Strong rule' was the only guide to policy. Wicker believed that gold also played a part. Wheelock (1991; 1992) also accepted the Strong rule as the primary guide to monetary policy.

8 It's interests, after all

1 The Board had only five members at the time. 'Academic economist' here corresponds to 'theorist'. Until the 1960s, the only academic economist at the Board (there were no

such Federal Reserve Bank presidents) was Adolph Miller (1914–36). From then until the 1990s, there were usually one or two. Board members with academic (and theorist) backgrounds were Ben Bernanke, Frederic Mishkin, and Randall Kroszner. The Philadelphia Reserve Bank President (Charles Plosser) was also an academic, as was Janet Yellen of the San Francisco Bank, who was not on the FOMC in 2008 but supported the Fed's response to the subprime mortgage crisis.

References

Acres, W.M. 1931. *The Bank of England from Within, 1694–1900*. Oxford University Press.
Acworth, A.W. 1925. *Financial Reconstruction in England, 1815–22*. P.S. King & Son.
Adair, J. 1976. *A Life of John Hampden*. MacDonald and Jane's.
Adams, G.B. 1912. *The Origin of the English Constitution*. Yale University Press.
Adams, J. 1765. *Instructions of the Town of Braintree to Their Representative*, in C.F. Adams, ed. 1851. *Works*, iii. Little, Brown.
Adams, S. 1961. *Firsthand Report: The Story of the Eisenhower Administration*. Harper.
Ahearn, D.S. 1963. *Federal Reserve Policy Reappraised, 1951–59*. Columbia University Press.
Akerlof, G. 2007. 'The missing motivation in macroeconomics', *American Economic Review*, March.
Aldrich, N. 1909. *The Work of the National Monetary Commission* (National Monetary Commission). US Government Printing Office.
——. 1911. 'Speech to the annual convention of the American Bankers Association', in Warburg (1930).
Aldrich, W. 1903. *Money and Credit*. Grafton.
Almon, J. 1792. *Anecdotes of the Life of the Right Honourable William Pitt, Earl of Chatham, and of the Principal Events of His Time, with His Speeches in Parliament, from the Year 1736 to the Year 1778*. J.S. Jordan.
Andersen, L.C. 1969. 'Money market conditions as a guide for monetary management', in K. Brunner. 1969. *Targets and Indicators of Monetary Policy*. Chandler.
Anderson, B.L. and Cottrell, P.L., eds. 1974. *Money and Banking in England: The Development of the Banking System, 1694–1914*. David & Charles.
Anderson, C.J. 1968. *A Half-Century of Federal Reserve Policymaking, 1914–64*. Federal Reserve Bank of Philadelphia.
Anderson, G.M. 1986. 'The U.S. federal deficit and national debt: A political and economic history', in J.M. Buchanan, C.K. Rowley, and R.D. Tollison, eds. 1986. *Deficits*. Basil Blackwell.
Anonymous. 1797. *Note on the Suspension of Cash Payments at the Bank of England in 1797*, in J.R. McCulloch. 1857. *Select Collection of Scarce and Valuable Tracts on Paper Currency and Banking*; reprinted A.M. Kelley, 1966.
Aronson, E. 1980. *The Social Animal*. Freeman.
Arrow, K.J. and Hahn, F.H. 1971. *General Competitive Analysis*. Holden-Day.
Ashley, W.J. 1903. *The Adjustment of Wages*. Longmans, Green.
Asso, P.F., Kahn, G.A., and Leeson, R. 2007. 'The Taylor rule and the transformation of monetary policy', *Working Paper*, Federal Reserve Bank of Kansas City, December.

References

Auerbach, A.J. 2002. 'Is there a role for discretionary fiscal policy'? in Federal Reserve Bank of Kansas City (2002).
Ayer, A.J. 1952. 'Introduction' to A.J. Ayer and R. Winch, eds. *British Empirical Philosophers: Locke, Berkeley, Hume, Reid, and J.S. Mill*. Routledge & Kegan Paul.
Bacon, F. 1603. *Valerius Terminus or the Interpretation of Nature*, in B. Montagu, ed. 1844. *Works*, i. Carey and Hart.
Bagehot, W. 1866. 'What a panic is and how it might be mitigated', *Economist*, 12 May; reprinted in M. Collins, ed. 1993. *Central Banking in History*, i. Edward Elgar.
———. 1873. *Lombard Street*. Henry King; reprinted John Murray, 1917.
Bain, A. 1882. *John Stuart Mill: A Criticism with Personal Recollections*. Longmans, Green and Co.
Balke, N.S. and Gordon, R.J. 1984. 'Historical data', in Gordon (1984).
Barber, W.J. 1996. *Designs within Disorder: Franklin D. Roosevelt, the Economists, and the Shaping of American Economic Policy, 1933–45*. Cambridge University Press.
Baring, F. 1797. *Observations on the Establishment of the Bank of England and on the Paper Circulation of the Country*. Minerva Press; reprinted with *Further Observations*, A.M. Kelley, 1967.
Barro, R.J. 1979. 'On the determination of the public debt', *Journal of Political Economy*, October.
———. 1984. 'The behavior of U.S. deficits', in Gordon (1984).
———. 1987. 'Government spending, interest rates, prices and budget deficits in the United Kingdom, 1730–1918', *Journal of Monetary Economics*, September.
Beard, C.A. 1913. *An Economic Interpretation of the Constitution of the United States*. Macmillan; 2nd edn 1935.
Benavie, A. 1998. *Deficit Hysteria: A Common-Sense Look at America's Rush to Balance the Budget*. Praeger.
Bentham, J. 1838. *Manual of Political Economy*, in J. Bowring, ed., *Works*, 1838–43, iii; reprinted Russell & Russell, 1962.
Berkeley, G. 1710. *A Treatise Concerning the Principles of Human Knowledge*, in A.M. Lindsay, ed. 1910. *A New Theory of Vision and other Select Philosophical Writings*. J.M. Dent & Sons.
Bernanke, B.S., Laubach, T., Mishkin, F.S., and Posen, A.S. 1999. *Inflation Targeting: Lessons from International Experience*. Princeton University Press.
Beveridge, W. 1909. *Unemployment: A Problem of Industry*. Longmans, Green; 2nd edn 1930.
Bierce, A. 1911. *The Devil's Dictionary*. Neale Publishing Co.
Binney, J.E.D. 1958. *British Public Finance and Administration, 1774–92*. Clarendon Press.
Black, R.D.C. 1972. 'W. S. Jevons and the foundation of modern economics', *History of Political Economy*, Fall.
Blaug, M. 1996. *Economic Theory in Retrospect*, 4th edn. Cambridge University Press.
Blinder, A.S. 1988. 'The fall and rise of Keynesian economics', *Economic Record*, December.
———. 1994. 'Overview', in Federal Reserve Bank of Kansas City, *Reducing Unemployment: Current Issues and Policy Options*.
———. 1996. 'Central banking in a democracy', Federal Reserve Bank of Richmond *Economic Quarterly*, Fall.
———. 1997a. 'What central bankers could learn from academics – and vice versa', *Journal of Economic Perspectives*, Spring.

——. 1997b. 'A core of macroeconomic beliefs?' *Challenge*, July/August.
—— and Holtz-Eakin, D. 1984. 'Public opinion and the balanced budget', *American Economic Review*, May.
Bolles, A.S. 1894. *The Financial History of the United States*, 4th edn. D. Appleton; reprinted A.M. Kelley, 1969.
Bordo, M.D. 1987. 'Bimetallism', in J. Eatwell, M. Milgate, and P. Newman. *The New Palgrave: A Dictionary of Economics*. Macmillan.
——, Goldin, C., and White, E.N., eds. 1998. *The Defining Moment: The Great Depression and the American Economy in the Twentieth Century*. University of Chicago Press.
Boswell, J. 1791. *The Life of Samuel Johnson*. Charles Dilly.
Boulding, K.E. 1956. *The Image: Knowledge and Life in Society*. University of Michigan Press.
——. 1966. 'The economics of knowledge and the knowledge of economics', *American Economic Review*, May.
Bowen, W.G. 1960. *The Wage–Price Issue: A Theoretical Analysis*. Princeton University Press.
Brackenridge, H.M. 1859. *History of the Western Insurrection in Western Pennsylvania Commonly Called the Whiskey Insurrection*. W.S. Haven.
Brands, H.W. 2000. *The First American: The Life and Times of Benjamin Franklin*. Doubleday.
Bratton, K.A. 1994. 'Retrospective voting and future expectations: the case of the budget deficit in the 1988 election', *American Politics Quarterly*, July.
Bremner, R.P. 2004. *Chairman of the Fed. William McChesney Martin, Jr., and the Creation of the Modern American Financial System*. Yale University Press.
Brimmer, A.F. 1989. 'Central banking and systemic risks in capital markets', *Journal of Economic Perspectives*, Spring.
British Parliamentary Papers. 1969. Irish University Press.
Brougham, H. 1839. *Historical Sketches of Statesmen who Flourished in the Time of George III*. Lea and Blanchard.
Brown, A.J. 1955. *The Great Inflation of 1939–1951*. Oxford University Press.
Brown, P.H. 1902. *History of Scotland*. Cambridge University Press.
Brunner, K. and Meltzer, A.H. 1964a. *Some General Features of the Federal Reserve's Approach to Policy*, for US Congress (1964).
——. 1964b. *The Federal Reserve's Attachment to the Free Reserves Concept*, for US Congress (1964); reprinted in Brunner and Meltzer, eds. 1989. *Monetary Economics*. Blackwell.
——. 1968. 'What did we learn from the monetary experience of the United States in the Great Depression?' *Canadian Journal of Economics*, May.
Buchanan, J.M. and Wagner, R.E. 1977. *Democracy in Deficit: The Political Legacy of Lord Keynes*. Academic Press.
Bullion, J.L. 1982. *A Great and Necessary Measure: George Grenville and the Genesis of the Stamp Act, 1763–65*. University of Missouri Press.
Burke, E. 1774. 'Speech on American taxation', House of Commons, 19 April, in *Selected Works*, i.
——. 1790. *Reflections on the Revolution in France*, in *Selected Works*, ii.
——. 1874. *Selected Works*, E.J. Payne, ed. Clarendon Press; reprinted Liberty Fund, 1999.
Burnet, G. 1724–1734. *History of His Own Time*. J. Hyde, R. Gunne, R. Owen, and E. Dobson.

Burtt, E.A., ed. 1939. 'Introduction', *The English Philosophers from Bacon to Mill*. Random House.
Calomiris, C.W., ed. 2000. *U.S. Bank Deregulation in Historical Perspective*. Cambridge University Press.
—— and Wheelock, D.C. 1998. 'Was the Great Depression a watershed for American monetary policy'? in Bordo *et al*. (1998).
Camp, R.A. 1977. *The Role of Economists in Policy-Making: A Comparative Case Study of Mexico and the U.S.* Institute of Government Research, University of Arizona.
Cannan, E. 1925. *The Paper Pound of 1797–1821*, 2nd edn. P.S. King & Son; reprinted Frank Cass, 1969.
——. 1922. *A Review of Economic Theory*. P.S. King & Son.
Capie, F., ed. 1993. *History of Banking*. William Pickering.
——, ed. 1994. *The Future of Central Banking: The Tercentenary Symposium of the Bank of England*. Cambridge University Press.
Caplan, B. 2001. 'What makes people think like economists? Evidence on economic cognition from the "Survey of Americans and Economists on the Economy"', *Journal of Law and Economics*, October.
Carlson, K.M. 1979. 'Formulating economic policy for 1979 and beyond: old problems and new constraints', Federal Reserve Bank of St Louis *Review*, April.
Carpenter, W.B. 1874. *Principles of Mental Physiology with Their Applications to the Training and Discipline of the Mind, and the Study of its Morbid Conditions*. D. Appleton.
Carpenter, W.S. 1924. 'Introduction' to Locke (1690b).
Catterall, R.C.H. 1902. *The Second Bank of the United States*. University of Chicago Press.
Chandler, L.V. 1958. *Benjamin Strong, Central Banker*. Brookings Institution.
Churchill, W.S. 1956. *A History of the English-Speaking Peoples*, ii. *The New World*. Dodd, Mead & Co.
Clapham, J.H. 1944. *The Bank of England: A History*. Cambridge University Press.
Clarendon, Earl of. 1648. *The History of the Rebellion and Civil Wars in England Begun in the Year 1641*, written 1646–48, printed at the Theatre, Oxford, 1702–1704.
Clarida, R., Galí, J., and Gertler, M. 2000. 'Monetary policy rules and macroeconomic stability: evidence and some theory', *Quarterly Journal of Economics*, February.
Clarke, M.S. and Hall, D.A. 1832. *Documentary History of the Bank of the United States*. Gales and Seaton.
Clarke, P. 1988. *The Keynesian Revolution in the Making, 1924–36*. Clarendon Press.
Clower, R.W. 1965. 'The Keynesian counter-revolution: a theoretical appraisal', in F.H. Hahn and F.P.R. Brechling, eds. *The Theory of Interest Rates*. Macmillan.
Coats, A.W. 1993. 'Economics as a profession', in Coats, *The Sociology and Professionalization of Economics*. Routledge.
Cobb, J. 1986. 'What makes the Fed tick?' *Wall Street Journal*, 2 June.
Coke, E. 1628. *The First Part of the Institutes of the Laws of England*, 1st American edn (from 16th English edn). Jackson and Warner, 1812.
Coon, D. 1986. *Introduction to Psychology*, 4th edn. West Publishing Co.
Cornford, F.M. 1935. *Plato's Theory of Knowledge: Theaetetus and Sophist Translated with a Running Commentary*. Kegan Paul, Trench, Trubner & Co.
Cottrell, A.F., Lawlor, M.S., and Wood, J.H. 1995. 'What are the connections between deposit insurance and bank failures?' in Cottrell, Lawlor, and Wood, eds. *The Causes and Consequences of Depository Institution Failures*. Kluwer.

Cox, A.H. 1966. *Regulation of Interest Rates on Bank Deposits*. Bureau of Business Research, University of Michigan.
Cuddihy, W.J. 1979. '"A man's house is his castle": new light on an old case', *Reviews in American History*, March.
D'Abernon, E.V. Viscount. 1931. *Portraits and Appreciations*. Hodder and Stoughton.
Darwin, C. 1887. *Life and Letters*, ed. F. Darwin. D. Appleton & Co.
Davies, G. 1938. *The Early Stuarts, 1603–1660*. Clarendon Press.
Davis, W.W.H. 1899. *The Fries Rebellion, 1798–99*. Doylestown Publishing Co.; reprinted Arno Press, 1969.
Debreu, G. 1959. *Theory of Value: An Axiomatic Analysis of Economic Equilibrium*. Yale University Press.
DeLong, J.B. 1997. 'America's peacetime inflation: the 1970s', in C. Romer and D. Romer, eds. *Reducing Inflation: Motivation and Strategy*. University of Chicago Press.
Descartes, R. 1637. *Discourse on Method*, in E.S. Haldane and G.R.T. Ross, eds. 1931. *The Philosophical Works of Descartes*. Cambridge University Press.
Dewey, D.R. 1928. *Financial History of the United States*, 10th edn. Longmans, Green.
Dewey, J. 1916. *Democracy and Education*. Macmillan.
——. 1927. *The Public and its Problems*. Henry Holt.
Dicey, A.V. 1908. *Introduction to the Study of the Law of the Constitution*, 7th edn. Macmillan.
——. 1914. *The Law and Public Opinion in England*, 2nd edn. Macmillan.
Dickerson, O.M. 1951. *The Navigation Acts and the American Revolution*. University of Pennsylvania Press.
Dietz, F.C. 1928. 'The receipts and issues of the exchequer during the reigns of James I and Charles I', *Smith College Studies in History*, xiii, no. 4.
Douglas, R. 1999. *Taxation in Britain since 1660*. Macmillan.
Dowell, S.A. 1888. *History of Taxation and Taxes in England*, 3rd edn. Longmans Green; reprinted A.M. Kelley, 1965.
Dunbar, C.F. 1904. *Economic Essays*. Macmillan.
Eccles, M. 1951. *Beckoning Frontiers*. Knopf.
Eichengreen, B.J. 1992. *Golden Fetters: The Gold Standard and the Great Depression, 1919–1939*. Oxford University Press.
Eisner, R. 1969. 'Fiscal and monetary policy reconsidered', *American Economic Review*, December.
——. 1986. *How Real Is the Federal Deficit?* Free Press.
Elliot, J., ed. 1859. *The Debates in the Several State Conventions on the Adoption of the Federal Constitution as Recommended by the General Convention at Philadelphia in 1787, together with the Journal of the Federal Convention, etc.* J.B. Lippincott.
Elliott, D.C. 1960. 'The Federal Reserve System, 1914–29', in H.V. Prochnow, ed. *The Federal Reserve System*. Harper & Brothers.
Elzinga, K.G. 1992. 'The eleven principles of economics', *Southern Economic Journal*, April.
Employment Policy. Presented by the Minister of Reconstruction to Parliament, Cmd. 6527. HMSO, May 1944.
Evanoff, D.D. 1985. 'Priced services: the Fed's impact on correspondent banking', Federal Reserve Bank of Chicago *Economic Perspectives*, September/October.
Fair, R.C. 1996. 'Econometrics and presidential elections', *Journal of Economic Perspectives*, Summer.
Feavearyear, A.E. 1931. *The Pound Sterling*. Clarendon Press.

Federal Open Market Committee (FOMC). 1952. *Report of the* Ad hoc *Subcommittee on the Government Securities Market*, in US Congress (1954).
Federal Reserve Bank of Kansas City. 2002. *Stabilization Policy*.
Federal Reserve Board. 1943, 1975. *Banking and Monetary Statistics*.
Feer, R.A. 1988. *Shays's Rebellion*. Garland.
Feldstein, M.S. 1994. 'American economic policies in the 1980s: a personal view', in Feldstein, ed. *American Economic Policies in the 1980s*. University of Chicago Press.
Ferguson, E.J. 1961. *The Power of the Purse*. University of North Carolina Press.
Fetter, F.A. 1967. 'A historical confusion in Bagehot's *Lombard Street*', *Economica*, February.
Firestone, J.M. 1960. *Federal Receipts and Expenditures during Business Cycles*. Princeton University Press.
Fischer, D.H. 2004. *Washington's Crossing*. Oxford University Press.
Fisher, I. 1922. *The Purchasing Power of Money*, 2nd edn. Macmillan; reprinted A.M. Kelley, 1963.
——. 1926. 'A statistical relation between unemployment and price changes', *International Labor Review*, June; reprinted as 'I discovered the Phillips Curve', *Journal of Political Economy*, March–April 1973.
——. 1930. *The Theory of Interest*. Macmillan.
Fitzpatrick, E.A. 1918. *Budget Making in a Democracy*. Macmillan.
Fleming, W.L. 1957. 'Nullification', *Encyclopaedia Brittanica*.
Fonseca, E.G. da. 1991. *Beliefs in Action: Economic Philosophy and Social Change*. Cambridge University Press.
Franklin, B. 1962. *Papers*, ed. L.W. Labaree. Yale University Press.
Friedman, M. 1957. *A Theory of the Consumption Function*. Princeton University Press.
——. 1959. *A Program for Monetary Stability*. Fordham University Press.
——. 1970. 'A theoretical framework for monetary analysis', *Journal of Political Economy*, March/April.
——. 1993. 'A tale of Fed transcripts', *Wall Street Journal*, 20 December.
——. 1997. 'John Maynard Keynes', Federal Reserve Bank of Richmond *Economic Quarterly*, Winter.
—— and Schwartz, A.J. 1963. *A Monetary History of the United States, 1867–1960*. Princeton University Press.
Friedman, N. 2000. *The Fifty-Year War: Conflict and Strategy in the Cold War*. Naval Institute Press.
Gallatin, A. 1830. 'Considerations on the currency and banking system of the United States', *American Quarterly Review*, December; reprinted in Henry Adams, ed. 1879. *Writings*, iii. Lippincott.
——. 1967. *Selected Writings*, E.J. Ferguson, ed. Bobbs-Merrill.
Gardiner, S.R. 1906. *The Constitutional Documents of the Puritan Revolution, 1625–1660*, 3rd edn. Clarendon Press.
Geelhoed, E.B. 1959. *Charles E. Wilson and Controversy in the Pentagon, 1953–57*. Wayne State University Press.
Gibbons, J.S. 1859. *The Banks of New York, Their Dealers, the Clearing House, and the Panic of 1857*. D. Appleton.
Gilbert, B.B. 1992. *David Lloyd George: Organizer of Victory*. Batsford.
Gilmour, J.B. 1990. *Reconcilable Differences, the Budget Process and the Deficit*. University of California Press.
Glass, C. 1927. *An Adventure in Constructive Finance*. Doubleday, Page.

References

Godwin, W. 1798. *Enquiry Concerning Political Justice and its Influence on Morals and Happiness*, 3rd edn. G.G. and J. Robinson; reprinted F.E.L. Priestley, ed. 1946. University of Toronto Press.

Goff, B.L. and Tollison, R.D. 2002. 'Explaining U.S. deficits: 1889–1998', *Economic Inquiry*, July.

Golembe, C.H. 1960. 'The deposit insurance legislation of 1933: an examination of its antecedents and its purposes', *Political Science Quarterly*, June.

Goodfriend, M. 1986. 'Monetary mystique: secrecy and central banking', *Journal of Monetary Economics*, January.

——. 1993. 'Financial theory and central bank policies', in S.F. Frowen, ed., *Monetary Theory and Monetary Policy: New Tracks for the 1990s*. St Martin's Press.

—— and Lacker, J.M. 1999. 'Limited commitment and central bank lending', Federal Reserve Bank of Richmond *Economic Quarterly*, Fall.

Gordon, J.S. 1998. *Hamilton's Blessing*. Penguin Books.

Gordon, R.J., ed. 1974. *Milton Friedman's Monetary Framework: A Debate with His Critics*. University of Chicago Press.

——, ed. 1984. *The American Business Cycle*. University of Chicago Press.

——. 1990. 'What is new-Keynesian economics?' *Journal of Economic Literature*, September.

Gouge, W.M. 1833. *A Short History of Paper Money and Banking in the United States*. Grigg & Elliott; reprinted A.M. Kelley, 1968.

Graydon, A. 1846. *Memoirs of His Own Time with Reminiscences of the Men and Events of the Revolution*. Lindsay & Blakiston.

Green, E.J. 2005. 'Review', *Journal of Economic Literature*, March.

Green, J.R. 1887. *History of the English People*. Bedford, Clarke & Co.

Greenspan, A. 1992. 'Statement to Senate Committee on Banking, Housing, and Urban Affairs', 21 July, in *Federal Reserve Bulletin*, September.

——. 1993. 'Statement to Senate Committee on Banking, Housing, and Urban Affairs', 19 February, in *Federal Reserve Bulletin*, April.

——. 1994a. 'Discussion', in Capie (1994).

——. 1994b. 'Statement to Senate Committee on Banking, Housing, and Urban Affairs', 20 July, in *Federal Reserve Bulletin*, September.

——. 1996. 'Speech to American Enterprise Institute', *Wall Street Journal*, 6 December.

Greenstein, F.I. 1994. *The Hidden-Hand Presidency: Eisenhower as Leader*, 2nd edn. Johns Hopkins University Press.

Gregory, T.E., ed. 1929. *Select Statutes, Documents and Reports Relating to British Banking, 1832–1928*. Oxford University Press.

Greider, W. 1987. *Secrets of the Temple: How the Federal Reserve Runs the Country*. Simon & Schuster.

Grellier, J.J. 1810. *The History of the National Debt from the Revolution in 1688 to the Beginning of 1800*; reprinted Burt Franklin, 1971.

Grigg, J. 1985. *Lloyd George: From Peace to War, 1912–16*. University of California Press.

Grubb, F. 2003. 'Creating the U.S. dollar currency union, 1748–1811: a quest for monetary stability or a usurpation of state sovereignty for personal gain?' *American Economic Review*, December.

Hahn, F.H. 1984. 'Economic theory and Keynes's insights', University of Cambridge, Department of Applied Economics Discussion Paper no. 72.

Hamilton, A. 1790. *Report on a National Bank, Papers*, vii.

———. 1791. *Report on the Subject of Manufactures*, Papers, x.
———. 1851. *Works*, J.C. Hunter, ed. Charles Francis.
———. 1987. *Papers*. Harold C. Syrett, ed. Columbia University Press.
Hamilton, J.D. 1987. 'Monetary factors in the Great Depression', *Journal of Monetary Economics*, March.
Hammond, P.Y. 1962. 'NSC-68: prologue to rearmament', in Schilling *et al.* (1962).
Hammond, W.B. 1957. *Banks and Politics in America from the Revolution to the Civil War*. Princeton University Press.
Hankey, T. 1867. *The Principles of Banking, its Utility and Economy; with Remarks on the Working and Management of the Bank of England*. Effingham Wilson.
Hansen, A.H. 1939. 'Economic progress and declining population growth', *American Economic Review*, March.
———. 1955. 'Monetary policy', *Review of Economics and Statistics*, May.
Hargrove, E.C. and Morley, S.A. 1984. *The President and the Council of Economic Advisors: Interviews with CEA Chairmen*. Westview Press.
Harris, S.E. ed. 1947. *The New Economics: Keynes' Influence on Theory and Public Policy*. Knopf.
———. 1964. *Economics of the Kennedy Years*. Harper & Row.
Havrilesky, T. 1993. *The Pressures on American Monetary Policy*. Kluwer.
Hawtrey, R.G. 1913. *Good and Bad Trade*. Constable; reprinted A.M. Kelley, 1962.
———. 1932. *The Art of Central Banking*. Longmans, Green.
———. 1938. *A Century of Bank Rate*. Longmans, Green; 2nd edn. Frank Cass, 1962.
Hayek, F.A. 1952. *The Counterrevolution of Science: Studies on the Abuse of Reason*. Free Press.
———. 1960. *The Constitution of Liberty*. University of Chicago Press.
———. 1967. *Studies in Philosophy, Politics and Economics*. University of Chicago Press.
———. 1973. 1976. 1979. *Law, Legislation, and Liberty*. University of Chicago Press.
Hayes, A. 1970. 'The 1966 credit crunch', in D. Eastburn, ed. *Men, Money, and Policy: Essays in Honor of Karl Bopp*. Federal Reserve Bank of Philadelphia.
Healy, K.T. 1944. 'Development of a national system of transportation', in H. Williamson, *Growth of the American Economy*. Prentice-Hall.
Heller, W.W. 1966. *New Dimensions of Political Economy*. Harvard University Press.
Hepburn, A.B. 1903. *History of Coinage and Currency in the United States and the Perennial Contest for Sound Money*. Macmillan.
Hetzel, R.L. 2008. *The Monetary Policy of the Federal Reserve: A History*. Cambridge University Press.
Hicks, J.R. 1936. 'Mr. Keynes' theory of employment', *Economic Journal*, June.
———. 1937. 'Mr. Keynes and the "Classics"', *Econometrica*, April.
Highfield, R.A., O'Hara, M., and Wood, J.H. 1991. 'Public ends, private means: central banking and the profit motive, 1823–32', *Journal of Monetary Economics*, October.
Hill, C. 1961. *The Century of Revolution, 1603–1714*. Thomas Nelson and Sons.
Hofstadter, R. 1955. *The Age of Reform*. Knopf.
Holmans, A.E. 1961. *United States Fiscal Policy, 1945–1959*. Clarendon Press.
Holmes, O.W., Jr. 1870. 'Codes, and the arrangement of the law', *American Law Review*, October.
———. 1881. *The Common Law*. Little Brown.
———. 1897. 'The path of the law', *Harvard Law Review*, March.
Holt, M.F. 1999. *The Rise and Fall of the American Whig Party*. Oxford University Press.

Hoover, H. 1952. *Memoirs: The Great Depression, 1929–41*. Macmillan.
Horsefield, J.K. 1960. *British Monetary Experiments, 1650–1710*. Harvard University Press.
House of Commons. 1832. *Report from the Committee of Secrecy on the Bank of England Charter*; reprinted *British Parliamentary Papers (1969), Monetary Policy, General*, 4.
——. 1840. *Report from the Select Committee on Banks of Issue*; reprinted *British Parliamentary Papers* (1969), *Monetary Policy, General*, 5.
House of Lords. 1848. *Report from the Secret Committee to Inquire into the Causes of the Distress which has for Some Time Prevailed Among the Commercial Classes, and How Far It Has Been Affected by the Laws for Regulating the Issue of Bank Notes Payable on Demand*; reprinted *British Parliamentary Papers* (1969), *Monetary Policy, Commercial Distress*, 3.
Hubbard, K. 1920. *Abe Martin's Almanack*. Abe Martin.
Hume, D. 1739. *A Treatise of Human Nature*; reprinted L.A. Selby-Bigge, ed. 1978. Clarendon Press.
——. 1748. *An Enquiry Concerning Human Understanding*; reprinted C.W. Hendel, ed. 1955. Bobbs-Merrill.
——. 1752. 'Of money', *Political Discourses*; in E. Rotwein, ed. 1955. *David Hume: Writings on Economics*. University of Wisconsin Press,
Hutchison, T.W. 1964. *'Positive' Economics and Policy Objectives*. Harvard University Press.
——. 1994. 'The Jevonian revolution and economic policy in Britain', in T.W. Hutchison, *The Uses and Abuses of Economics*. Routledge.
Ifft, R.A. 1985. 'Treason in the early republic: the federal courts, popular protest, and federalism during the Whiskey Rebellion', in S.R. Boyd, ed. *The Whiskey Rebellion: Past and Present Perspectives*. Greenwood Press.
Irwin, D.A. 1998. 'From Smoot-Hawley to reciprocal trade agreements: changing the course of U.S. trade policy in the 1930s', in Bordo *et al.* (1998).
James, J.A. 1976. 'The conundrum of the low issue of national bank notes', *Journal of Political Economy*, April.
James, W. 1890. *The Principles of Psychology*. Henry Holt.
——. 1896. 'The will to believe', *New World*, June.
——. 1901. *Talks to Teachers on Psychology and to Students on Some of Life's Ideals*. Henry Holt.
——. 1907. *Pragmatism, A New Name for Some Old Ways of Thinking: Popular Lectures on Philosophy*. Longmans, Green.
Jenks, E. 1904. 'The myth of Magna Carta', *Independent Review*, November.
Jennings, I. 1965. *Magna Carta and its Influence in the World Today*. British Information Services.
Jevons, W.S. 1866. 'Brief account of a general mathematical theory of political economy', *Journal of the Royal Statistical Society*, June.
——. 1871. *The Theory of Political Economy*. Macmillan.
——. 1882. *The State in Relation to Labour*. Macmillan; reprinted A.M. Kelley, 1968.
Johnson, S. 1755. *A Dictionary of the English Language*. W. Strahan.
Joplin, T. 1822. *An Essay on the General Principles and Present Practice of Banking*. Baldwin, Cradock and Joy.
Juglar, C. 1893. *A Brief History of Panics and Their Periodical Occurrence in the United States*, trans. and updated by D. Thom, 3rd edn. 1916; reprinted A.M. Kelley, 1966.

Kane, E.J. 1996. 'De jure interstate banking: why only now?' *Journal of Money, Credit and Banking*, May.
Kanter, H. 1982. 'The defense budget process', in A. Wildavsky and M. Boskin, eds. *The Federal Budget: Economics and Politics*. Institute for Contemporary Studies.
Kaysen, C. 1968. 'Model-makers and decision-makers: economists and the policy process', *Public Interest*, Summer.
Keech, W.R. 1995. *Economic Politics: The Costs of Democracy*. Cambridge University Press.
Kemmerer, E.W. 1910. *Seasonal Variations in the Relative Demand for Money and Capital in the United States* (National Monetary Commission). US Government Printing Office.
Kennedy, W. 1913. *English Taxation, 1640–1799: An Essay on Policy and Opinion.* G. Bell; reprinted A.M. Kelley, 1964.
Keynes, J.M. 1919. *Economic Consequences of the Peace*. Macmillan.
——. 1923. *A Tract on Monetary Reform*. Macmillan.
——. 1933. 'A monetary theory of production', *Writings*, xiii.
——. 1936. *The General Theory of Employment, Interest and Money*. Macmillan.
——. 1937. 'The general theory of employment', *Quarterly Journal of Economics*, February.
——. 1971–89. *Collected Writings*, ed. D.E. Moggridge. Macmillan.
—— and Henderson, H.D. 1929. *Can Lloyd George Do It? The Pledge Examined*. The Nation and Athenaeum.
King, J.E. 1995. *Conversations with Post Keynesian Economists*. Macmillan.
Kissinger, H. 1959. 'The policy maker and the intellectual', *The Reporter*, 1959.
Klein, L.R. 1947. *The Keynesian Revolution*. Macmillan.
Knight, F.H. 1921. *Risk, Uncertainty and Profit*. Hart, Schaffner & Marx; reprinted A.M. Kelley, 1964.
Kolko, G. 1963. *The Triumph of Conservatism: A Reinterpretation of American History, 1900–1916*. Macmillan.
——. 1965. *Railroads and Regulation, 1877–1916*. Princeton University Press.
Kolodziej, E.A. 1966. *The Uncommon Defense and Congress, 1945–1963*. Ohio State University Press.
Krooss, H.E., ed. 1969. *Documentary History of Banking and Currency in the United States*. Chelsea House.
Kuhn, T.S. 1962. *The Structure of Scientific Revolutions*. University of Chicago Press.
Kydland, F.E. and Prescott, E.C. 1977. 'Rules rather than discretion: the inconsistency of optimal plans', *Journal of Political Economy*, June.
Labaree, B. 1964. *The Boston Tea Party*. Oxford University Press.
Lachmann, L.M. 1959. 'Professor Shackle on the economic significance of time', *Metroeconomica*, September.
Laffont, J. 2000. *Incentives and Political Economy*. Oxford University Press.
LaRoche, R.K. 1993. 'Bankers acceptances', in T. Cook and R.K. LaRoche, eds. *Instruments of the Money Market*, 7th edn. Federal Reserve Bank of Richmond.
Laughlin, J.L. 1912. *Banking Reform*. National Citizens League for the Promotion of a Sound Banking System; reprinted Arno, 1980.
——. 1933. *The Federal Reserve Act: Its Origin and Problems*. Macmillan.
Lawlor, M.S. 1994. 'On the historical origin of Keynes's financial market views', in N. de Marchi and M.S. Morgan, eds. *Higgling: Transactors and Their Markets in the History of Economics*. Duke University Press.

——. 2000. 'Modern macroeconomics: theory, policy, and events', *Journal of Post Keynesian Economics*, Summer.

——. 2005. 'William James's psychological pragmatism: habit, belief and purposive human behaviour', *Cambridge Journal of Economics*.

——. 2006. *The Economics of Keynes in Historical Context: An Intellectual History of the General Theory*. Palgrave Macmillan.

Lawson, T. 1997. *Economics and Reality: Economics as Social Theory*. Routledge.

Leijonhufvud, A. 1968. *On Keynesian Economics and the Economics of Keynes*. Oxford University Press.

LeRoy, S.F. and Singell, L.D., Jr. 1982. 'Knight on risk and uncertainty', *Journal of Political Economy*, April.

Lincoln, Abraham. 1907. *Life and Works*, ed. Marion M. Miller. Current Literature Publishing Co.

Lindsay, A.D., ed. 1910. *Socratic Discourses by Plato and Xenaphon*. J.M. Dent & Sons.

Livingston, J. 1986. *Origins of the Federal Reserve System: Money, Class, and Corporate Capitalism, 1890–1913*. Cornell University Press.

Locke, J. 1690a. *An Essay Concerning Human Understanding*; reprinted A.G. Fraser, ed. 1894. Clarendon Press.

——. 1690b. *Two Treatises of Civil Government*; reprinted J.M. Dent, 1924.

Lown, C.S. and Wood, J.H. 2003. 'The determination of commercial bank reserve requirements', *Review of Financial Economics*, 1.

Loyd, S.J. 1844. *Thoughts on the Separation of the Departments of the Bank of England*. Pelham Richardson; reprinted in Capie (1993 vii).

Lucas, R.E., Jr. 1976. 'Econometric policy evaluations: a critique', in K. Brunner and A. Meltzer, eds. *The Phillips Curve and Labor Markets*. North-Holland.

—— and Sargent, T.J. 1978. 'After Keynesian economics', in *After the Phillips Curve: Persistence of High Inflation and Unemployment*. Federal Reserve Bank of Boston; reprinted in Lucas and Sargent, eds. 1981. *Rational Expectations and Econometric Practice*. University of Minnesota Press.

Macaulay, T.B. 1855. *History of England from the Accession of James II*, 2nd edn. Macmillan.

McCallum, B.T. 1981. 'Price level determinacy with an interest rate rule and rational expectations', *Journal of Monetary Economics*, November.

——. 2002. 'Recent developments in monetary policy analysis: the roles of theory and evidence', Federal Reserve Bank of Richmond *Economic Quarterly*, Winter.

McCulloch, J.R. 1858. 'Treatise on Metallic and Paper Money and Banks', *Encyclopedia Britannica*, 8th edn.

McFarland, L. 2001. *Cold War Strategist: Stuart Symington and the Search for National Security*. Praeger.

McGuire, R.A. 2003. *To Form a More Perfect Union. A New Economic Interpretation of the United States Constitution*. Oxford University Press.

McKechnie, W.S. 1914. *Magna Carta: A Commentary on the Great Charter of King John*, 2nd edn; reprinted Burt Franklin, 1958.

McLellan, D., ed. 1981. *Karl Marx: Interviews and Recollections*. Barnes & Noble.

McNamara, R.S. 1995. *In Retrospect: The Tragedy and Lessons of Vietnam*. Times Books.

Macy, J. 1909. *The English Constitution: A Commentary on its Nature and Growth*. Macmillan.

Madigan, B.F. and Nelson, W.R. 2002. 'Proposed revision to the Federal Reserve's discount window lending programs', *Federal Reserve Bulletin*, July.

Magee, S.P., Brock, W.A., and Young, L. 1989. *Black Hole Tariffs and Endogenous Policy Theory: Political Economy in General Equilibrium*. Cambridge University Press.
Maisel, S.J. 1973. *Managing the Dollar*. Norton.
Maitland, F.W. 1902. 'The growth of jurisprudence, 1154–1273', in H.D. Traill and J.S. Mann, eds. *Social England: A Record of the Progress of the People*, i. Cassell.
Malone, D., ed. 1930. *Correspondence between Thomas Jefferson and Pierre Samuel Du Pont de Nemours*. Houghton Mifflin.
Marshall, A. 1885. *The Present Position of Economics*, Inaugural Lecture; reprinted Marshall (1925).
———. 1887. 'Remedies for fluctuations of general prices', *Contemporary Review*, March; reprinted Marshall (1925).
———. 1920. *Principles of Economics*, 8th edn. Macmillan.
———. 1925. *Memorials*, ed. A.C. Pigou. Macmillan.
——— and Marshall, M.P. 1879. *The Economics of Industry*. Macmillan.
Marshall, J. 1807. *The Life of George Washington*. C.P. Wayne; reprinted Chelsea House, 1983.
Matusow, A. 1998. *Nixon's Economy*. University Press of Kansas.
Matthews, R.C.O. 1990. 'Marshall and the labour market', in J.K. Whitaker, ed., *Centenary Essays on Alfred Marshall*. Cambridge University Press.
Mayer, T., ed. 1990. 'Minimizing regret: cognitive dissonance as an explanation of FOMC behavior', in Mayer, *The Political Economy of American Monetary Policy*, Cambridge University Press.
Medhurst, M.J. 1993. *Dwight D. Eisenhower: Strategic Communicator*. Greenwood Press.
Meerman, J.P. 1963. 'The climax of the Bank War: Biddle's contraction, 1833–34', *Journal of Political Economy*, August.
Meltzer, A.H. 1993. 'Commentary', in *Changing Capital Markets: Implications for Monetary Policy*. Federal Reserve Bank of Kansas City.
———. 2003. *A History of the Federal Reserve, 1913–51*. University of Chicago Press.
Menand, L. 2001. *The Metaphysical Club*. Farrar, Straus and Giroux.
Mill, J.S. 1838. 'Bentham', *London and Westminster Review*, August; *Works*, x.
———. 1848. *Principles of Political Economy, with Some of their Applications to Social Philosophy*, 7th edn. 1871; reprinted, W.J. Ashley, ed. 1909. Longmans, Green.
———. 1861. *Considerations on Representative Government*. Parker, Son, and Brown; *Works*, xix.
———. 1989. *Collected Works*. J.M. Robson and J. Stillinger, eds. University of Toronto Press.
Mints, L.W. 1945. *A History of Banking Theory in Great Britain and the United States*. University of Chicago Press.
Miron, J.A. 1986. 'Financial panics, the seasonality of the nominal interest rate, and the founding of the Fed', *American Economic Review*, March.
Mises, L. von. 1962. *Liberalism*, trans. by R. Raico. Princeton University Press.
Mitchell, B.R. 1962. *Abstract of British Historical Statistics*. Cambridge University Press.
Mitchell, W.C. 1913. *Business Cycles*. University of California Press.
Modigliani, F. and Brumberg, R.E. 1954. 'Utility analysis and the consumption function: an interpretation of cross-section data', in K.K. Kurihara, ed. *Post-Keynesian Economics*. Rutgers University Press.

References

Moggridge, D.E. 1969. *The Return to Gold, 1925.* Cambridge University Press.

——. 1992. *Maynard Keynes.* Routledge.

Moore, S. 2000. 'Testimony before the House Judiciary Committee on the line item veto', *Cato Congressional Testimony*, Cato Institute, 23 March.

Morgan, E.S. and Morgan, H.M. 1995. *The Stamp Act Crisis*, 2nd edn. University of North Carolina Press.

Mosak, J.L. 1945. 'Forecasting postwar demand: III', *Econometrica*, January.

Neikirk, W.R. 1987. *Volcker: Portrait of the Money Man.* New Congdon and Weed.

Nelson, R. 1987. 'The economics profession and the making of public policy', *Journal of Economic Literature*, March.

Nelson, R.R. and Winter, S.G. 1982. *An Evolutionary Theory of Economic Change.* Harvard University Press.

Nettels, C.P. 1962. *The Emergence of a National Economy, 1775–1815.* Holt, Rinehart, and Winston.

Nevins, A. 1954. *Ford: The Times, the Man, the Company.* Scribner.

—— and Commager, H.S. 1945. *A Short History of the United States.* Modern Library.

North, D.C. and Weingast, B. 1989. 'Constitutions and commitment: the evolution of institutions governing public choice in seventeenth-century England', *Journal of Economic History*, December.

Nourse, E.G. 1953. *Economics in the Public Service: Administrative Aspects of the Employment Act.* Harcourt, Brace.

Noyes, A.D. 1909. *Forty Years of American Finance. A Short Financial History of the Government and People of the United States since the Civil War, 1865–1907.* G.P. Putnam's Sons.

——. 1938. *The Market Place: Reminiscences of a Financial Editor.* Little, Brown.

Office of Management and Budget. 2001. *A Citizen's Guide to the Federal Budget.*

Ogg, D. 1955. *England in the Reigns of James II and William III.* Clarendon Press.

Olson, J.C. 2003. *Stuart Symington: A Life.* University of Missouri Press.

O'Neill, T.P., Jr. 1994. *All Politics is Local and Other Rules of the Game.* Times Books.

Orphanides, A. 2003. 'Historical monetary policy analysis and the Taylor rule', *Journal of Monetary Economics*, July.

——. 2006. 'The road to price stability', Working paper, Federal Reserve Board, January.

Paley, W. 1814. *The Principles of Moral and Political Philosophy*, 20th edn. R. Faulder.

Parliamentary History of England from the Earliest Period to the Year 1803. 1813. T.C. Hansard.

Pasquet, D. 1925. *An Essay on the Origins of the House of Commons*, trans. by R.G.D. Laffan. Cambridge University Press.

Peirce, C.S. 1878. 'How to make our ideas clear', *Popular Science Monthly*, January; reprinted in C.J.W. Kloesel, ed. 1982. *Writings of C.S. Peirce*, iii. Indiana University Press.

Pepys, S. *Diary*, R. Latham and W. Matthews, eds. University of California Press, 1983.

Perry, R.B. 1935. *The Thought and Character of William James: As Revealed in Unpublished Correspondence and Notes, together with His Published Writings.* Little, Brown.

——. 1948. *The Thought and Character of William James: Briefer Version.* Harvard University Press.

Peterson, M.D. 1987. *The Great Triumvirate: Webster, Clay, and Calhoun.* Oxford University Press.

Petty, W. 1682. *Quantulumcunque Concerning Money*; reprinted Petty, *Economic Writings*, Charles Hull, ed. A.M. Kelley, 1963.
Phelps, C.W. 1917. *The Foreign Expansion of American Banks*. Ronald Press.
Phelps, E.S. 1969. 'The new microeconomics in employment and inflation theory', *American Economic Review*, March.
Phillips, A.W. 1958. 'The relation between unemployment and the rate of change of money wage rates in the United Kingdom, 1861–1957', *Economica*, November.
Pickering, D., ed. 1807. *Statutes at Large from Magna Carta to the End of the Eleventh Parliament of Great Britain*. anno 1761, continued to 1806. Cambridge University Press.
Pierce, J.L. 1980. 'Comments on the Lombra-Moran paper', *Carnegie-Rochester Conference Series on Public Policy*, Autumn.
Pigou, A.C. 1908. *Economic Science in Relation to Practice*. An Inaugural Lecture given at Cambridge University. Macmillan.
———. 1936. 'Mr. J.M. Keynes' General Theory of Employment, Interest and Money', *Economica*, May.
Plato. 1991. *Protagoras*, J. Wright, trans. with notes. Clarendon Press.
Polanyi, M. 1958. *The Study of Man*. University of Chicago Press.
———. 1964. *Personal Knowledge: Towards a Post-Critical Philosophy*. Harper and Row.
———. 1966. *The Tacit Dimension*. Routledge & Kegan Paul.
Popper, K. 1972. *Objective Knowledge*. Clarendon Press.
Posen, A.S. 1995. 'Declarations are not enough: financial sector sources of central bank independence', in B. Bernanke and J. Rotemberg, eds. *NBER Macroeconomics Annual*. MIT Press.
Posner, R.A. 2003. 'Dewey and democracy: a critique', *Economic Education Bulletin*, American Institute for Economic Research, January.
Ricardo, D. 1821. *On the Principles of Political Economy and Taxation*, 3rd edn. John Murray.
Riedl, B.M. 2005. 'What's wrong with the federal budget process?' *Backgrounder #1816*. Heritage Foundation.
Riezman, R. and Wilson, J.D. 1995. 'Politics and trade policy', in J. Banks and E. Hanushek, eds. *Modern Political Economy*. Cambridge University Press.
Rivlin, A.M. 1984. 'Reform of the budget process', *American Economic Review*, May.
Robbins, L. 1934. *The Great Depression*. Macmillan.
———. 1952. *The Theory of Economic Policy in English Classical Political Economy*. Macmillan.
Robertson, D.H. 1915. *A Study of Industrial Fluctuation*. P.S. King & Son.
———. 1926. *Banking Policy and the Price Level*. P.S. King & Son.
———. 1928. *Money*. Cambridge University Press.
———. 1938. 'Mr. Keynes and "finance"', *Economic Journal*, June.
Rogers, J.E.T. 1909. *The Industrial and Commercial History of England*, 6th edn. T. Fisher Unwin.
Romer, C.D. and Romer, D.H. 2002. 'The evolution of economic understanding and postwar stabilization policy', in Federal Reserve Bank of Kansas City (2002).
Romer, D.H. 1993. 'The New Keynesian synthesis', *Journal of Economic Perspectives*, Winter.
Sack, B. and Wieland, V. 2000. 'Interest-rate smoothing and optimal monetary policy: a review of recent empirical evidence', *Journal of Economics and Business*, January/April.

Salant, W.S. 1989. 'The spread of Keynesian doctrines and practices in the United States', in P.A. Hall, ed. *The Political Power of Economic Ideas: Keynesianism across Nations*. Princeton University Press.

Samuelson, P.A. 1946. 'Lord Keynes and the General Theory', *Econometrica*, July; reprinted in Harris (1947).

——. 1951. 'Principles and rules in modern fiscal policy: a neo-classical reformulation', *Money, Trade, and Economic Growth: Essays in Honor of John Henry Williams*. Macmillan.

——. 1958. *Economics*, 4th edn. McGraw-Hill.

—— and Solow, R. 1960. 'Analytical aspects of anti-inflation policy', *American Economic Review*, May.

Santoni, G.J. 1986. 'The effects of inflation on commercial banks', Federal Reserve Bank of St Louis *Review*, March.

Sapir, E. 1927. 'The unconscious patterning of behavior in society', in E.S. Dummer, ed. *The Unconscious: A Symposium*. A.A. Knopf.

Sargent, T.J. and Wallace, N. 1975. '"Rational" expectations, the optimal monetary instrument, and the optimal money supply rule', *Journal of Political Economy*, April.

Savage, J.D. 1988. *Balanced Budgets & American Politics*. Cornell University Press.

Sayers, R.S. 1951. 'The development of central banking after Bagehot', *Economic History Review*, vol. 4, no. 1; reprinted in Sayers, 1957. *Central Banking after Bagehot*, Clarendon Press.

——. 1953. 'Ricardo's views on monetary questions', *Quarterly Journal of Economics*, February; reprinted in Sayers and T.S. Ashton, eds. 1953. *Papers in English Monetary History*. Clarendon Press.

Schattschneider, E.E. 1935. *Politics, Pressures and the Tariff. A Study of Free Private Enterprise in Pressure Politics, as Shown in the 1929–1930 Revision of the Tariff.* Prentice-Hall.

Scheffler, I. 1974. *Four Pragmatists: A Critical Introduction to Peirce, James, Mead, and Dewey*. Humanities Press.

Schilling, W.R. 1962. 'The politics of national defense: fiscal 1950', in Schilling *et al.* (1962).

——, Hammond, P.Y., and Snyder, G.H. 1962. *Strategy, Politics, and Defense Budgets*. Columbia University Press.

Schlesinger, A.M. 1918. *The Colonial Merchants and the American Revolution*. Columbia University.

Schumpeter, J.A. 1911. *The Theory of Economic Development*; trans. by Redvers Opie. 1934. Harvard University Press.

——. 1954. *History of Economic Analysis*. Oxford University Press.

Schwartz, A.J. 1992. 'The misuse of the Fed's discount window', Federal Reserve Bank of St Louis *Review*, September/October 58–69.

Sek, L. 2001. 'Fast-track authority for trade agreements: background and developments in the 107th Congress', *Congressional Research Service Issue Brief for Congress*, 14 May.

Seligman, E.R.A. 1908. 'The crisis of 1907 in the light of history', *The Currency Problem and the Present Financial Situation*. Columbia University Press.

Shackle, G.L.S. 1962. 'To the *QJE* from Chapter 12 of the *General Theory*: Keynes's ultimate meaning', *The Years of High Theory: Invention and Tradition in Economic Thought, 1926–1939*. Cambridge University Press.

Shoven, J.B. 1984. 'The behavior of United States deficits: comment', in Gordon (1984).

Siklos, P.L. 2008. 'The Fed's reaction to the stock market during the great depression: fact or artifact?' *Explorations in Economic History*, April.
Simmons, R.C. and Thomas, P.D.G. 1983. *Proceedings and Debates of the British Parliaments Respecting North America, 1754-1783*, vol. 2, *1765-68*. Kraus International Publications.
Simon, H.A. 1957. *Models of Man*. Wiley.
——. 1959. 'Theories of decision-making in economics and behavioral science', *American Economic Review*, June.
Simons, H. 1936. 'Rules versus authorities in monetary policy', *Journal of Political Economy*, February.
Skaggs, N.T. 1984. 'A theory of the bureaucratic value of Federal Reserve operating procedures', *Public Choice*, vol. 43, no. 1.
Skidelsky, R. 1983, 1992, 2000. *John Maynard Keynes*. Penguin.
Slaughter, T.P. 1986. *The Whiskey Rebellion: Frontier Epilogue to the American Revolution*. Oxford University Press.
Smith, A. 1776. *An Inquiry into the Nature and Causes of the Wealth of Nations*; reprinted Random House, 1937.
——. 1759. *The Theory of Moral Sentiments*; reprinted Liberty Fund, 1982.
Smith, D.L. 1999. *The Stuart Parliaments, 1603–1689*. Arnold.
Smith, V. 1936. *The Rationale of Central Banking and the Free Banking Alternative*. P.S. King & Son.
Smithies, A. 1945. 'Forecasting postwar demand: I', *Econometrica*, January.
——. 1960. 'The balanced budget', *American Economic Review*, May.
Snyder, G.H. 1962. 'The "New Look" of 1953', in Schilling *et al.* (1962).
Sorensen, T.C. 1965. *Kennedy*. Harper & Row.
Sowell, T. 1987. *A Conflict of Visions*. William Morrow.
Spearman, D. 1957. *Democracy in England*. Rockliff.
Speck, W.A. 1988. *Reluctant Revolutionaries: Englishmen and the Revolution of 1688*. Oxford University Press.
Sprague, O.M.W. 1910. *History of Crises under the National Banking System*. (National Monetary Commission). US Government Printing Office; reprinted A.M. Kelley, 1968.
Sproul, A. 1980. *Selected Papers*, ed. L.S. Ritter. Federal Reserve Bank of New York.
Stein, H. 1969. *The Fiscal Revolution in America*. University of Chicago Press.
——. 1994. *Presidential Economics*, 3d edn. American Enterprise Institute.
Stigler, G.J. 1988. *Memoirs of an Unregulated Economist*. Basic Books.
——. 1971. 'The theory of economic regulation', *Bell Journal of Economics and Management Science*, Spring.
Stockman, D.A. 1986. *The Triumph of Politics: Why the Reagan Revolution Failed*. Harper & Row.
Strong, B. 1930. *Interpretations of Federal Reserve Policy*. Harper & Row.
Strouse, J. 1999. *Morgan: American Financier*. Random House.
Sullivan, M. 1935. *Our Times, 1900–1925*, vi. Charles Scribner's Sons.
Sumner, W.G. 1874. *A History of American Currency*. Henry Holt.
Taft, W.H. 1913. *Popular Government*. Yale University Press.
Tanner, J.R. 1928. *English Constitutional Conflicts of the 17th Century, 1603–1689*. Cambridge University Press.
Tarshis, L. 1947. *The Elements of Economics. An Introduction to the Theory of Price and Employment*. Houghton Mifflin.

Taus, E.R. 1943. *Central Banking Functions of the U.S. Treasury, 1789–1941.* Columbia University Press.
Taussig, F.W. 1931. *The Tariff History of the United States*, 8th edn. G.P. Putnam's Sons.
Taylor, J.B. 1993. 'Discretion versus policy rules in practice', *Carnegie-Rochester Conference Series on Public Policy*, December.
Thackeray, W.M. 1945. *Letters and Private Papers*, ed. G.N. Ray. Harvard University Press.
Theil, H. 1961. *Economic Forecasts and Policy*, 2nd edn. North-Holland.
Thomas, P.D.G. 1992. *Revolution in America: Britain and the Colonies, 1763–1776.* University of Wales Press.
Thornton, D.L. 2001. 'The codification of an FOMC procedure', Federal Reserve Bank of St Louis *Monetary Trends*, March.
——. 2006. 'When did the FOMC begin targeting the federal funds rate?' *Journal of Money, Credit and Banking*, December.
—— and Wheelock, D.C. 2000. 'A history of the asymmetric policy directive', Federal Reserve Bank of St Louis *Review*, September/October.
Timberlake, R.H. 1993. *Monetary Policy in the United States: An Intellectual and Institutional History.* University of Chicago Press.
Tinbergen, J. 1939. *Statistical Testing of Business Cycle Theories.* League of Nations.
Tobin, J. 1958. 'Defense, dollars, and doctrines', *Yale Review*, March; reprinted in Tobin. 1966. *National Economic Policy.* Yale University Press.
——. 1977. 'Macroeconomic models and policy', *Frontiers of Quantitative Economics*, M.D. Intrilligator, ed. North Holland.
——. 1987. 'Keynesian policies in theory and practice', in P.M. Jackson, ed., *Policies for Prosperity: Essays in a Keynesian Mode.* MIT Press.
Tocqueville, A. de. 1840. *Democracy in America*, trans. with intro. by H. Mansfield and D. Winthrop. 2000. University of Chicago Press.
Todd, W.F. 1992. 'FDICIA's discount window provisions', Federal Reserve Bank of Cleveland *Economic Commentary*, 15 December.
Truman, H.S. 1956. *Memoirs*, ii: *Years of Trial and Hope.* Doubleday.
US Bureau of the Census. 1975. *Historical Statistics of the United States, Colonial Times to 1970.* U.S. Government Printing Office.
US Congress. 1913. *Report on Concentration of Control of Money and Credit.* House doc. 504, Investigative (Pujo) Subcommittee of Committee on Banking and Currency, 62nd Congress, 2nd session.
——. 1922. *Agricultural Inquiry.* Hearings, Joint Commission of Agricultural Inquiry, 67th Congress, 1st session.
——. 1954. *United States Monetary Policy. Recent Thinking and Experience.* Hearings, (Flanders) Subcommittee on Economic Stabilization of the Joint Committee on the Economic Report, 83rd Congress, 2nd session.
——. 1956a. *Study of Airpower.* Hearings, Subcommittee on the Air Force of the Senate Committee on Armed Services, 85th Congress, 1st session.
——. 1956b. *Nomination of Wm. McC. Martin, Jr.* Hearings, Senate Banking Committee, 84th Congress, 2nd session.
——. 1957. *January 1957 Economic Report of the President.* Hearings, Joint Economic Committee, 85th Congress, 1st session.
——. 1961. *Review of the Annual Report of the Federal Reserve System for 1960.* Hearings, Joint Economic Committee, 87th Congress, 1st session.
——. 1962. *State of the Economy and Policies for Full Employment.* Hearings, Joint Economic Committee, 87th Congress, 2nd session.

———. 1964. *The Federal Reserve after Fifty Years*. Hearings, Subcommittee on Domestic Finance of the House Committee on Banking and Currency, 88th Congress, 2nd session.

———. 1969. *The 1969 Economic Report of the President*. Hearings, Joint Economic Committee. 91st Congress, 1st session.

Van Schreeven, W.J. and Scribner, R.L. 1973. *Revolutionary Virginia: The Road to Independence*. University Press of Virginia.

Veitch, G.S. 1913. *The Genesis of Parliamentary Reform*; reprinted Archon Books, 1965.

Velde, F.R. 2004. 'Poor hand or poor play? The rise and fall of inflation in the U.S.', Federal Reserve Bank of Chicago *Economic Perspectives*, 1Q.

Viner, J. 1937. *Studies in the Theory of International Trade*. Allen & Unwin.

———. 1944. 'The economist in history', in M. Shields, ed. *International Financial Stabilization*. Irving Trust.

Volcker, P.A. 1978. 'The role of monetary targets in an age of inflation', *Journal of Monetary Economics*, April.

———. 1994. 'Discussion', in Capie (1994).

——— and Gyohten, T. 1992. *Changing Fortunes*. Times Books.

Wald, A. 1936. 'On some systems of equations in mathematical economics', trans. by O. Eckstein for *Econometrica*, October, 1951.

Warburg, P.M. 1910. *The Discount System in Europe* (National Monetary Commission). US Government Printing Office.

———. 1930. *The Federal Reserve System: Its Origin and Growth*. Macmillan.

Warren, R.P. 1946. *All the King's Men*. Harcourt, Brace.

Washington, G. 1944. *Writings*, ed. John C. Fitzpatrick. US Government Printing Office.

Wedgwood, C.V. 1955. *The King's Peace, 1637–41*. Collins.

Weintraub, S. 1955. 'Monetary policy: a comment', *Review of Economics and Statistics*, May.

Weslager, C.A. 1976. *The Stamp Act Congress, with an Exact Copy of the Complete Journal*. University of Delaware Press.

West, R.C. 1977. *Banking Reform and the Federal Reserve, 1863–1923*. Cornell University Press.

Wetterau, B. 1998. *Desk Reference on the Federal Budget*. Congressional Quarterly.

Whale, P.B. 1944. 'A retrospective view of the Bank Charter Act of 1844', *Economica*, August.

Wheelock, D.C. 1990. 'Member bank borrowing and the Fed's contractionary monetary policy during the Great Depression', *Journal of Money, Credit, and Banking*, November.

———. 1991. *The Strategy and Consistency of Federal Reserve Policy, 1924–33*. Cambridge University Press.

———. 1992. 'Monetary policy in the Great Depression: what the Fed did, and why', Federal Reserve Bank of St Louis *Review*, March/April.

White, L.H. 1984. *Free Banking in Britain: Theory, Experience, and Debate, 1800–1845*. Cambridge University Press.

Wicker, E. 1969a. 'Brunner and Meltzer on Federal Reserve policy during the Great Depression', *Canadian Journal of Economics*, May.

———. 1969b. 'The World War II policy of fixing a pattern of interest rates', *Journal of Finance*, June.

Wicksell, K. 1898. *Interest and Prices*, trans. by R.F. Kahn. 1936. Royal Economic Society.

Wildavsky, A.B. 1987. *The New Politics of the Budgetary Process*. Scott, Foresman.

Wilkins, M. 1991. 'Foreign banks and foreign investment in the United States', in R. Cameron and V.I. Boykin, eds. *International Banking, 1870–1914*. Oxford University Press.
Williams, W.M.J. 1908. *The King's Revenue, Being a Handbook to Taxes and the Public Revenue*. P.S. King & Son.
Willis, H.P. 1915. *The Federal Reserve*. Doubleday, Page.
Wilson, W. *Papers*, ed. Arthur S. Link. Princeton University Press, 1966–94.
Winch, D. 1969. *Economics and Policy: A Historical Study*. Walker and Company.
Witte, J.F. 1985. *The Politics and Development of the Federal Income Tax*. University of Wisconsin Press.
Wood, J.H. 2001. 'More inflation in our future, Mr. Greenspan?' *Research Reports*, American Institute for Economic Research, 23 July.
———. 2003. 'Bagehot's lender of last resort: a hollow hallowed tradition', *Independent Review*, Winter.
———. 2005. *A History of Central Banking in Great Britain and the United States*. Cambridge University Press.
———. 2007. 'Prospects for an inflation-targeting Fed', *Central Banking*, November.
———. 2008a. 'The Fed's balance sheet', *Research Reports*, American Institute for Economic Research, 21 April.
———. 2008b. 'Monetary policy and the Great Depression', ms.
——— and Wood, N.L. 1985. *Financial Markets*. Harcourt Brace Jovanovich.
Woodford, M. 2003. *Interest and Prices. Foundations of a Theory of Monetary Policy*. Princeton University Press.
Woodham-Smith, C. 1962. *The Great Hunger*. E.P. Dutton.
Woods, R.L. 1951. *The Businessman's Book of Quotations*. McGraw-Hill.
Woodward, B. 2000. *Maestro*. Simon & Schuster.
Woolrych, A.H. 1958. 'The collapse of the Great Rebellion', *History Today*, September.
Woozley, A.D. 1957. 'Knowledge', *Encyclopaedia Britannica*, iii.
Yeager, L. 1962. 'Introduction', *In Search of a Monetary Constitution*. Harvard University Press.
Ziegler, P. 1988. *The Sixth Great Power: A History of Barings, 1762–1929*. Knopf.

Index

Acres, W.M. 87
Acworth, A.W. 86
Ad hoc Subcommittee of the FOMC 167–8
Adair, J. 12–14
Adams, G.B. 10
Adams, John 23, 34
Adams, John Quincy 34
Adams, S. 40
Advance Planning for Public Works Act 69
Ahearn, D.S. 168
Akerlof, G. 61
Aldrich, Nelson 103, 106–7, 109–10
Aldrich, W. 161
Aldrich plan 103–4
Aldrich-Vreeland Act 103
Almon, J. 10
Althorp, Lord 87
American Bankers Association 103, 106
American revolution 7, 11, 17, 29; *see also* Stamp Act
Andersen, L.C. 139, 167
Anderson, B.L. 158
Anderson, C.J. 167
Anderson, G.M. 71
Annapolis Convention 29
Area Redevelopment Act 70
Argyll, Earl of 19
Armstrong, Louis 143
Aronson, E. 139
Arrow, K.J. 134–5
Arthur, Chester A. 37
Articles of Confederation 28–9
Ashley, W.J. 48
Asso, P.F. 180
Attwood, Thomas 62
Auerbach, A.J. 70–1
automatic stabilizer 77
Axilrod, Steve 140

Ayer, A.J. 116

Bacon, F. 46
Bagehot, Walter 84, 87, 89–92, 102, 156–7, 170
Bain, A. 49
Baldwin, O.D. 109
Balke, N.S. 73, 77
Bank Charter Acts of 1833 and 1844 85–90
Bank of England: and Bank of the United States 93; and development of monetary policy 87–92; and Federal Reserve 106, 168; and interests 84–5; Monetary Policy Committee 120–1, 136, 142; and panics 156–8; and suspension of convertibility 85–7
bankers acceptances 106–7
Banking Acts: of 1933 109; of 1935 108, 163, 166
Banks of the United States 83–4, 188; behavior of 97–8; charters of 92–4, 96–8; constitutionality of 93–5; votes on 94–5, 97–9
Bannister, John 66
Barber, W.J. 67
Baring, F. 157–8
Baring, T.C. 127
Barro, R.J. 23, 68
Bartlett, Bruce 69
Beard, C.A. 29
Benavie, A. 2
Bentham, J. 48
Benton, Thomas 99
Berkeley, G. 122, 192n1
Berkeley, Justice Sir Robert 14
Bernanke, B.S. 163, 172, 174, 189, 193n1
Beveridge, W. 51
Bierce, A. 7

214 Index

bills only 168–9
bimetallism 88, 101
Binney, J.E.D. 33
Black, R.D.C. 49
Blaug, M. 49
Blinder, A.S. 2, 64, 72, 118, 122, 135–6, 141
Bolles, A.S. 18
booms and busts 155–62
Bordo, M.D. 88
Boston Tea Party 27
Boswell, J. 122, 191n1
Boulding, K.E. 121, 127
Bowen, W.G. 61
Brackenridge, H.M. 191n4
branch banking 110
Brands, H.W. 25
Bratton, K.A. 72
Bremner, R.P. 156, 170
Brimmer, A.F. 143
Brougham, H. 191n3
Brown, A.J. 161
Brown, P.H. 15
Brumberg, R.E. 61
Brunner, K. 138, 154, 167, 192n2
Bryan, William Jennings 101, 112
Buchanan, J.M. 71
budget: and economists' fears 74–5; full employment 70–1; military 75–9; models of 68; smoothing 71–2; US 67–8
Budget and Accounting Act of 1921 72, 77
Budget and Impoundment Control Act of 1974 40, 72, 77
Budget Enforcement Act of 1990 72
Bullion, J.L. 23–4
Bullion Report 86
bureaucracies *see* economic advice
Burke, E. 17, 27–8, 31, 149–50
Burnet, G. 19
Burns, Arthur 163, 170
Burtt, E.A. 116
Bush, George H.W. 70
Bush, George W. 70

Calhoun, John 97
Calomiris, C.W. 107, 167
Camp, R.A. 137
Cannan, E. 4, 86
Capie, F. 192n3
Caplan, B. 71
Carlson, K.M. 173
Carpenter, W.B. 125
Carpenter, W.S. 7
Carter, Jimmy 172

Catherine the Great 149
Catterall, R.C.H. 97–8
central bankers: credibility 92, 153, 157–8, 188; expectations 153, 157–70; knowledge and language 3–4, 112–14, 117–22, 137–45, 151–5, 181, 189; preferences 3–4, 189; *see also* Federal Reserve System
central banking: and independence, transparency, and accountability 1, 84, 87–8, 112, 153–5, 167, 170–2, 175, 183, 189; theory of 86–92; *see also* Federal Reserve System
Chamberlain, Joseph 51
Chandler, L.V. 164–5
Charles I 11–15, 18–20, 41, 84–5
Charles II 15–22, 84
Charles River Bridge v. *Warren Bridge* 98
Churchill, W.S. 12
Civil War (American) 28, 33, 36, 75, 77, 100–1, 103, 112, 190
Civil War of 1640s 8, 15, 19
Clapham, J.H. 85, 92
Clarendon, Earl of 14
Clarida, R. 153, 155, 171
Clark, Edgar 192n5
Clarke, M.S. 96–7
Clarke, P. 48
classical model and policies 2, 42, 48–53, 57–8, 155; and modern macroeconomics 59, 63; *see also* expectations
Clay, Henry 35, 83, 97, 99
Clements, Judson 192n5
Cleveland, Grover 143
Clinton, William 70
closed systems 117–23, 134–5, 142–4, 148–50
Clower, R.W. 64
Coats, A.W. 136
Cobb, Howell 100
Cobb, J. 140
Coe, George 108–9
cognitive dissonance 139–43
Coke, Justice Sir Edward 11
Cold War 28, 38, 67–8, 75–9
Commager, H.S. 105
commercial paper 100–3, 106–7, 110
Committees of Correspondence 25
Commonwealth *see* Cromwell, Oliver
communications: between economists 57–63, 114, 134–5; economists and policymakers 113–14, 117–21, 137–45; policymakers and the public 151–2; *see also* economic advice; ideas; knowledge

constrained vision *see* open systems
Coon, D. 118
corn laws 92
Cornford, F.M. 116
Cornwallis, General Lord 17
Cottrell, A.F. 110
Cottrell, P.L. 158
Council of Economic Advisors 1, 44, 65, 73–4, 77, 127, 137, 169
Cox, A.H. 109
Crawford, William 33, 95, 97
credibility *see* central bankers
credit crunch of 1966 169
crises: of 1819 156; of 1893 101; definition 161; history 101, 160; *see also* panics
Cromwell, Oliver 10, 13, 15, 18
Cuddihy, W.J. 31
Currency and Bank Notes Act of 1928 92

D'Abernon, E.V. Viscount 126
Daane, Dewey 169
Dallas, A.J. 96
Darwin, C. 46
Davidson, P. 134–5
Davies, G. 12
Davis, W.W.H. 30
Dawes, Charles 78
Debreu, G. 134–5
Declaration of Breda 15
Declaration of Independence 8, 23
Declaratory Act 26–7
deficit hysteria 2
deficits: British 33; early American 32–4; stability of 67–79
DeLong, J.B. 171
Democratic Party: and Federal Reserve Act 103; and national banks 99; and tariffs 37–8
Depository Institutions Deregulation and Monetary Control Act 108
Descartes, R. 115
Dewey, D.R. 18, 32, 35–8, 191n5
Dewey, J. 123, 145–8
Dicey, A.V. 49
Dickerson, O.M. 24
Dietz, F.C. 7
discount window *see* Federal Reserve
Douglas, R. 21
Dowell, S.A. 16, 24
Duane, James 28
Duesenberry, James 44
Dulles, John Foster 151
Dunbar, C.F. 158

East India Company 27
Eccles, M. 132–3, 163
Econometric Society 1944 Round Table 73
economic advice 1–4, 114, 127–37
economic philosophers 118–23
economical reformers 17
economics and politics vii, 1, 4
economists: and the Fed 139–43, 153–5, 161; *see also* classical, communications; Keynesian; new classical; new Keynesian
Edgeworth, F.Y. 191n1
Edward I 10
Eichengreen, B.J. 180
Eisenhower, Dwight 39–40, 69, 78, 151
Eisner, R. 2, 61
elastic currency 100–2
Elkins Act 105–6
Elliot, J. 31
Elliott, D.C. 173
Elzinga, K.G. 79
empiricists 4, 114–17, 123
Evanoff, D.D. 110
excess reserves 167
exchequer 12–13, 16–18, 21–2, 27
exclusion crisis 19
expectations: actuarial 54–5, 69; economists' 142; in *The General Theory* 54–7; Keynesian 69; rational 1, 62–3, 151; *see also* central bankers

Fair, R.C. 72
Feavearyear, A.E. 17, 84, 87, 89, 156
Federal Advisory Council 105, 107
Federal Deposit Insurance Corporation 109–10
Federal Deposit Insurance Corporation Improvement Act 110
Federal Reserve Act 86, 166; preamble 100; development of 103–5; features 106–12
Federal Reserve Banks directors 105
Federal Reserve Board 104–11, 166–7, 175, 178
Federal Reserve System 83–4, 188, 190; behavior 162–83; charter 111–2; discount window 109, 159–77; knowledge 155–61; origins 101–5; political pressure on 165–6, 169–75, 189–90; purposes 106–10, 144; reputation of 154–5; *see also* central bankers; monetary policy
Federal Trade Commission 105

Federalist Papers 29–30
Feer, R.A. 30
Feldstein, M.S. 127–8
Ferguson, E.J. 30
Fetter, F.A. 87, 156
Findlay, William 97
Firestone, J.M. 71
First Dutch War 14
fiscal policy: theory and practice 1–4; UK 33; US 67–79, 188
Fischer, D.H. 11
Fisher, I. 48, 51, 59, 61, 63, 69, 161, 179
Fitzpatrick, E.A. 3
Fleming, W.L. 191n6
Foley, Paul 21
Fonseca, E.G. da 44, 46–7
Ford, Henry 128
Franklin, Benjamin 23–5
free-reserves guide 164–8, 175–81, 192n2
free trade 4, 33, 37–8
Friedman, M. 42, 44, 60–1, 90, 100, 107, 112, 117, 151, 154, 168, 191n3
Friedman, N. 67
Fries' Rebellion 30
Frisch, Ragnar 60
full-employment surplus 70

Gallatin, Andrew 33, 94–6
Gardiner, S.R. 12, 14–15
Geelhoed, E.B. 40
General Theory, The: according to Keynes 53–7, 113, 135, 168; antecedents 47–53; inapplicable and illogical 61–3, 79, 130–1; and Keynesians 57–60, 131–5, 191; *see also* expectations; stagnation thesis
George III 10, 25
Gibbons, J.S. 159
Gilbart, J.W. 89
Gilbert, B.B. 130
Gilmour, J.B. 72
Glass, C. 103–4, 111
Glorious Revolution 8, 15–21, 84
Godwin, W. 149
Goff, B.L. 68, 77
gold: discoveries 37, 88, 158; reserves 86, 89, 91–2, 98–9, 103, 157, 164, 166, 176; standard 86, 88, 97, 101–2, 112, 165, 175–6, 179–80, 189
Gold Standard Act of 1900 101
Goldwater, Barry 40, 44
Golembe, C.H. 110
Goodfriend, M. 91, 151–2, 179, 186
Gordon, J.S. 33

Gordon, R.J. 60, 63, 73, 77
Gouge, W.M. 98
Gramm-Rudman (Balanced Budget and Emergency Deficit Control) Act 77
Graydon, A. 11
Great Deflation of 1873–96, 88
Great Depression 45, 67–8, 79, 90, 110, 164, 171, 173, 179–81, 190
Green, E.J. 153, 155
Green, J.R. 10
Greenback Party 101
greenbacks 101, 112
Greenspan, Alan 107, 136, 144, 162–3, 172, 174, 189
Greenstein, F.I. 151
Gregory, T.E. 89, 91–2
Greider, W. 110
Grellier, J.J. 22
Grenville, George 23–6
Grey, Thomas 13
Grigg, J. 130
gross domestic product 192n1
gross national product 74, 192n1
Grubb, F. 95
Guilford, Lord Keeper 20
Gulf War 67
Gyohten, T. 172

Hahn, F.H. 134–5
Hall, D.A. 96–7
Hamilton, Alexander 18, 28–30, 32–3, 35, 72, 93, 96, 105, 188
Hamilton, J.D. 180
Hammond, P.Y. 78
Hammond, W.B. 95–6, 98, 158–9
Hampden, John 10, 12–14
Hankey, T. 90, 92, 161
Hansard, T.C. 96
Hansen, A.H. 65, 154, 168
Harding, W.P.G. 105
Hargrove, E.C. 137
Harris, S.E. 43, 74
Harrison, William Henry 99
Harsch, Joseph 152
Havrilesky, T. 105, 173–4
Hawtrey, R.G. 51, 160, 168, 179
Hayek, F.A. 45, 121, 149–50
Hayes, A. 138, 169
Healy, K.T. 106
Heller, W.W. 1, 44, 74, 79, 137
Henderson, H.D. 130
Henry, Patrick 24–5
Henry II 9
Henry III 10

Hepburn, A.B. 102
Hepburn Act 105–6
Hetzel, R.L. 181
Hicks, J.R. 59, 191n4
Highfield, R.A. 98
Hill, C. 16–20
Hofstadter, R. 106
Holmans, A.E. 79
Holmes, O.W., Jr. 123, 126, 128–9, 150
Holt, M.F. 35, 99, 192n1
Holtz-Eakin, D. 72
Hooker, J.D. 46
Hoover, Herbert 37, 173
Horsefield, J.K. 84
House of Commons 11, 17, 19, 21–2, 24, 26, 85, 87, 89, 91, 157
House of Lords 10, 26, 91
Hubbard, K. 7
Hume, D. vii, 2, 46, 61–3, 113–16
Hutchison, T.W. 49, 51

ideas 2–4, 83–4; communication of 43–7; effects on policy 67, 79, 153; and impressions 113; *see also* interests; economists
Ifft, R.A. 32
impressions *see* ideas 113
inconsistency of optimal plans 90–1, 161
Independent Treasury 94, 99–100, 188, 190
institutions: complexity 72; and interests of monetary policy 83–112
interest rates: deposit ceilings 109; operation twist 169; peg 167–8; and reserve requirements 108; smoothing 111
interests 2–4, 7, 19, 23, 29, 35, 37, 41, 63–6, 83, 155, 172, 183; and democracy 7–8, 145–60, 190; and ideas 29, 33, 42, 66, 79, 146, 187–90; *see also* institutions; tax conflicts
International Acceptance Bank 107
Interstate Commerce Commission 104–6
IRAs 74
irrational exuberance 172
Irwin, D.A. 37–9

Jackson, Andrew 34–5, 83, 98–9, 105
Jackson, Henry 40
James, J.A. 192n4
James, W. 46, 123–5, 181
James I 15
James II 13, 16, 18–22, 41, 84
Jefferson, Thomas 32–4, 93–5, 191n6

Jenks, E. 10
Jennings, I. 8
Jevons, W.S. 49–50, 58
Job Appropriations Act 70
Job Creation and Worker Assistance Act 70
John, King 8–10, 16, 23, 41
Johnson, Lyndon 44, 74, 137, 169
Johnson, S. 16, 31, 122, 191n1, 192n1
Joplin, T. 87
Juglar, C. 161

Kane, E.J. 110
Kanter, H. 78
Kaysen, C. 137
Keech, W.R. 69–70, 72
Kemmerer, E.W. 101, 103
Kennedy, John F. 41, 69, 73–4, 137, 169
Kennedy, W. 16
Kennedy round 39
Keynes, J.M. 2–3, 36, 42–66, 68–9, 71, 73, 113, 121, 129–35, 168, 187, 192n5; *see also General Theory, The*; Keynesian
Keynes, J.N. 51
Keynesian 3, 42, 154–5, 191n3: advice 134–5, 168; and *The General Theory* 57–60, 131–5; model 65, 187; policies 1–2, 8, 43, 68–72; revolution 3, 45–8, 71
King, J.E. 134
Kissinger, H. 137
Klein, L.R. 60
Knight, F.H. 192n5
knowledge: personal 116, 122; tacit 121–2; theory of 114–7; of time and uncertainty 54–8, 120, 135, 192n5; transmission of 3, 113; *see also* central bankers; economic advice; empiricists; pragmatists; rationalists
Kolko, G. 103, 192n5
Kolodziej, E.A. 40, 78
Korean War 39, 67, 73, 75, 171
Krooss, H.E. 93–4, 96, 98–9, 111, 173
Kroszner, Randall 193n1
Kuhn, T.S. 43
Kydland, F.E. 91

Labaree, B. 27
Lachmann, L.M. 120
Lacker, J.M. 91, 151
Laffont, J. 4
laissez faire 48–9, 53, 88, 98
language 46–7, 101, 121; *see also* central bankers; policymakers

LaRoche, R.K. 107
Laughlin, J.L. 103, 106, 112
Lawlor, M.S. 57, 64, 124–5
Lawson, T. 118
leaning against the wind 154, 168
Leijonhufvud, A. 64
lender of last resort 84, 87, 90–2, 102, 156, 162
LeRoy, S.F. 192n5
Lincoln, Abraham 83, 99–100, 105
Lindsay, A.D. 117
liquidity preference 55–6, 59
Livingston, J. 101–2
Lloyd George, D. 129–30
Locke, J. 7, 29, 115
Louis XIV 17, 20, 84
Louisiana Purchase 33, 191n5
Lown, C.S. 108
Loyd, S.J. 91–2, 126, 157–8
Lucas, R.E., Jr. 61–3
Lucas critique 63
Lyell, Charles 46

MacArthur, General Douglas 171
Macaulay, T.B. 16, 19–20, 22
McCallum, B.T. 1, 151
McCracken, Paul 169
McCulloch, Hugh 159
McCulloch, J.R. 85
McCulloch v. *Maryland* 93
McFadden Banking Act 94, 112
McFarland, L. 40–1
McGuire, R.A. 29
McKechnie, W.S. 9–10
McLellan, D. 45
Macmillan Committee on Finance and Industry 52
McNamara, R.S. 41
Macy, J. 14
Madigan, B.F. 110
Madison, James 29, 34, 93, 96, 191n6
Magee, S.P. 1
Magna Carta 8–12, 23
Maisel, S.J. 136, 141, 145, 169–70
Maitland, F.W. 9
Malone, D. 95
Mansfield, Harvey 146
Marshall, A. vii, 4, 48–9, 51, 88, 191n1
Marshall, J. 93
Marshall, M.P. 4
Martin, William McChesney, Jr 154–6, 158, 161, 163, 168–71, 174–5, 189
Martin, William McChesney 156
Marx, Karl 45, 191n1

Mary: of Modena 20; princess 20; queen 84
Mason, George 31
Matthews, R.C.O. 51
Matusow, A. 170
Mayer, T. 139–44
Medhurst, M.J. 41
Meerman, J.P. 98
Meltzer, A.H. 86, 90, 120–1, 138, 154, 167, 192n2
Menand, L. 125
Meredith, William 24
military spending 67–8, 75–9
Mill, J.S. 44, 49, 57–9, 62, 116, 149, 191n1
Mill, James 191n1
Miller, Adolph 193n1
Mints, L.W. 86
Miron, J.A. 111
Mises, L. von 45
Mishkin, Frederic 193n1
missile gap 8, 39–41
Mitchell, B.R. 23, 48, 88
Mitchell, W.C. 51
Modigliani, F. 61
Moggridge, D.E. 48, 129–33
monetarists 42, 60–1
monetary mystique 151
monetary policy: in early monetary institutions 83, 86, 90, 100, 110, 112; gradualism 169; Keynes's 56–7; by littles 118; theory and practice 1–4, 113–14, 188; *see also* Bank of England; classical model and policies; Federal Reserve System; Keynesians
money market myopia 3
Monk, General George 15
Monmouth, Duke of 19
Monroe, James 34
Moore, S. 40
Morgan, E.S. 25
Morgan, H.M. 25
Morgan, J.P. 143
Morganthau, H. 133
Morley, S.A. 137
Mosak, J.L. 73

Napoleon 86
Nasser, President 151
National Banking System 101–2, 107
National Bureau of Economic Research 69–70
National Citizens League 103, 106
National Monetary Commission 103

National Reserve Association 103
National Security Council Paper NSC-68, 78
National Sound Money League 102
Neal, Stephen 173–4
Neikirk, W.R. 169
Nelson, R. 136
Nelson, R.R. 118
Nelson, W.R. 110
Nettels, C.P. 96
Neville, John 32
Nevins, A. 105, 128
new classical synthesis 1
New Classics 2, 42, 60–3, 155
New Economics 73–4, 136
New Freedom 83
New Keynesians 2, 63
New Liberalism 47–8
New York Clearing House Association 108–9
Nixon, Richard 79, 169–70
Nobel Prize in Economic Science 60
Norman, George Warde 89, 91
Norman, Montagu 92
North, D.C. 21
Nourse, E.G. 136–7
Noyes, A.D. 159–60
nullification principle 35, 191n6

O'Neill, T.P., Jr 13
Office of Management and Budget 72
Ogg, D. 13, 19, 21
Olson, J.C. 40–1
open systems 117–22, 134–5, 142, 147–52
operation twist 169
opinion surveys 71–2
Orphanides, A. 163, 181
Otis, James 31
Overstone, Lord *see* Loyd
Owen, Robert 112

Paine, Thomas 11
Paley, W. 46
Palmer, Horsley 91
Palmer rule 89, 110
panics: of 1825 86–7, 156–7; of 1847 92; of 1857 159; of 1873 159; of 1893 156; of 1907 103, 160; *see also* crises
paradigm 42
paradox of thrift 71
Parliament: and Charles I 12–14; Commonwealth 15; Convention 21; long 15; Pension 16, 21; short 15; terms 22

Pasquet, D. 11
Patman, Wright 154–5
Peirce, C.S. 123
Pell, Senator 138
pensions 16–18, 191n1
Pepys, S. 84
permanent income hypothesis 69
Perry, R.B. 47
Peterson, M.D. 35
Petty, W. 84
Phelps, C.W. 107
Phelps, E.S. 51
Phillips, A.W. 61
Phillips curve 51, 61–3, 135, 142, 144, 171, 181, 188
Pickering, D. 24, 26
Pierce, J.L. 141
Pigou, A.C. 51, 57, 191n1
Pitt, William (Lord Chatham) 10, 23, 26, 31, 191n3
Plato 115–17, 124, 149
Plosser, Charles 193n1
Polanyi, M. 121–2, 124, 127
policymakers: and economists 1–4, 73, 113–4; and the public 145–8, 151–2; *see also* central bankers
political economy vii, 4
Popper, K. 127
Posen, A.S. 112
Posner, R.A. 147–8
Post-Keynesians 134–5
pragmatists 4, 46, 114, 119, 122–7
Prescott, E.C. 91
price fixing 108
price level: variations in 48–52, 88; *see also* Federal Reserve System
Progressive Era 37, 103–6
propensities to consume and invest 54–5
Prouty, Charles 192n5
public choice 4
Public Works Impact Program 70
Pujo investigation 103
Pure Foods and Drug Act 105

rationalists 4, 114–17
Reagan, Ronald 1, 67, 70, 72, 75, 127–8, 137, 173
real bills 158, 166
real bills doctrine 86
Report on the Subject of Manufactures 33
Republican Party: and tariffs 37–8
reserve requirements 107–8, 164, 166–7, 176
Resumption Act of 1875 101
Reuss, Henry 110

Reynolds, George 106
Ricardian equivalence 69, 76
Ricardo, D. 50, 69, 191n1
Riedl, B.M. 72
Riezman, R. 4
Rivlin, A.M. 72
Robbins, L. 45, 48, 52–3
Robertson, D.H. 51, 58–9, 161
Robertson, J.L. 169
Rogers, J.E.T. 126–7
Romer, C.D. 1
Romer, D.H. 1, 63
Roosevelt, F.D. 129, 133
Rouse, Robert 137
rule of law 10, 14

Sacheverell, William 21
Sack, B. 179
Salant, W.S. 69
Samuelson, P.A. 3, 44, 61, 71, 120–1, 154
Santoni, G.J. 112
Sapir, E. 121
Sargent, T.J. 42, 61–2
Savage, J.D. 7
Sayers, R.S. 59, 92
Schattschneider, E.E. 33, 37–8
Scheffler, I. 124
Schilling, W.R. 39–40
Schlesinger, A.M. 28
Schumpeter, J.A. 63, 119–20, 156, 181
Schwartz, A.J. 90, 100, 107, 110, 112, 154
Scribner, R.L. 25
Sek, L. 39
Seligman, E.R.A. 160
Seven Years War 23
Seward, William 36
Shackle, G.L.S. 54, 135
Shaw, G.B. 43
Shaw, Leslie 100
Shays's Rebellion 30, 32
ship money 8, 11–15
Shirley, William 191n2
Shoven, J.B. 68
Siklos, P.L. 180
silver interests 86, 101
Simmons, R.C. 27
Simon, H.A. 118
Simons, H. 120
Singell, L.D., Jr. 192n5
Skaggs, N.T. 179
Skidelsky, R. 51, 57, 60, 63, 130
Slaughter, T.P. 32
Smith, A. 48, 55, 71, 108–9, 116, 124, 133, 145, 148

Smith, D.L. 19, 21
Smith, V. 89
Smithies, A. 71, 73
Snyder, G.H. 39
Solow, R. 61
Sorensen, T.C. 41
Sowell, T. 148–9
Spatz, General Tooey 78
Spearman, D. 48
Speck, W.A. 18
Sprague, O.M.W. 101, 103, 109
Sproul, A. 137
sputnik 40
stability: of Federal government deficits 67–79; of monetary policy
stabilization: policies 3–4, 63–6, 68–72; theory of 42–63; *see also* fiscal policy; monetary policy
stagnation thesis 65, 73–4
Stamp Act 8, 23–6, 41; Congress 23, 25
Stein, H. 129
Stigler, G.J. 47, 111
stimulus package of 2008 70
Stockman, D.A. 72, 75, 128
Strong, B. 158, 162–4, 169, 174, 181, 189
Strong rule *see* free-reserves guide
Strouse, J. 143
Stuarts 14–15, 23
Stumpf, Carl 46
Sugar Act 24–5
Sullivan, M. 79
Sumner, W.G. 156
Surface Transportation Assistance Act 70
Symington, Stuart 40–1
symmetallism 88

Taft, W.H. 29, 37
tallies 84, 192n2
Tanner, J.R. 12, 14–18
Tariff Board of 1910 37–8
Tariff Commission of 1882 37; of 1916 38
tariffs 8, 24, 27, 30, 33–9; Act of 1789 30, 33; Act of 1864 37; compromise of 1833 35; Dingley 37; General Agreement on Tariffs and Trade 38–9; Payne–Aldrich 37; Reciprocal Trade Agreements Act 38–9; Smoot-Hawley 37–8; Underwood 37
Tarshis, L. 44, 79
Taus, E.R. 100
Taussig, F.W. 35–8
tax conflicts 2–3, 7–8; *see also* Magna Carta; missile gap; ship money; Stamp Act; tariffs; Whiskey Rebellion

tax smoothing 33, 67, 71, 75–8
taxes: customs 24, 27, 33–9; excise 15–16, 30–3, 84; hearth 16; income 74, 192n2; land 15–16, 20, 22; scutage and inheritance 8; stamp 23–6; stimulus cuts and rebates 69; window 30
Taylor, J.B. 180
Taylor rule 120, 155, 180–2
Temple, Sir William 28
Thackeray, W.M. 126
Theil, H. 60
Thirty Years War 11
Thomas, P.D.G. 25–7
Thornton, D.L. 152, 179
Tilden, Samuel J. 146
Timberlake, R.H. 86, 98, 100, 167
Tinbergen, J. 60
Tobin, J. 69, 122, 154
Tocqueville, A. de 145–7
Todd, W.F. 110
Tollison, R.D. 68, 77
tone and feel 114, 137–9
tontine 84, 192n2
Tooke, Thomas 157
tories 19–21
Townshend, Charles 27
Treasury accounts 17–18
Triennial Act of 1694 22
Truman, H.S. 39–40, 69, 73, 137
Tudors 14, 22
Tunnage Act 85
Tyler, John 99
Tyler, R. 60

United States Congress *see* Federal Reserve System; fiscal policy
United States Supreme Court 93, 98, 106
USSR 74
uncertainty 43, 55–64; *see also* central banking; expectations
unconstrained vision *see* closed systems

Van Schreeven, W.J. 25
Veitch, G.S. 17
Velde, F.R. 171
Vietnam War 169
Viner, J. 66, 101
Volcker, P.A. 111, 122, 142, 144, 152, 162–3, 169, 172–3, 189
Voltaire 149

Wagner, R.E. 71
Wald, A. 134
Wallace, N. 42

War of 1812 33
War on Terror 67–8, 78, 174
Warburg, P.M. 102–3, 105, 107, 192n6
Warren, R.P. 187
Washington, George 11, 32, 34, 66, 93
Webster, Daniel 35
Wedgwood, C.V. 12–13
Weingast, B. 21
Weintraub, S. 154, 168
Weslager, C.A. 25
West, R.C. 103
Wetterau, B. 72
Whale, P.B. 92
Wheelock, D.C. 152, 167, 179, 192n2
Whig Party 83, 99, 192n1
whigs 11, 19–21
Whiskey Rebellion 30–2
White, L.H. 89
Wicker, E. 164, 168, 192n2
Wicksell, K. 59, 179
Wieland, V. 179
Wildavsky, A.B. 78–9
Wilkins, M. 107
William and Mary 84
William III 20–2, 84
William the Conqueror 10
Williams, W.M.J. 16
Willis, H.P. 103, 111
Wilson, J.D. 4
Wilson, Woodrow 38, 83, 99, 103–5
Winch, D. 69
Winter, S.G. 118
Winthrop, Delba 146
Witte, J.F. 73
Wood, J.H. 77, 85, 90, 92, 100, 108–9, 144, 169, 174, 180, 189–90, 192n1
Wood, N.L. 77, 109
Woodford, M. 153–5
Woodham-Smith, C. 49
Woods, R.L. 128
Woodward, B. 136
Woolrych, A.H. 15
Woozley, A.D. 115
Wordsworth, William 191n2
World Trade Organization 39, 191n7
World War I 67–8, 75–9, 88, 156, 172, 188
World War II 1, 38–9, 67–9, 73–9, 108, 168, 173

Yeager, L. 143
Yellen, Janet 193n1

Ziegler, P. 127

eBooks – at www.eBookstore.tandf.co.uk

A library at your fingertips!

eBooks are electronic versions of printed books. You can store them on your PC/laptop or browse them online.

They have advantages for anyone needing rapid access to a wide variety of published, copyright information.

eBooks can help your research by enabling you to bookmark chapters, annotate text and use instant searches to find specific words or phrases. Several eBook files would fit on even a small laptop or PDA.

NEW: Save money by eSubscribing: cheap, online access to any eBook for as long as you need it.

Annual subscription packages

We now offer special low-cost bulk subscriptions to packages of eBooks in certain subject areas. These are available to libraries or to individuals.

For more information please contact webmaster.ebooks@tandf.co.uk

We're continually developing the eBook concept, so keep up to date by visiting the website.

www.eBookstore.tandf.co.uk